Survival and Resistance in
Evangelical America

Survival and Resistance in Evangelical America

Christian Reconstruction in the Pacific Northwest

CRAWFORD GRIBBEN

OXFORD
UNIVERSITY PRESS

OXFORD
UNIVERSITY PRESS

Oxford University Press is a department of the University of Oxford. It furthers
the University's objective of excellence in research, scholarship, and education
by publishing worldwide. Oxford is a registered trade mark of Oxford University
Press in the UK and certain other countries.

Published in the United States of America by Oxford University Press
198 Madison Avenue, New York, NY 10016, United States of America.

© Oxford University Press 2021

Library of Congress Cataloging-in-Publication Data
Names: Gribben, Crawford, author.
Title: Survival and resistance in Evangelical America / by Crawford Gribben.
Description: New York, NY, United States of America. :
Oxford University Press, [2021] |
Includes bibliographical references and index.
Identifiers: LCCN 2020032350 (print) | LCCN 2020032351 (ebook) |
ISBN 9780199370221 (hb) | ISBN 9780199370245 (epub)
Subjects: LCSH: United States—Church history—20th century. |
Evangelicalism—United States—History—20th century. |
United States—Church history—21st century. |
Evangelicalism—United States—History—21st century. |
Migration, Internal—United States. |
Evangelism—United States—Forecasting.
Classification: LCC BR526 .G76 2021 (print) |
LCC BR526 (ebook) | DDC 277.308/3—dc23
LC record available at https://lccn.loc.gov/2020032350
LC ebook record available at https://lccn.loc.gov/2020032351

DOI: 10.1093/oso/9780199370221.001.0001

1 3 5 7 9 8 6 4 2

Printed by Sheridan Books, Inc., United States of America

For Scott Spurlock

The future has never been shaped by majorities but rather by dedicated minorities

—R. J. Rushdoony, *The messianic character of American education*, p. 334

Then let them which be in Judaea flee into the mountains

—Matthew 24:16

Contents

Preface   ix
Map   xiii

Introduction   1

1. Migration   10

2. Eschatology   33

3. Government   59

4. Education   90

5. Media   114

Conclusion   136

Glossary   151
Notes   155
Bibliography   189
Index   205

Preface

When a world disintegrates, nothing more quickly becomes contempt-
ible than its dead values, nothing more dead than its fallen gods, and
nothing more offensively fetid than its old necessities. This will be no
less true of the values of this dying age.[1]

This book sets out to trace some important trends in evangelical views of
politics, society, and culture at the "end of white Christian America."[2] Some
very important demographic shifts are providing contexts for new iterations
of conservative religion. In one respect, the changing face of evangelicalism
is hardly surprising. "Each time the modern religious right has seemed to be
in decline," one historian of the movement has noted, "it has reemerged in
a new form."[3] This is certainly true of the controversial religious and political movement known as Christian Reconstruction. While this movement
has generated waves of critical commentary, it has generated hardly any serious scholarly attention. Historians of modern American evangelicalism
routinely refer to a number of its key thinkers, but only Molly Worthen, Julie
J. Ingersoll, Michael J. McVicar, Brian Auten, Frances Fitzgerald, and Gillis
J. Harp have offered substantial accounts of its principal themes or thought
leaders, or of the influence they have commanded.[4] This lack of discussion
may be related to the fact that almost everyone who writes about the movement argues that it declined, and perhaps died, in the 1990s.[5] This book makes
a different case. In a social history of theological ideas, which draws upon
ethnographic and literary critical approaches, this book sets out to explain
why, how, and to what effect increasing numbers of born-again Protestants
are moving away from political activity to push for preparedness for survival
or cultural reform, while describing elements of the "reconstructed" communities and culture that, in advancing this agenda, they have created in the
Pacific Northwest. In the context of this broader migration of religious and
political conservatives into states such as Idaho, Christian Reconstruction
has been revived, modified, and tempered, and, as its advocates develop

savvy and strategic use of the tools of American mass culture, its ideas have a greater cultural purchase than ever before.[6]

In preparing this work, I have accumulated a great many debts to my colleagues and friends. This book is dedicated to Scott Spurlock. Put most simply, I could not have written it without him. The idea for this book emerged in spring 2010, from conversations that we shared during our employment at Trinity College Dublin, and our discussions of its content continued as we each moved into new positions elsewhere. The project took a major step forward during our often unpredictable road trip around eastern Washington and northern Idaho in the hot, combustible summer of 2015, during which we conducted many of the interviews upon which this book is based, and discussed many of what would become the book's central ideas. In making this project possible—for being a great conversation partner and for much else besides—I owe Scott an enormous debt. I am also grateful for support and encouragement from many colleagues at Queen's University Belfast, especially Andrew Holmes, David Livingstone, and Tristan Sturm, and for advice on Christian Reconstruction from John Larkin QC, the Attorney General for Northern Ireland. I have benefited a great deal from conversations with friends and colleagues in other institutions, particularly Anne Brunon-Ernst, R. Scott Clark, Ian Clary, Catherine Clinton, D. G. Hart, Jordan Haug, Jacob Hickman, Steve Knowles, Ryanne Pilgeram, Jeff Sanders, Rebecca Scofield, Adam Sowards, Matthew Avery Sutton, Guillaume Tusseau, and Joe Webster. I have been grateful for the opportunity to discuss this project in seminars and conferences in my own university, at conferences of the Irish Association for the Academic Study of Religions and the British Association for the Study of Religion, as well as in seminar groups at the University of Idaho, Washington State University, Brigham Young University, and Sciences Po, Paris. And I have learned a huge amount from the undergraduate students who have taken my course on the history and anthropology of the end of the world, especially Lucy Wray, and from graduate students working on related themes, especially Benjamin Huskinson, whose sharing of his experience of living in Moscow, Idaho, has been invaluable.

I record my thanks to the many individuals and institutions who were willing to become the subjects of my investigation. While I have been following the literary output of this movement since the mid-1990s, my conversations were carried out in a sequence of long-distance interviews that began in 2013 and in intensive fieldwork that was conducted in the summers of 2015 and 2016. I interviewed a large number of individuals, spent time with some small communities that preferred to remain anonymous, and followed the ethical guidelines of my university in handling the records of these conversations.[7] Readers may wonder why so many of the voices in this book are male—the simple answer is that male voices overwhelmingly predominate within the cultures that this book describes, and I have tried to compensate for this by promoting women's perspectives whenever the sources permitted me to do so, which was not nearly as often as I would have preferred.[8] Following a sometimes controversial anthropological practice, I have occasionally created composite characters for interviewees who preferred to remain anonymous, in order to protect their privacy.[9] Other individuals were prepared to go on record, and in this respect I gratefully acknowledge the assistance of Gary North; James Wesley Rawles; Mark Rushdoony, who very kindly granted access to the private papers of his father, R. J. Rushdoony; and members of the faculty and student body of New Saint Andrews College, Moscow, Idaho, especially Timothy Edwards, Chris Schlect, and Douglas Wilson.[10]

The completion of this book was not without its challenges. One of the most complex things to consider, while completing fieldwork, was whether my own activity of gathering data was connecting individuals, families, congregations, and other social units in ways that complicated their existing relationships. I was also aware of the ways in which some of the more occluded communities that became subjects of this research could repurpose its conclusions for their own ends.[11] In addition, while I have been following this movement for over two decades, I have written this book as an outsider, and have not felt required to take positions on the controversies about theology, plagiarism, and pastoral care that have embroiled a number of the individuals and congregations that are discussed in this book. But the most substantial challenge to complete this book was knowing how best to deal with the unexpected result of the presidential election of November 2016. In my fieldwork, in the summers of 2015 and 2016, my interviewees spoke with sustained dismay about the future of American politics, society, and culture. While their attitudes toward Donald Trump varied from scorn to serious concern, none of my interviewees predicted his success, and they responded to his election with ambivalence, and only very occasionally hope, a series of tensions that I have done my best to reflect in the following pages. Ironically, as this book went to press, in October 2020, President Trump tweeted that the congregation that is its subject has been persecuted—and that this persecution showed that Democrats wanted to "shut down" other evangelical churches too.[12]

This book is an attempt at historical analysis, rather than a policy intervention or the sounding of an alarm.[13] The religious culture that is the subject of this book has drawn attention, in its earlier manifestations, from critics in evangelical and mainstream cultures who have focused on its political arguments and their legal implications—particularly in relation to the massive extension of the death penalty that was proposed by the first generation of Christian Reconstructionists, an element of a broader program of public policy that McVicar has described as "nauseous" and "disturbing," and which is one element of the theonomist vision that its modern legatees have tended to adapt or abandon.[14] This book attempts to do something different. It adopts an interdisciplinary method, qualifying some of the conclusions of this earlier body of work while thinking more holistically about the controversial character and likely impact of my subjects' social, cultural, and political claims. While other work in the field has adopted biographical, institutional, or thematic approaches, this book attempts to combine all three.[15] And, while a great deal of previous work on these believers has been polemical, I have chosen to follow Ingersoll's approach, attempting to be descriptive and analytical, while allowing my subjects to speak for themselves.[16] I recognize that many readers will find material in this book to be disturbing, but they will agree with the advocates of Christian Reconstruction on this, at least—that there is no such thing as intellectual neutrality. I have my own interpretive presuppositions, which I have discussed elsewhere, but in writing this book I have tried to present my subjects as objectively as I can. Any errors that remain are my own responsibility.

As always, I am especially grateful to my editor, Cynthia Read, whose early enthusiasm for this project was matched by the patience with which she oversaw its completion. But my deepest debts of gratitude are to my family, and especially to Pauline, Daniel, Honor, Finn and Samuel. *Mar is uaidh agus is tríd agus is chuige atá gach ní dá bhfuil ann. Moladh go deo leis.*

Crawford Gribben
Tulaigh na Mullán, June 2019

Map

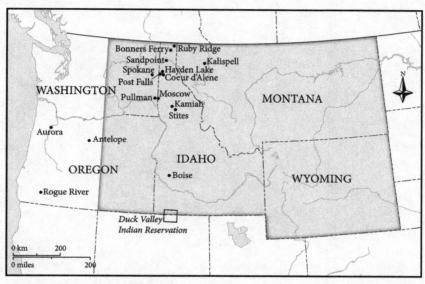

Map 0.1 The American Redoubt

Introduction

There are times when we must regroup, take stock, and start over.[1]

The doctrine of the priesthood of all believers . . . is a program for not only survival but victory.[2]

American religion is changing. This book documents some important shifts in evangelical political thinking during a period of significant demographic and cultural change, which has provided a context for the revitalization of one of the most controversial religious and political movements in recent American history. This book describes a migration into the Pacific Northwest of religious and political conservatives, among whom and from whom the claims of Christian Reconstruction, or "theonomy," as this movement of ideas is often known, are beginning to circulate in modified forms more widely and more effectively than ever before. From their base in northern Idaho, these latter-day theonomists are developing the work of R. J. Rushdoony, Gary North, and others of the first generation of the writers of Christian Reconstruction, reiterating their optimistic view of the future, an eschatological position known as postmillennialism, as well as their expectation that the expansion of Christian influence around the world will be marked by changes in government and by a widespread return to the demands of Old Testament law. While the first generation of Reconstructionists had to fight for the right to provide a distinctively Christian education in private or home schools, the new theonomists have established some very successful educational programs while supporting a liberal arts college that directs students into graduate studies in elite European universities as well as the Ivy League. While the first generation of Reconstructionists promoted their arguments in a media culture of photocopied newsletters and books that appeared under the auspices of minor evangelical publishers, the

Survival and Resistance in Evangelical America. Crawford Gribben, Oxford University Press (2021). © Oxford University Press. DOI: 10.1093/oso/9780199370221.003.0001

new theonomists have created a vibrant, generically varied and far-reaching media culture with connections to publishers such as HarperCollins, Penguin, Random House, and Simon & Schuster, and vehicles of mass culture such as Amazon Prime video and Netflix. And while the first generation of Reconstructionists drew its intellectual firepower from the two think tanks that were associated with its principal leaders, the new theonomists draw from a proliferating and innovating series of ideas institutions in locations across and beyond the United States. Their arguments are certainly making an impact. In the run-up to the 2016 election, candidates for the Republican presidential nomination offered policy suggestions that had long been discussed by Rushdoony's Chalcedon Foundation, including a 10 percent flat tax and punishment for women who had abortions.[3] And, in the last few years, the hostility to abortion that this suggestion represented has been reflected in the trend across Southern states to radically restrict its provision. Theonomists have long predicted that a new America would emerge out of widespread social crisis. Perhaps they are making their own predictions come true. With a more professional presentation, with its ideological edges rubbed smooth, and with significant intellectual centers and increasingly viable communities in the Pacific Northwest, the movement of Christian Reconstruction may never have been as important as it is today.

The revival and modification of Reconstruction is, in many ways, surprising.[4] Since the 1970s, and in the aftermath of the "third disestablishment," the general trend in evangelical politics has been for believers to accept the liberal political order and their place within it by using rights-based arguments to defend their situation as a moral minority.[5] This trend has been partially reversed in the last decade, during which period believers have thought in ambivalent ways about their relation to mainstream culture. My previous book, *Writing the Rapture: Prophecy Fiction in Evangelical America* (2009), considered the best-selling Left Behind novels and the literary tradition from which they emerged in order to document a cultural mood at the end of the Bush administration.[6] This mood, at least in its popular cultural manifestations, seemed to prefer end-times escapism or sentimental piety to strategies of resistance and survival, despite the cultural power suggested by the sales of over sixty-five million Left Behind novels and the relative strength of evangelicalism in political terms.[7] At the end of the Bush era, paradoxically, the literary culture of evangelicalism suggested that, in their imaginative work at least, born-again

Protestants had no aspiration to retain significant political power. And so, as evangelicals emoted and sat back in anticipation of the rapture, they witnessed a new phase in the polarization of American politics with the election of Barack Obama (2008), a polarization that contributed in no small measure to the election of Donald Trump (2016) and the tensions that it, in turn, precipitated. But evangelical popular culture continues to be paradoxical.[8] Even as the Supreme Court moves in a more conservative direction, and the prospect of its striking down *Roe v. Wade* no longer seems impossible, born-again Protestants continue to think of themselves as a vulnerable and beleaguered remnant. Reinforcing this identity, believers consume products that argue for an alternative view of the future and of the ethical responsibilities that it demands—magazines, novels, curricula, preparedness manuals, and websites that emphasize their marginal status and the many ways in which they may need to resist, in order to survive, the cultural conditions that mark the "failure" of liberalism at the "end of white Christian America."[9] Drawing on central themes in the tradition of Reformed theology, those evangelicals who are turning to this alternative view of their responsibility share a high view of culture as well as a keen interest in issues concerning government and law. But, the spokespersons for this new movement insist, the cultural resistance to which believers are called is not to be political. Believers are moving away from the political style of the Religious Right, and from urban centers, as the *Economist* and the *Washington Post* have noted, in order to build something more credible and sustainable in the Pacific Northwest—reconstructed subcultures out of which there will develop a global hegemony of Christian faith.[10]

This turn among conservative Christians toward themes of survival, resistance, and reconstruction has had some unexpected and occasionally tragic consequences. Among the many graduates of the growing number of Christian home schools there appear to have numbered the racially motivated perpetrators of the serial bombings in Austin in 2018 and the Passover synagogue shootings in San Diego in 2019. Preachers within evangelical communities have consistently condemned these outrages, while commentators in some of their most important media networks have begun to critique the ideological, ethical, political, and theological arguments that, they worry, connect this violence to social, cultural, and religious convictions that have long been circulating within their religious world.[11] This is not merely an in-house conversation. Discussions about the links between evangelical homeschooling, Reformed theology, and racial violence now appear in some very telling barometers of popular opinion, which have begun to show an interest in parsing the theological claims that underpin this cultural turn.[12] Amid continuing debates about gun ownership, evangelicals and their critics share a common concern about the lengths to which some believers will take the new emphasis upon resistance to broader cultural trends. For the situation is complex. These observers are not dealing with a simple case of cause and effect, as if believers are growing more radical as their cultural status declines. Instead, believers are growing more radical as their cultural power increases, as the Supreme Court has begun to move in a more conservative direction. They are embracing marginality at precisely the moment when their cultural power may be at its height. This book considers the paradox, and shows how trends in the wider political landscape are shaping, even as they are being shaped by, opinion-formers within the variety of conservative Protestantism that has become one of the most powerful forces in evangelical America.

For American evangelicalism is changing. Commentators on this definition-bending religious movement have for some time noticed that the political cultures of born-again Protestants, which were never homogenous, are becoming much less predictable.[13] Of course, as D. G. Hart has noted, it was always the case that its single denominator belied the extent to which evangelicalism existed as a series of interrelated but competing religious communities.[14] Recent work has focused attention on the dominant narratives within these competing contexts, paying special attention to the growth of the evangelical left.[15] This book, by contrast, focuses on the emergence of communities that remain skeptical of the theological and cultural assumptions both of the Religious Right and of its principal alternatives. Since the 1990s, these consolidating political options have been subjected to a powerful critique by a small, geographically concentrated, sometimes well-connected, and surprisingly influential group of polemicists and activists, who, despite their sometimes diffuse convictions, share a critique of the dominant trends in evangelical politics and, as part of their solution, promote various kinds of internal migration into the Pacific Northwest in an effort to bolster the formation of communities that, among other things, respect the obligations of the Ten Commandments. These entrepreneurs of faith-based relocation benefit from connections that range from well-known children's authors and celebrity preppers to major media figures such as the late Christopher Hitchens.[16] Their thought leaders include several best-selling authors, with major publishing deals, whose interests range from cultural engagement by means of the liberal arts to paramilitary preparedness for a second American civil war. In the heartland of this movement, in northern Idaho, the pursuit by migrating evangelicals of something akin to Adorno's "strategy of hibernation" may look like disengagement from the cultural mainstream, but it reflects an effort to achieve a more revolutionary objective than was ever imagined by the Religious Right.[17] And this effort can be formidably high-brow. In an email exchange in 2013, for example, one of the principal and most widely published proponents of these new emphases in evangelical social theory, Gary North, suggested that the titles that might best explain his perspective included the classic sociological account of *The Quest for Community* (1953) by Robert Nisbet, who served on North's UCLA PhD committee; Martin Van Creveld's analysis of *The Rise and Decline of the State* (1999); and Jacques Barzun's cultural history of Western civilization, *From Dawn to Decadence* (2001).[18] As North's note suggests, theonomic writers have been able to draw down considerable and varied ideological resources to create materials for different kinds of audiences, and to serve different kind of agendas, in order to redirect evangelicals toward strategies of survival, resistance, and reconstruction.

This new evangelical critique of religious politics and its principal born-again alternatives is most developed in a series of intentional communities in north Idaho. The location, though far from the most obvious centers of political or cultural influence, should not be especially surprising. The advocacy of rural living has a long history in American popular culture, and these believers might at first glance appear to be moving in search of the good life, into what might quite properly be regarded as one of the most breathtaking landscapes—as well as one of the least racially or culturally diverse regions—in North America.[19] However, according to their advocates, the communities into which these believers are being gathered will be guided by the demands of Old Testament law, and will expand organically, over generations and through normal democratic means, in sometimes incompatible visions, to determine the shape and size of government, and to renew or replace the American Constitution, and the system of liberal democracy that it assumes. These are extraordinary objectives, but the extent to which they have gained traction in some localities shows why their advocates do not regard them as entirely implausible. This strategy is proving to be successful: the migration movement is growing, its ideals are becoming more clearly articulated, and its agenda is now on the national stage where, in the aftermath of recent episodes of race-based violence, as we have seen, some of its subcultures are subject to uncertain and sometimes confusing analysis. Investigating the achievements of this internal migration, this book traces the texts, cultures, and communities that an increasing number of born-again Protestants have developed as means to consolidate their religious life in the short term, and in the longer term to reconstruct the wider society of which they are at present only a tiny constituent part, as they plan to construct a radically conservative and authentically Christian America.[20]

Of course, despite the recent revival of modified forms of Christian Reconstruction, these themes of survival, resistance, and reconstruction are not foreign to the long history of evangelical political thinking, and believers who represent themselves as existing on the social margins are well within the historic mainstream of American religion.[21] For much of their history, whether in creating or in losing the mainstream—if that is indeed what they achieved—born-again Protestants have reiterated the tradition of jeremiad that was developed in Puritan New England, reinscribing its moralistic dualism in the changing contexts of the nineteenth, twentieth, and early twenty-first centuries. Born-again Protestants were certainly important in the emergence of modern conservatism in the suburbs of Cold War California.[22] But evangelicals may have become most aware of their paradise lost as the circumstances of the middle and later twentieth century contributed to the restructuring of national politics, a "third disestablishment" that accentuated their sense of marginal status.[23] Since the late 1960s, a small number of conservative evangelicals have been discussing the need to survive and resist an impending crisis in American society, while hoping for, if not always actually planning for, the reversal of the ideology that some of their most prominent writers have described as "secular humanism."[24] Reflecting the sometimes considerable intellectual capital of their thought leaders, these believers have constructed secular humanism in terms of the ideology and political practice that were popularized by critical theorists associated with the Frankfurt School, and are more confident than most of their evangelical brethren that the dogmas of what they often describe as "cultural Marxism" will implode to precipitate the establishment of a Christian nation. This discussion has recently intensified. After the embarrassments associated with the efforts of the Religious Right and the scandals of the televangelist media empires upon which it depended, conservative evangelicals experienced a "generational reversal" under President Barack Obama, some of whose priorities confirmed their dismay with the immediate direction of

American politics and culture.[25] Their frustration with this sense of marginality pushed a large majority of born-again Protestants to swing toward Donald Trump, a candidate who shared few of their values, in the presidential election of 2016.[26] Trump's surprise victory, the religious politics of which have yet to be thoroughly analyzed, was both hailed and lamented among evangelical communities in the Pacific Northwest. Their responses marked out a division between those who believed that the system could be reformed from within, under the iconoclastic leadership of a politically inexperienced and morally dubious celebrity, a position that was widely articulated on militia-related websites and which gestured toward the strategies of the old Religious Right, and those who argued that the election offered further evidence of all that was wrong with America, the next act in the unfolding drama of divine judgment upon the nation, a position more popular among the heirs of Christian Reconstruction and other advocates of godly government.

In these confusing times, the subjects of this book are not unique in articulating and acting upon their variety of political dismay. Christians from other traditions have shared their concerns about the prevailing cultural conditions, and ambivalence at the unexpected and sometimes ambiguous rightward turn in national politics. Shortly after Trump's inauguration, conservative commentator Rod Dreher published what the New York Times described as the "most discussed and most important religious book of the decade."[27] Catapulted to the top of bestseller lists, The Benedict Option (2017) described attempts by Catholics and Orthodox Christians to pursue a new monasticism in groups of families and congregations that have sought to live apart from the cultural mainstream, thereby to renew the virtues by which an earlier and better society had been sustained. Dreher had planned to include in his survey of intentional movements one of the Reformed communities that this book describes, but pulled this material from his book over concerns as to how leaders in that community had responded to a serious pastoral problem that had arisen among their members.[28] In so doing, Dreher omitted the possibility of his critical consideration of a religious community that, despite its very specific and ostensibly limiting geographical and ideological contexts, has done a great deal to channel the social, cultural, and political aspiration of born-again Protestants. This community has developed the materials and infrastructure through which other groups may be protected and reinvented, not least by means of the very substantial audience among homeschoolers and classical Christian educators for the curricula and marriage advice materials produced by their publishing house, as well as the substantial audiences for their programming on Amazon Prime video and Netflix, the products of which promote the strategies of survival, resistance, and reconstruction that might shape conservative evangelicalism into the middle part of this century. Whatever Dreher's concerns, these believers were respectable, if sometimes radical, "crunchy" conservatives, with concerns similar to those interviewed in his earlier work, and "countercultural conservatives," similar to those described by Alex Schäfer.[29]

As might be expected, there are significant differences among the individuals, families, congregations, and communities in the single geographical area that is the focus of this book. But these are differences within a broad and diverse series of communities that pursue their many quests for community from a common ideological source. This book traces the origins of this migration movement and its distinctive critique of religious politics to its roots in "one of the most controversial and poorly understood religious and political movements to emerge in the United States during the twentieth century."[30] "More a school of thought than an organization," Christian Reconstruction was developed by R. J. Rushdoony and his son-in-law Gary North in the late 1960s, but it has evolved over time, and has variegated in that evolution.[31] Its success, one critic has observed, depends upon the "simplicity and radicalism of the proposal . . . read the law and do it."[32] Proponents of Christian Reconstruction differ from other advocates of the benefits of Mosaic law by arguing that it should provide a national legal code, as well as moral guidance for individuals. Its scope is expansive: Rushdoony's *Institutes* argues for the abolition of prisons, strict limits on lending and debt, the control of capitalism, and other apparently progressive policies, as well as the massive extension of the death penalty with which his name is more often associated. Scholars vary in their assessment of this movement's importance. For some, like Daniel K. Williams, in his history of *God's Own Party: The Making of the Christian Right* (2010), Christian Reconstruction is worthy only of passing reference. Others, including Steven P. Miller, argue that the importance of the movement has been exaggerated in the (anti-?) moral panic that seems to have followed upon the discovery of the influence of ultra-conservative religion on recent American politics. For others, including Max Blumenthal, the movement has shaped in fundamental ways the *Republican Gomorrah* (2009).[33] Frances Fitzgerald identified Rushdoony as one of the two most important thinkers of the Religious Right—the other being Francis Schaeffer, whose ideas were (to put it mildly) indebted to those of Rushdoony.[34] Benjamin Huskinson has identified Rushdoony as a crucial node in the promotion of creation science.[35] Despite the significance of Christian Reconstruction, the movement has been the subject of only two research monographs, by Michael J. McVicar and Julie J. Ingersoll. The latter historian has argued that the movement's "core is regional," but while she has traced its cultures in the American South, I found reconstructed communities in their most concentrated form in eastern Washington and northern Idaho.[36] There, the ideas of Christian Reconstruction have been put to multiple, proliferating, and innovating uses in families, in churches, and even occasionally in local and national government.[37] In Idaho, as elsewhere in the United States, the advocates of this system look past an occasional variety of perspectives to embrace a common concern to survive, resist, and then to reconstruct wider society. From their base in the Pacific Northwest, reconstructed Christians expect to witness and participate in the recovery of America.

In this book, I explore the impact of these controversial religious ideas in the modern heartland of American theonomy by drawing on an extensive print culture and interviews, conducted over several years, over long distances and face-to-face, with leaders of and participants within these communities. While I have been reading the publications of some of my subjects since the mid-1990s, I completed much of the fieldwork for this project during the reconfiguration of American conservatism in the period immediately before the 2016 election, while remaining in touch with several of these communities in its aftermath. While describing the narratives of tragedy and hope that shape these varieties of evangelical response, I also explore the significance of President Trump's unexpected electoral success—which the subjects of this book, with various degrees of confidence, tend to represent as the postponement, rather than the reversal, of cultural decline. As their political circumstances grow ever more ambiguous, American evangelicals are increasingly interested in strategies of survival and resistance at "the end of white, Christian America." After all, there may be trouble ahead.

1
Migration

It is those who have a faith, and a hope for the future, in time and eternity, who survive.[1]

It is sometime in the very near future. A financial panic has generated massive inflation and political crisis, and American citizens are increasingly uneasy. As prices rise and government mechanisms break down, the welfare system collapses and riots erupt in major cities. Society rushes toward an inevitable tipping point. Police departments lose manpower as employees choose to stay at home to defend their families and properties, and urban centers are engulfed in a chaos of looting and murder. A lucky few escape the cities, risking everything to reach remote locations in which they have prepared for this eventuality. Among their number are two evangelical Christians, whose foresight, skills, and courage enable them to escape the East Coast and to move slowly and painfully across the continent toward safe havens in the West. Many others are making similar journeys. Individually and in groups, these survivalists evade unscrupulous locals and vicious criminal gangs, and confront hostile militias and invading armies from Europe and China. But Joshua Kim and Megan La Croix finally reach their destination. This mixed-race couple finds community in Moscow, Idaho, and employment in Christ Church, one of its larger congregations, as they prepare to resist the horrors to come. For it is from their redoubt in the Pacific Northwest that Kim and La Croix begin the war to save America.[2]

The plot of *Liberators* (2014), by best-selling author, prolific blogger, and former military intelligence officer James Wesley Rawles, refers to themes and geographical locations that have energized many of the recent discussions of survival and resistance in evangelical America. Taking advantage of the rising interest in survivalism and "prepping," which sustains popular television shows on homesteading, frontier living magazines such as *The Backwoodsman* (est. 1980) and *The New Pioneer* (est. 2010), and more

Survival and Resistance in Evangelical America. Crawford Gribben, Oxford University Press (2021). © Oxford University Press. DOI: 10.1093/oso/9780199370221.003.0002

militaristically orientated titles such as *Offgrid* (est. 2013), Rawles's novels have overlapping plots that chart the journeys of his protagonists from Seattle, Chicago, Florida, England, Iraq, and other overseas locations to an area of the Pacific Northwest that he and many others have come to describe as the "American Redoubt." His novels combine fact and fiction, inserting imaginary characters into real-life religious communities in an effort to help his readers do the same for themselves. These communities may neither have sought nor given permission for their inclusion within his work. Some may be entirely unaware of his writing, and others may be embarrassed by their proximity to his advice about arms procurement and militia-training tips.[3] But the leaders and members of these congregations may share Rawles's concern about the short-term future, even if they do not share his strategies for survival and resistance: it is no accident that the heroes of *Liberators* end up working with a new, growing, and nationally influential congregation that is led, in reality, by Douglas Wilson, one of the most erudite and controversial of the evangelical theorists of American cultural decline, and one of the most important promoters of religious migration and other familial, ecclesiastical, and cultural strategies for survival, resistance, and reconstruction.

Rawles began to theorize the concept of the American Redoubt in 2011. In a blog post that he has repeatedly updated, he has described the Redoubt as an enclave including Idaho, Montana, Wyoming, eastern Oregon, and eastern Washington, in which a new community of religious conservatives could survive and resist an impending crisis in American society.[4] In an interview, which I recorded in 2013, Rawles emphasized that the "Redoubt movement is not a political movement, but merely a very informal trans-migration project. The goal is to solidify a conservative Christian worldview through a demographic shift. Thus far it has been successful, and . . . with passing years we will further solidify a conservative Christian redoubt within the United States."[5] In his publications, Rawles has laid out the principles upon which the new community should be established. "I am a separatist, but on religious lines, not racial lines," he has explained, insisting that he welcomes as his neighbors "Christians of all races," as well as Orthodox and Messianic Jews who "share the same moral framework." His writing encourages "people with the same outlook to move to the Redoubt States, to effect a demographic solidification. We're already a majority here. I'd just like to see an even stronger majority."[6] His novels and blog posts identify the (mainly Reformed Protestant) congregations in which he believes migrants to the Redoubt would be welcomed.[7] And Rawles is clear as to what this migration should achieve—a "demographic solidification" supporting limited government, on the basis that "governments tend to expand their power to the point that they do harm," and upholding divine law, on the basis that the "foundational morality of the civilized world is best summarized in the Ten Commandments."[8] Rawles's program for action may appear extreme, but it is this combination of libertarian politics and the idealization of Old Testament law that, over the last forty years, has driven a quiet revolution in evangelical social theory in which the creation of a redoubt is only one element of a much larger program for defensive action in the hope of broader social change. The eventual significance of this religious ferment may be as yet unclear, but, in secluded towns in the Pacific Northwest, where "refugees to the American Redoubt" are "relieved" to arrive, its exponents are imagining new strategies to contest American modernity.[9]

Rawles is correct—his strategy is succeeding. The political and religious migration to the Pacific Northwest that has continued for forty years has recently picked up speed. In the last few years, media reports have suggested that a significant number of individuals have heeded the call to migrate, driving up local property prices and reprofiling political participation, especially in areas such as the north Idaho panhandle, where one leading religious community has published advice for those of the "discontented of Judah" who are considering relocating to its town.[10] These individuals and the communities that they form work at some distance from but sometimes in dependence upon Rawles's vision of the near future in which Christian values and the American Constitution must be defended, if necessary, by force, and a vision of the longer-term future in which American society will be rebuilt according to Old Testament law. Drawing on Reformed theology, the social theory of Christian Reconstruction, and libertarian politics, these believers are projecting significant soft power, publishing books with Penguin, Simon & Schuster, HarperCollins, and Random House, achieving best-selling status in the *New York Times*, while engaging with coauthors and interlocutors of the status of Christopher Hitchens, promoting their work on Netflix and Amazon Prime video, and enjoying coverage in the *Economist* and the *Washington Post*.[11]

As this media network suggests, the strategy of religious migration is gaining momentum, as the values and arguments of the migrants and those who identify with them make an impact in local political and economic life, while being repackaged for a wider audience in publications by a broader coalition of conservative commentators. These believers who are moving to the

Pacific Northwest may recognize that they have lost the culture war—despite or sometimes even because of the election of Donald Trump—and that another kind of conflict is beginning. This book examines the origins, evolution, and cultural reach of the migration that might tell us most about the future of American evangelicalism, describing the "strategy of hibernation" that offers telling insights into the recent development of "American religious nationalism," the strategies of survival and resistance upon which it depends, at the "end of white Christian America."[12]

The "strategies of hibernation" that are being popularized by influential evangelicals present a stage in the renaissance of conservative political thinking that began with the Barry Goldwater campaign in 1964 but that came into public prominence in the mid-1970s.[13] This political re-engagement of evangelicals was associated with the controversial interventions and ambitions of well-known political figures, and associated fears that believers were organizing to impose a conservative right-wing social agenda on the wider American public. But not all evangelicals have been persuaded by this vision of the American future, nor of the strategies by which it may be attained. In recent years, an influential evangelical left has also appeared, generally, but not consistently, maintaining the movement's broader critique of abortion and same-sex marriage, while pursuing an agenda that focuses on local issues of exclusion and marginality.[14] Other evangelicals have found these alternatives to be unsatisfactory. Disappointed by the achievements of the Religious Right, and worried by the emergence of an evangelical left, these believers have developed deliberate and reflective strategies of tactical (and, they hope, temporary) retreat, which have often been justified by the rhetoric of surviving and ultimately resisting the dark days of late Christendom, pursuing "Benedict options" long before Rod Dreher had theorized or advertised that possibility. Some of these believers continue to adopt quietism and political passivity with the purpose of surviving in the period preceding the "rapture" (an approach especially popular among the dispensational premillennialists that make up the overwhelming majority of American evangelicals). Others have adopted more ambitious varieties of cultural retreat, with the intention of building alternative communities and institutions designed to resist and eventually to redeem or replace the culture of their "secular" counterparts (an approach especially popular among postmillennialists, but which is also now growing in popularity among premillennialists, and which has been especially influential among thought leaders who encourage cultural participation, artistic expression, and political involvement). Disenchanted with the direction of the American mainstream, and disappointed by the strategy and vision of prominent evangelical politicians, many born-again Protestants are now planning for the near future under the rubrics of survival and resistance.

Of course, conservative Protestants have always argued for withdrawal from "the world," which earlier generations of fundamentalists often understood to signify a rejection of mainstream media culture and such vices as alcohol and tobacco. But an influential minority of contemporary evangelicals is pushing beyond this traditional exhortation for a distinctively godly lifestyle while overturning some widely held earlier assumptions. Sometimes the withdrawal for which they argue is ecclesiastical, in which the traditional fundamentalist appeal to retreat from corrupt or compromising denominations is evolving into the formation of a loose network of "home churches," or unincorporated "free churches." Sometimes the withdrawal for which they argue is educational, as in the rhetoric surrounding the rapidly increasing popularity of homeschooling and the establishment of new liberal arts colleges friendly to homeschool graduates. At its most radical, the withdrawal for which they argue is geographical, as advocated by secessionist organizations, including the Christian Exodus movement, which encourages evangelicals to relocate to South Carolina, in the hope of seceding from the union—an idea so compelling that it is hard to believe that no one has ever thought of it before—and in Rawles's campaign to have "god-fearing [sic] Americans" evacuate to the "American Redoubt." The subjects of this book draw repeatedly on Reformed theology, though often in an eclectic manner, rarely without qualification, and sometimes to unfortunate ends. But it is these evangelicals' concern to rebuild the world from which they are withdrawing that so radically differentiates them from the politically passive pietists and politically engaged fundamentalists whom they have succeeded. For while they may argue on the basis of rights, as a tactic in the political short term, their goal is to reconstruct the liberal political order in its entirety. For many of these migrants, democracy is not an uncontested good.

While they are not entirely unrepresentative, the subjects of this book do not participate in any kind of religious mainstream, although they do exercise significant clout in some areas in which they have concentrated numbers, and their soft power extends into the bestseller lists of major newspapers and movement profiles in journals of record. Their developing agendas are redefining key features of American evangelicalism, as spokespersons within the larger movement adopt their rhetoric of survival and resistance, if not their expectation of renewal. The individuals, groups, and institutions discussed in this book are often rejecting politics itself, withdrawing from established forms of evangelical activism in the expectation of a faith-driven social and cultural renaissance, in their role as a remnant that imagines itself as a vanguard. The subjects of this book are not necessarily advocating a coherent agenda as part of their strategy for social change. Like the broad-based, diffuse, and contradictory evangelical movement from which they emerge and which they continue to critique, the individuals, groups, and institutions described in this book draw on shared intellectual roots to present a range of sometimes incompatible strategies and objectives. But these believers share a concern to identify the issues that are compromising larger communities of born-again Protestants in late Christendom. In that sense, this book offers further evidence for the fragmentation of American evangelicals. But it also suggests that this fragmentation reveals deep disillusion among many evangelicals with the political and cultural futures advocated by those public figures who are often assumed to be the leaders of their "movement"—and further proof for the inappropriate use of a singular noun to describe several different "evangelical" things. The subjects of this book may be unrepresentative, but they are hardly as marginal as they sometimes believe. This book argues that their voices—projected from isolated homesteads and small towns in the Pacific Northwest—are successfully challenging the influence of those national religious leaders who have done the most to facilitate the political re-engagement of American evangelicals. Perhaps the future of American evangelicalism may be best observed on its margins.

I

It is difficult to define the boundaries or the center of the migration movement this book describes. While its intellectual roots may be relatively easy to trace, its contemporary demographic is not so easily identified or quantified, and not always easy to distinguish within the broader migration movement of which it is a part. This is certainly true in terms of race: the migrants I encountered were almost always white, though some prominent advocates of migration are African Americans, and among my most rewarding interviewees were a mixed-race couple. Some of the groups I encountered in north Idaho appeared to have few links outside their family homestead, making a virtue of self-sufficiency. Other multi-family units appeared to be very small: the membership of several of the congregations I encountered likely amounted to no more than a few families, some of them autonomous congregations and others a part of tiny denominational networks, some of which had moved into the area as a preexisting congregational unit (one such group had moved *en masse* from New York State). Other groups were much more substantial: the community associated with a liberal arts college and several congregations in Moscow, Idaho, may amount to almost two thousand individuals, representing around 10 percent of the permanent population of their area. This congregation might come closest to identifying the movement's center. While its membership varies from gun-rights homesteaders in artisan employment to highly educated academics, writers, and software engineers, it is held together by a robust set of theological commitments that include Reformed theology, postmillennial eschatology, and the expectation of short-term tribulation. But while it is possible to estimate the size of individual communities, it is impossible to calculate the total size of the migration movement of which they are a part.

One reason the demographic question is so difficult to answer is that many of these migrants, following Rawles's guidance about "operational security," prefer to live under the radar (while often presenting on social media far more information about themselves than they might realize). Of course, the question of the size of the migration is something that also interests its participants. Some of my better-informed subjects suggested that the number of those who had relocated to the Redoubt amounted to "many thousands."[15] Another informant, a well-connected gun-rights activist who had lived in the region for over twenty years, believed that around 10,000 individuals had migrated to the Redoubt by 2015, basing his calculation on the growth of his own congregation, one of the largest in the area, which, when I visited, had around 800 attendees.[16] But no one can be certain. This lack of verifiable data generates an interesting methodological problem for journalists and social scientists, who might find it challenging to write about a movement with no formally appointed spokespersons or any recognizable boundaries of membership, but which is significant enough to push up property values, be featured in the international press, and earn a place on major bestseller lists.[17] Julie J. Ingersoll has already observed this problem of quantification in her work on Christian Reconstruction: if the precise number of adherents of this movement must remain elusive, she observes, the influence of theonomist ideas is much easier to trace.[18] This demographic problem may therefore be better addressed using the tools of historical, cultural,

and rhetorical studies, which would help focus critical analysis of this nu-
merically elusive population on its shared conversation, rather than on an
agreed manifesto or membership lists. Historians in other fields have wres-
tled with the same problem of identifying a complex and permeable subject.[19] In the Redoubt, as David Sabean has argued of another context, "what
is common . . . is not shared values or common understanding so much as
the fact that members of a community are engaged in the same argument,
the same *raisonnment*, the same *Rede*, the same discourse, in which alternative strategies, misunderstandings, conflicting goals and values are thrashed
out."[20] The spikes in property values that coincide with the media boom in
discussions of the Redoubt may indicate where migrants have settled, and
they can be cross-referred to the locations of the congregations that are
recommended on Rawles's website, survivalblog.com, which cluster around
Boise, Post Falls, and Bonners Ferry.[21] But the significance of this movement
may not lie in the numbers or precise locations of its adherents, for these
communities have developed powerful strategies to reach far beyond their
localities and to address a national or global audience, disseminating their
distinctive views of eschatology, government, and education in an ambitious,
entrepreneurial, and expanding media culture. Even if the numbers involved
in the migration are small, or must remain unknown, its advocates have
drawn on familiar themes in Reformed theology and in the history of the
American West to enjoy significant cultural reach on popular websites and
bestseller lists, using the tools of American mass culture to propose a radical
alternative to its norms.

The extent of this cultural reach can be illustrated in the popularity of
Rawles's writing. His projects in fiction and nonfiction, in print and online,
are complementary. They invoke the same narrative structure, and reiterate
the same leading themes: America is facing an emergency, its government
is driving the nation toward a crisis, and individuals should take responsibility for their own safety and that of their family and neighbors. Rawles's
publications rely heavily on technical description, whether of weaponry,
investments, or mechanics. They function as a primer for the political and religious ideas that underpin his work, providing a justification for government
by biblical law, which he presents as a libertarian ideal. But his publications
also serve a geographical and cultural purpose, calling attention to the
benefits of living in northwestern states, and encouraging his readers to relocate. There is safety only in the right kind of community and in the right kind
of place, Rawles argues. And a large number of people are paying attention to

his message. His "preparedness" website, survivalblog.com, claims to attract upward of 320,000 unique hits every week, totaling almost 85 million unique hits since 2005. As traffic to his website has increased, he has developed his ideas about "preparedness" in a series of novels and handbooks that have achieved remarkable success. His first novel, *Patriots: Surviving the Coming Collapse* (2006), was self-published, but its sequels, *Survivors: A Novel of the Coming Collapse* (2011), *Founders: A Novel of the Coming Collapse* (2013), *Expatriates: A Novel of the Coming Global Collapse* (2013), and *Liberators: A Novel of the Coming Global Collapse* (2014), were picked up by Penguin and Simon & Schuster imprints. Rawles has capitalized on his success as a writer of fiction by developing more formally constructed survivalist manuals. *How to Survive the End of the World as We Know It* (2009), which became a *New York Times* bestseller, was followed by *Tools for Survival: What You Need to Survive When You're on Your Own* (2015), both of them published by Penguin. Rawles is certainly making an impact. And many of his readers are making the preparations he recommends. So too are some of those who compete with Rawles for influence—including some whose websites advertise their relation to various militia. Despite the best guesses of participants, and movement profiles in newspapers of record, no one knows how many individuals should be identified with the migration. But if the millions of hits on survivalblog.com are any indication, or if the achievement of *New York Times* bestseller status is any kind of clue, the widespread consumption of the very idea of the Redoubt, and its representation in popular culture, may be as significant as its lived experience. The media of the Redoubt creates a virtual "imagined community" that large numbers of its participants find compelling.

II

Whatever the power of this literary culture, many of those who are drawn to the idea of the Redoubt prefer their community to be actual rather than virtual—and they are not alone. These recent settlers, driven by their concern about the direction of American culture, and inspired by attempts to renew it, are not the first to seek a better life in the Pacific Northwest. For the last two centuries, migrants have been attracted by Idaho's reputation as a "sanctuary for religious dissenters and experimenters."[22] Much of this history has been taken for granted, perhaps because of the normativity of Mormon migration into the area, but also because the religious history of Idaho is "still a frontier," as Jill K. Gill has put it, and remains as neglected as other aspects of the state's history, as Adam Sowards has noted.[23] With the exception of work by James Aho and a small number of other scholars, some of which is now quite dated, the religious cultures of the Panhandle and Palouse have been better served by travel memoirs than by historical or social scientific scholarship: in fact, very little of the region's religious history has been explored beyond the history of its far-right organizations.[24] But utopian, millennial, and communitarian movements, many with trans-Atlantic connections, have a long history of moving into the region, or of using it as a base for national or international organizations.[25] As is the case elsewhere, some millennial communities have "endured for generations." Numbers of Latter-day Saints, whose religious cultures dominate in southern Idaho, have grown from the 26 settlers who moved to the Salmon River in 1855 to the 456,496 members currently residing in state, as reported by the Mormon Newsroom.[26] But other groups have been less successful in finding a permanent home in the Pacific Northwest.

Some of these transient religious communities have made important—if almost always controversial—contributions to the religious history of the region. One of the most interesting of the short-lived movements was led by Wilhelm Keil, a Pietist who left Prussia in 1836. Keil crossed the Atlantic, eventually settling in Pittsburgh, where he transferred his loyalties into Methodism and thence into a highly individualistic mystical millennialism. He gathered followers around his apocalyptic convictions, which closely resembled those of William Miller, whose calculations were being recovered after the "Great Disappointment," and the group moved *en masse* to northern Missouri, where they established a community called "Bethel," before forming a more enduring base of operations in Aurora, Oregon, in 1856. The Aurora community pursued its interest in German folk music and agricultural innovation while waiting, for several decades thereafter, for the millennium.[27] Other short-lived groups were less conventionally Christian. In 1929, Frank Bruce Robinson established an entirely new religious movement in Moscow, Idaho. "Psychiana," which began as an experiment in New Thought, grew through newspaper advertisements to become "perhaps the most successful mail-order religion in the world," employing at its peak around 100 local people to handle on a daily basis up to 50,000 letters from adherents, until the demise of the organization shortly after the death of its founder in 1948.[28] Robinson's religious entrepreneurialism sustained a networked community that demonstrated the potential of savvy marketing in popular media, a lesson not lost on other religious and political communities operating in the area. In the early 1970s, conservative Catholics congregated in northern Idaho in communities that evidenced frustration with the reforms of Vatican II, forming congregations including the Tridentine Latin Rite Church that was established in Coeur d'Alene and later moved into Spokane, Washington.[29] The region has also sustained smaller communities. The Exclusive Brethren Bible readings that Garrison Keillor recalled in *Lake Wobegon Days* (1985) were held in Sandpoint.[30] And it was in the same town that Michael Travesser gathered the members of his controversial Lord Our Righteousness Church, which migrated in 2000 to New Mexico, when it became embroiled in accusations of sexual exploitation, and was the subject of some very critical journalism.[31]

In the same period, in southern Oregon, a number of survivalist communities emerged, many of them with a distinctive religious complexion. Mel Tappan published *Survival Guns* (1976), wrote articles for *Soldier of Fortune* and *Guns and Ammo*, and edited his personal survival newsletter while living in Rogue River. In the late 1970s, Larry and Peg Letterman developed over 200 plots for survivalist homesteads in Ponderosa Village, none of which rivaled for sophistication the underground complex of 240 condominium units developed as the Terrene Ark, near La Verkin, in southwest Utah, in 1981.[32] The most visible of these alternative communities, and perhaps the most controversial, was the Rajneeshpuram community that flourished in Wasco County, Oregon, in the 1980s. This controversial new religious movement, which was known for its members' famous orange jumpsuits as well as its financial reach, met its demise amidst allegations of bioterrorism.[33] Religious migrants have been moving in and out of Idaho for 200 years—and some of their visions have been aggressive.

This aggression has been most obvious in the explicitly racist organizations that, over the last fifty years, have enabled the "consolidation" of the White Power movement in the Pacific Northwest.[34] In the mid-1970s, the followers of Richard Butler, a leader of the Church of Jesus Christ, Christian, and an immigrant from California, gathered at his compound on Hayden Lake, Idaho, to participate in conferences that become notorious as meetings of the Aryan Nations, and the epicenter of racist activity that escalated from unwelcome graffiti to terrorist atrocities in Coeur d'Alene and Boise.[35] Many of these advocates of racial separatism argued for the creation of a white homeland in Washington, Oregon, Idaho, Montana, and Wyoming, and pushed for migration into the territory that would later be described as the American Redoubt. "All we heretics ask for, is the Northwestern part of the USA," one of Butler's newsletters put it. "The enclave of the Aryan Nations in Idaho should be expanded to include the sparsely populated states of Washington, Oregon, Idaho, Montana and Wyoming."[36] As might be expected, the "Northwest imperative" his publicity encouraged had some violent consequences in the region.[37] In August and September 1986, five bombs were planted in Coeur d'Alene: within weeks a spy within Butler's compound had provided the information that led to arrests and prosecutions, for the Aryan Nations compound was riddled with informants, including agents of the FBI and the Bureau of Alcohol, Tobacco and Firearms, Idaho State troopers, and multiple undercover journalists.[38] Several academics were also attending the racist rallies: Raphael S. Ezekiel, who interviewed Butler while making no effort to conceal his scholarly intentions, found the Hayden Lake rallies among the "most dramatic" demonstrations of *The Racist Mind* (1995), while James Mitchel, who attended the rallies in disguise, found the Aryans to be absurd, boring, and bored, and described participants "strutting earnestly about as if wanting to look like what they cannot ever possibly be: warriors, leaders, legends, participants in a great cause."[39] Nevertheless, the investigation against white supremacist criminality was fatal for Butler's group: Aryan Nations members dispersed, Butler moved to Sandpoint, and the Hayden Lake compound was bulldozed in 2001.[40] But, in the region, its legacy is widely remembered.

This history of racist communalism has provided a context for more recent attempts at religious survival and resistance. One local resident who was briefly drawn into the Hayden Lake community was Randy Weaver, a Special Forces veteran who moved his family to the Idaho Panhandle as a consequence of his fears that America was about to face the judgment of God in a cataclysmic race war. Weaver socialized with members of the Aryan Nations compound, and was identified by government agents as a potential informant within the group. When he refused to provide intelligence on the community, Weaver became the victim of entrapment, and the subject of aggressive and illegal action from the government agents, which led to the siege in August 1992 that cost the lives of his son Sammy, his wife Vicki, and Deputy U.S. Marshal William Francis Degan.[41] The modern militia movement was in some senses born at Ruby Ridge, as gun-rights advocates, skinheads, patriots, and Christian conservatives joined in a well-publicized protest at the hostile action by government agents that a court case later identified as illegal over-reach.

The siege at Ruby Ridge was concluded through the intervention of Bo Gritz, the presidential candidate of the Populist Party, who negotiated the surrender by gaining Randy Weaver's trust: the men shared a background in Special Forces, and a conspiratorial and apocalyptic worldview that called for relocation to the Pacific Northwest. Shortly after the conclusion of the siege, Gritz established his own end-times survivalist community, purchasing 200 acres near Kamiah, Idaho, which he subdivided and sold for homesteads to "interested patriots."[42] The community was preparing for the worst. Gritz imagined his "covenant community" in apocalyptic terms:

> I observed a pouring out of virtuous people from the metropolitan centers into the hinterlands. I beheld covenant communities standing separate from a tyrannical government. . . . It was Armageddon. Millions of massed soldiers—both men and women—were slaughtered, but the homeland was spared.[43]

Despite the bombastic rhetoric and survivalist instincts, Gritz's aspirations were utopian. This community, which he advertised as "Almost Heaven," boasted a "multiracial social base, and a vigorous commitment to eco-systems such as solar power and organic building materials such as hay and wood."[44] Nevertheless, Gritz was satirized by the documentary maker Louis Theroux, and eventually left the community, which continues to the present day. But his project, and the publicity it attracted, may have encouraged the formation of more ambitious attempts at intentional relocation into the Pacific Northwest.

The migration of evangelicals into Idaho gathered pace after the "twi-light of the American Enlightenment," in the 1950s and 1960s.[45] The number of migrants increased in the 1970s, inspired by what Michael Barkun has identified as that decade's "disaster obsessions," when "large numbers of people" became convinced that they lived in "an insecure world on the verge of cataclysmic events."[46] This was particularly the case among born-again Protestants: "the civil rights movement, Vietnam, the Cold War, and the . . . oil crisis inspired visions of disaster and doom among a new crop of evangelical writers," and their warnings and prognostications "provided a populist, grassroots challenge to the increasingly staid evangelicalism of the second half of the twentieth century."[47] The best-known example of this genre of prophetic literature was Hal Lindsey's *The Late Great Planet Earth* (1970), a popular exposition of prophetic beliefs that provided an explanatory narrative for these "disaster obsessions" in its 28 million copies sold by 1990.[48] These evangelical publications appeared alongside another literature of despair prepared by activists, academics, and public intellectuals, including Barry Commoner's *The Closing Circle* (1971), Donella H. Meadows et al.'s *The Limits to Growth* (1972), Robert Heilbroner's *An Inquiry into the Human Prospect* (1974), and Howard Ruff's *How to Prosper during the Coming Bad Years* (1979), which "prophesied imminent calamity, and possibly the extinction of all human life" by means including "nuclear war, environmental pollution, overpopulation, and energy shortages." In these and other titles, Barkun argues, Americans were "saturated in doom-laden visions, the future seen under the aspect of disaster."[49]

Over the last forty years, these migrants have consolidated Idaho's religious culture, which is now distinctive within the Pacific Northwest, though little understood.[50] Gill has complained that researchers "base generalizations about Idaho's religious character on that of its neighbors," the "none states" of Oregon and Washington, with their famously high percentages of irreligious inhabitants. But the differences between Oregon, Washington, and Idaho are now striking. Only 36.7 percent of the inhabitants of Oregon and Washington report a religious affiliation, against 50 percent of the inhabitants of Idaho.[51] Those who have participated in this migration, many of them from California, have driven "a political realignment" in Idaho, making it "one of the nation's most conservative [states]," propelling it to "the forefront of America's culture wars" and, as conservative politics have gained ground within the state, contributing to what scholars have described as the "southernization" of its politics.[52] In 2006, for example, Steven Thayne, a father of eight homeschooled children, ran for office as a State Representative, and worked to restore 1950s-style family values to the state, sometimes in controversial circumstances.[53] (In 2019, Matthew Shea gained notoriety when, as an elected official in eastern Washington, he was investigated by the FBI for his statements in favor of replacing constitutional government with a theocracy.[54]) And the migration continues. One of the larger beneficiary congregations now publishes carefully considered guidance for those among the "discontented of Judah" who wish to relocate to the region.[55] The leaders of this influential congregation warn migrants not to take at face value the area's representation in the media—or by other migrants. For, despite the impact of evangelical political culture, there are disappointments in Moscow and other utopias.

III

The most ambitious and influential movement in this long history of religious migration into the Pacific Northwest is gathering pace. Its roots are also in the "disaster obsessions" that marked the "twilight of the American Enlightenment." In the 1960s, a small group of Californian evangelicals began to make practical preparations for an expected crisis in American society, while considering how that society should be renewed or, sometimes, replaced. Political and religious readings of the problem and its solution became mutually reinforcing. These believers began to develop a new theological movement, centered around its leading theorist. R. J. Rushdoony (1916–2001) was the son of immigrants fleeing the genocide that had destroyed the ancient Christian culture of Armenia.[56] After his studies in UC Berkeley (BA 1938, MA 1940), and theological studies at the Pacific School of Religion (BD 1944), Rushdoony entered the Presbyterian ministry, determined that the fate that had fallen upon the Armenian church should not fall upon American evangelicals. His first role was to serve as missionary on the Duck Valley Indian Reservation, which straddled Nevada and Idaho. His earliest writing, including a 1949 article in the *Westminster Theological Journal*, reflected upon the lessons he learned from his work among the Indians.[57] In the 1950s, he was drawn into the emerging evangelical renaissance, and wrote occasionally for *Christianity Today*, but also began to develop a social theory and sense of eschatological optimism that were deeply at odds with contemporary evangelical norms and that would make him "one of the most controversial ministers of the twentieth century" as well as "one of the most frequently cited intellectuals of the American right wing."[58] In the 1960s, his emerging program was identified with Cold War cultural warriors, and his writing took on an urgent, often apocalyptic, tone as it looked for a critical distance from the American conservatism that it also wanted to protect. "Always predisposed to accept the contemporary mythologies," he feared, the American church had become a "particularly devout exponent of and adherent to the myth of the age. Only occasionally do pockets of resistance appear."[59]

In an effort to establish a "pocket of resistance," Rushdoony founded the Chalcedon Foundation in 1965, a bootstrap think tank that in the 1970s and 1980s became one of the most influential sources of conservative opinion, and a key if almost always unacknowledged part of the infrastructure of the Religious Right.[60] Chalcedon existed to promote his alternative to the revivalism of the evangelicals, and the philosophical analysis of the Reformed. Rushdoony wanted to push for survival as well as reconstruction. In the mid-1960s, he set up a rural retreat near San Luis Obispo, California, and encouraged like-minded supporters to invest in it, but the project failed before any of the participants had relocated to the site.[61] Significantly, Rushdoony's commitment to survivalism came before his delineation of a program for Christian Reconstruction. And he supported his survivalist plans in print. *Preparation for the Future* (1966) considered widespread fears on the right that the United States would be taken over by communists, and insisted that, "in some form, an economic collapse is certain; the only question is, in what form?"[62] The pamphlet advised readers to invest in tangible assets, especially silver and gold, as well as in developing skills such as gardening and car mechanics.[63] "What a man wants in the way of skills and implements in a time of crisis, he had better have now. They will not be obtainable then."[64] And Rushdoony's advice focused upon location. The social changes of the 1960s were pushing conservatives out of major urban centers, he believed. "Federal legislation to limit the right of sale of private property, in the name of 'fair housing,' is likely to do further harm to property values," he insisted, even as he imagined that cities would come to suffer "increasing racial and leftist revolutionary violence . . . arson, sniping, terrorism, and the destruction of lines of communication will be practiced. Eight major dams provide most of America's electricity: these will be targets of action. Gasoline will be poured into the sewer systems and ignited to burn out a city's communication lines."[65] It was time for those who wished to survive the impending catastrophe to remove themselves from urban centers, to purchase a small amount of agricultural land and to live in proximity to it.[66] Working the land, those who intended to survive the impending crisis would enjoy "good health, which rests on exercise, good foods, and a sound spiritual condition." Rushdoony's message was ultimately religious: "it is those who have a faith, and a hope for the future, in time and eternity, who survive."[67] Michael J. McVicar notes that Rushdoony's newsletters in the later 1960s "read like dispatches from some post-apocalyptic dystopian future—riots; mass killings; government-sponsored torture; food shortages; scientific planners run amok."[68] Rushdoony was certainly pessimistic about the political and cultural short term. Nevertheless, trusting in God's sovereignty, and his blessing of the obedient, Rushdoony advised his readers to prepare "not for survival but for victory."[69]

In the early 1970s, Rushdoony articulated these ideas deliberately to counter the sensationalist pessimism of *The Late Great Planet Earth*, even as he was briefly associated with Hal Lindsey, and a regular, if unlikely, speaker at his Los Angeles "Jesus People" mission house, as we will later see. Rushdoony's program for Christian Reconstruction drew on themes that resonated within the Reformed tradition, arguing that properly organized societies should be governed by the laws of the Ten Commandments, and advancing the postmillennial eschatology that sustained the expectation that this kind of Christian society would one day encompass the globe. Rushdoony's theology was in many respects antithetical to that of Lindsey, although if it did not capture the imagination of evangelicals as effectively as *The Late Great Planet Earth*, it may have exercised comparable political influence: Rushdoony's theology shaped the ideals of the Religious Right (and not just because the hugely influential evangelical culture warrior Francis Schaeffer may have extensively borrowed ideas that had been developed by Rushdoony and other Reconstructionists).[70] This is one reason why Christian Reconstruction has become such a source of controversy, both within and outside evangelicalism. While most historians of modern evangelicalism offer brief but sober observations of Rushdoony's influence, popular warnings against the Religious Right offer shrill warnings that its advocates may be fomenting a coup, forgetting that Rushdoony was entirely opposed to a top-down restructuring of secular society, any idea of revolution, and, necessarily, any attempt to use his ideas to justify violence. America would not be changed through politics, he argued, but through transformed individuals, and as these transformed individuals impacted families, towns, and eventually counties. Rushdoony's work was never quietist, but neither did it affirm the top-down political strategies of the leaders of religious conservatism by whom it was quietly and selectively co-opted. As his biographer notes, Rushdoony was "one of the most frequently cited intellectuals of the American right," yet his work and the movement it inspired "remain understudied and fundamentally underappreciated in the religious, political, and cultural history of the twentieth century."[71] It was certainly "underappreciated" within the denominations in which he held ministerial credentials: the mainstream Presbyterian Church (USA) in which he began his career provided a very cold house for his ideas, but the Orthodox Presbyterian Church into which he moved in 1958 was also largely resistant to his arguments.[72] The influence of Christian Reconstruction would be most obvious outside the existing denominational networks—more evident, perhaps, in the world of politics than in the world of religion, and most evident, perhaps, in the Pacific Northwest. All that it needed was a suitable moment of crisis.

That moment seemed to come in the late 1990s. After the failed attempt to impeach President Bill Clinton, and as technological disaster loomed in the so-called millennium bug, Gary North, Rushdoony's son-in-law, identified the area around Moscow, Idaho, as a secure location in which to plan for survival. One of the most prominent advocates for Y2K preparedness, North had long expected the catastrophic disruption of modern society and saw in the crisis a very viable possibility of its occurrence.[73] Since the mid-1980s, he had been suggesting that the turn into the twenty-first century would be marked by a significant eschatological step-change, and perhaps even the beginning of the biblical millennium.[74] In the run-up to the expected crisis, North advocated for paramilitary-style survivalism with such force that it divided the Christian Reconstruction movement.[75] At the end of the 1990s, he operated a website that warned readers of the dangers of the "millennium bug," and his strategies for survival also included migration to the Pacific Northwest.[76] Among those who followed North's advice to move into the region was James Wesley Rawles, a former military intelligence officer whose published work would do most to popularize the idea of skills acquisition, arms procurement, and religious migration to the area that he would describe as the "American Redoubt."[77]

IV

Twenty years later, this migration continues. The recent migrants fit few stereotypes, and evidence an "anti-establishment, separatist, or agrarian off-the-grid . . . that overlaps with back-to-the-land hippie counterculture."[78] Their motivations or aspirations are not always clear. In fieldwork among recent arrivals, I heard many different kinds of stories. Migrants came alone, in families, in groups, which they sometimes described as "clans," or as entire congregations. They came from California, the Midwest, New England, from the Caribbean, and from several parts of Europe. They were black and white, advocates of racial segregation, members of mixed-race families and churches, and—to my surprise—segregationists who found fellowship in mixed-race congregations. Evangelical, Catholic, and Orthodox Christians worked alongside people of no fixed religious affiliation. They were encouraged to relocate by reading homesteading websites, militia websites, theological textbooks, and by consuming alternative news sources like "Radio Free Redoubt." Some had been guided in their planning by advice from the leaders of a church, listed as being friendly to preppers in a list of Reformed and Messianic congregations hosted on survivalblog.com. Some wanted to live visibly in communities, building businesses on Main Street, while others preferred isolation, pursuing the ideals of a new agrarianism. Some were comfortably ensconced in traditional housing in attractive towns, others were collecting their own energy in expensive off-grid developments, or working, hand-to-mouth, in isolated homesteads, while others were planning for collective defense in a community of hundreds that would come to be known as "the Citadel."[79] Some had purchased defensible off-grid property through businesses with names like "American Redoubt Realty" or "Survival Realty," preparing to respond to violence, while others were expecting to live in peace. Some were building weapons and others foreswore their use. Some were theocrats, others were libertarians, and a very small number self-identified as anarchists. Some wanted to escape from moral relativism of recent social policy, while others were content to live beside anyone, gay or straight, who would leave them alone. Some were hostile to technology, while others were using it to build social media empires. Some were suspicious of researchers, and failed to respond to contact of any kind, while others were very willing to talk, preferring to be interviewed by email or telephone, and some welcomed me into their homes or places of employment, and initiated further contact after the fieldwork had concluded. Almost all of my informants were deeply concerned about gender roles, but, among their number, some men were working for the renewal of family life, while some women had established prominent positions in militia communities. These migrants were members of overlapping communities, and did not subscribe to an agreed arrangement of religious, political, or activist doctrines. They did not often know about each other, or have an awareness of how others within the Redoubt may have conceived of them. Some wished to connect with existing communities, or to keep themselves at a critical distance from them. Some wished to build a family or a congregation, while others wished to build a fortress. Some were preparing for tribulation while others were pursuing the millennium. All of them wanted to resist, and almost all of them expected to survive.

As this variety suggests, there is much more to this migration than a concern to consolidate a "backwoods nationalism" by means of constructing a "backwoods utopia."[80] Very few of the migrants would subscribe to the "bucolic" fascism that Christopher Hitchens discovered in the American South.[81] Instead, their concern is to escape, resist, and ultimately survive an impending crisis in American politics and society. For some, that survival will be made possible by their withdrawal from blue states and urban centers to stockpile heirloom seeds and literary classics. For others, that survival will be made possible by their fighting for constitutional rights—if necessary, by bearing arms. But even here there are important differences. Most migrants expect to survive the crisis, in order to rebuild a better—either a godlier or more libertarian—culture. But some of those most prominent in the militia cultures of the Redoubt expected to resist the crisis while privately admitting that they had no real expectation of surviving it.

While it would be misleading to think of the migrants as representing a monolithic community, they do share sufficient common features to warrant their being regarded as a category.[82] My interviewees shared what Richard T. Hofstadter rather unfairly dismissed as a "paranoid style," a conviction that American society is declining at a precipitous rate, and that they will find their best chance of surviving and resisting within the Pacific Northwest.[83] This performance of anxiety returns to several themes. Each of the groups we encountered narrated their concerns within an eschatological register, in discourse that represented something more than a fundamentalist "love affair with the last days."[84] Even those who anticipated the long-term triumph of Christian civilization expected to endure a generational reversal of their hopes. Their explanatory narratives often built upon the politics of suspicion that has come to divide Americans since the turn to conspiracy theory in popular culture during the 1990s.[85] These narratives were also regularly anti-urban. For many of our interviewees, the flight to Idaho was a flight from the culture of cities: the Redoubt is sustained by the ambivalence about the city that runs deep within conservative religion and some versions of libertarian politics.[86] For some of the critics of this movement, this hostility to the city is necessarily racist, but this claim must be balanced against the rhetoric's reinscription of the ideals of the "new pioneers" of the 1960s, as well as the mixed-race background of the migrants themselves, and it is not clear that the participants in the Redoubt understand these references as racist dog-whistling; while thought leaders like Douglas Wilson and James Wesley Rawles regularly denounce any hint of segregationist politics, the racism that exists in the Redoubt is often explicit.[87] These migrants share a commitment to action—whether advanced on libertarian principles or, more often, those of biblical law—and aspire to survive, resist, and rebuild American modernity. Their ideas are provincial, their goals are national, but their reach is often global.[88]

This description suggests that these migrants live in a constant state of readiness, as if their eschatological expectations defined every aspect of their lives. Of course, I did not find that to be the case. For all of their commitment to agendas of survival and resistance, the migrants I encountered also live very normal lives. They hold down jobs, raise families, go shopping, and, often, are happy to consume the products of mass culture. There could be jarring differences between the quotidian and the ideal, or commitments to routine that suggested that normalcy trumped any heightened sense of crisis.

These differences—and others like them—continue to be important. There are serious disagreements among rival groups of migrants, which are often documented online, and direct threats are not uncommon, especially on the blogs connected to militia culture. There are differences between the recent wave of migrants and earlier waves: some migrants to the Redoubt come with an appreciation of existing communities even as they adopt a critical distance from them. For life imitates art: when Joshua Kim and Megan La Croix, the protagonists of Rawles's novel *Liberators*, reach Moscow, they integrate with a congregation that does already exist, the Reformed congregation that is led in reality by Douglas Wilson.[89] Whatever their intentions, aspirations, or expectations, however they arrived, and despite the tensions that their arrival may create, the migrants' attempt to resist and survive the corrosion of American modernity ends in Moscow and other utopias in the American Redoubt.

V

This book provides the first full-length description and analysis of the cultures of survival, resistance, and reconstruction that are emerging in evangelical America. While the importance of evangelical prophetic belief has been clearly signaled in popular culture and media, writing from within the academy has been slow to address the significance of the range of its possible ethical or lifestyle implications, so that journalists have been quicker than scholars to pick up on the significance of this cultural turn. This omission in scholarly description and analysis continues despite growing interest in fundamentalism as a global phenomenon, especially in the aftermath of 9/11, and despite growing awareness of the influence in American politics of born-again Protestants. The subjects of the book are among those that still suffer in scholarly discussions by being what Susan Harding has described as a "repugnant cultural other."[90] While a number of accounts of the growth of the Religious Right have been published, authors have overwhelmingly focused on evangelical aspirations to control wider society, rather than their aspiration to withdraw in the expectation of rebuilding it. This book will address these themes within its wider consideration of the significance of differing and sometimes competing patterns of cultural withdrawal and reconstruction in evangelical America, focusing on those individuals, groups, and institutions that are working to promote cultural withdrawal, while hoping for a faith-driven social and cultural renaissance, which they expect to lead. The chapters of this book describe how my subjects' plans for survival and resistance have been developed, articulated, and disseminated, and consider what might be the likely consequences of their work.

In this extraordinarily beautiful region of the Pacific Northwest, Moscow—a city once known as "Paradise"—is not an unlikely utopia. The region is idyllic: Marilynne Robinson, in her fictional memoir of her childhood in the northern part of the state, observed "how nearly the state of grace resembled the state of Idaho."[91] Many of those who have migrated to the area in which Robinson grew up have hoped to discover it to be a "state of grace." But they have discovered that the Redoubt is also a state of conflict. To move into the Redoubt is to move into a world that retains something of the enchantment of early modern Reformed theology, where Calvinist resistance theory retains its political urgency, but also to move into a world in which, at least in Rawles's fiction, every problem has a technical solution. As his preparedness manuals suggest, the migration movement is a flight from modernity that is made possible by modernity's tools. And as a product of modernity, the migration also witnesses to the clash between the conceptual worlds of contemporary Americans. The efforts to reform society by the application of divine law is voluntarist and libertarian until it achieves a substantial electoral mandate—for, as even some of its libertarian advocates admit, the program to turn American citizens into citizens of the kingdom of heaven must at some tipping point become a program of "coercive re-enchantment."[92] But the widespread appeal of this kind of thinking is evidence that some of the new Redoubt communities represent something that is both residual to American history and threatening to assumptions about the linearity of that history and the character of the modernity that many, perhaps most, Americans take for granted. The communities described in this book offer an alternative modernity, which reinscribes the habits and assumptions of an earlier age, to craft a culture that must, by the logic of postmillennial eschatology, inevitably replace it.

So perhaps it is not insignificant that Joshua Kim and Megan La Croix should find their way to Moscow, or that they should seek refuge in Douglas Wilson's Christ Church, the most successful congregation in the Redoubt. For, as this book suggests, those who are writing resistance can help us understand the hopes, fears, and achievements of those believers who are thinking about survival, resistance, and reconstruction in evangelical America.

2

Eschatology

Everyone talks about eschatology, but almost nobody studies it very thoroughly.[1]

On a hot summer afternoon, in a popular coffee shop in an attractive north Idaho resort town, we met two smart and articulate thirty-something men. Fashionably presented, and with an impressive range of reference in cultural and critical theory, these men were members of a small but deeply committed community of Reformed Protestants that balanced their need for publicity with an acute fear of what that publicity might bring. The men and their families had "fled" from California, as they put it, as the state was being swamped by illegal immigrants and the progressive politics of the left.[2] In the late 1990s, they had found a home in a congregation of Christian Reconstructionists in Spokane, Washington, but they had since moved to establish a new fellowship in the Idaho Panhandle. This move had allowed these men, with their wives and children, to realize a simpler life—to move from urban locations and technology-enabled careers into small towns and employment in traditional arts and crafts, a decision that had occasioned significant financial challenges. The men wanted to understand our motives in approaching them, and our first attempt to make contact, through the congregation's website, had failed. The men explained that they were wary of approaches from strangers, believing that they had been the subjects of government surveillance. It was not difficult to imagine why government agents might want to know about this group: they met for worship in a remote location in the woodlands; they followed a religious teacher who was accused of Holocaust denial and who argued against "racial inter-breeding . . . with inferior stock"; and they attended public events on the theme of resistance to government.[3] Their paranoia made them look suspicious: some of this activity was uncomfortably similar to that of the neo-Nazi groups that had been established around Hayden Lake two decades previously.[4] But, while

Survival and Resistance in Evangelical America. Crawford Gribben, Oxford University Press (2021). © Oxford University Press. DOI: 10.1093/oso/9780199370221.003.0003

talking quite candidly about race, politics, and demographic change, these men took pains to dissociate themselves from the religion, politics, and expectations of the racist far-right. Their concern was to survive the onslaught of American modernity, in the hope, if not quite in the expectation, of seeing its reconstruction.

The small congregation of which these men were part was organized around a distinctive set of ideas. They were, they believed, R. J. Rushdoony's most authentic disciples. They preferred his earlier work, which commented on racial difference, disapproved of the struggle for African-American civil rights, permitted "racial and cultural discrimination of various sorts," and generated some hasty accusations of Holocaust denial, to the ambiguity of his later work. In making this distinction, they may have overlooked the fact that Rushdoony presided over a mixed-race family—he was, after all, an ethnic Armenian with an Anglo-American wife and an adopted Native American son—as well as his occasional condemnations of racist prejudice.[5] But they were right to observe that the later Rushdoony was more ambiguous, officiating at a mixed-race wedding, and commending the African-American minister Rev. E. V. Hill, alongside whom he would later serve on the Council for National Policy, as "one of the great pastors of America" whose "work of Christian reconstruction is one of the more exciting stories of our time."[6] Carefully selecting their sources within the literature of Christian Reconstruction, these men were "kinists," theorists of racial difference and advocates of a particular variety of religious ethno-nationalism that argues for the Christian duty to prefer the members of one's family and, by extension, one's *ethnos*. Rushdoony, they insisted, had been a kinist before his time, despite what they believed to be his gerontological wobbles.[7] The kinists did not believe in racial supremacy, unlike the Hayden Lake skinheads. Instead, they claimed, the gospel would redeem races as it preserved their differences, and Christians should sustain these differences in racially homogeneous families, congregations, and in distinctive social and perhaps even national spheres.

Racial theory was only one part of this congregation's critique of American modernity, and, as the conversation continued, the men grew more expansive in their concern about the direction of American culture. They had moved from southern California, to eastern Washington, and then to northern Idaho to escape the challenges posed by what they identified as the pervasive influence on the West Coast of the cultural theory of the Frankfurt School, which had destroyed the American norms and made evangelicalism a "lazy thing." In the Pacific Northwest, however, they were discovering that modernity could not so easily be escaped. Gay pride marches were now being held in Spokane, they lamented, and Somali immigrants could be seen on the streets of Coeur d'Alene. The men had fled from western cities but could not escape the influence of cultural Marxism as the conditions of American modernity pushed further into the Redoubt.

Yet, for all of their negativity, the men insisted that they were hopeful. Following Rushdoony, they expected the influence of Reformed Protestantism to revive throughout America and to sweep across the globe, with, they added, a new emphasis on the preservation of one's *ethnos* coming in its train. But they found it hard to balance hope against dismay. One of the men admitted that he "envied" dispensational premillennialists, who, at least, had the satisfaction of seeing their expectations of cultural decline be realized. The kinists' reading of eclectic sources supported an often sophisticated account of American enervation, which called for radical actions, which they were prepared to make. The men found guidance on Rawles's survivalblog.com, and drew from Douglas Wilson's publications, despite both authors' denunciation of this brand of racial politics. The lived reality of these interviewees was of course more complex—one of the men, I later discovered, also attended a mixed-race congregation in the town—but, like many other migrants to the Pacific Northwest, lamenting the decline and fall of Christendom, these kinists were considering "how to survive the end of the world as we know it," planning for survival and resistance at the "end of white, Christian America," in the hope that the religious and cultural conditions of the Old South would eventually rise again.

My conversations with the kinists illustrated a broader pattern in the recent migration to the Pacific Northwest. American evangelical strategies of survival and resistance are driven by expectations of both failure and success—expectations that many believers, like the kinists, struggle to hold in balance. The declinism at the center of much of this discussion, as my interviewees noted, is a ubiquitous theme in evangelical culture, and so, in the eyes of many observers, its participants are driven by fear, by the eclipse of traditional religious nationalism in a moment of destabilizing demographic and political change, conditions that make new brands of ethnonationalism attractive for many believers. But it is not their apprehensions about the American future that makes these migrants distinctive. Instead, they may be distinguished from other born-again Protestants by their several varieties of hope. It is hope that makes their movement, and the wider migration to the Pacific Northwest, so controversial—because eschatology, insofar as it imagines a better world, is necessarily involved in critique of the present, and is therefore fundamental to the project of survival, resistance, and reconstruction. Recognizing that dispensational premillennialism continues to dominate American evangelical rhetoric and institutions, this chapter will describe the reification and recasting of evangelical eschatological narratives in the 1970s. Tracing the emergence, evolution, and effect of a new and radically political postmillennialism, which now circulates widely in north Idaho, this chapter will consider the formulation of the new eschatological style that characterizes the social engagement and political disengagement of a growing number of American evangelicals, explaining their aspiration to survive and resist an impending crisis in society and culture, and to build community in the Pacific Northwest in order to rescue the world beyond. This chapter describes the varieties of hope that sustain strategies of survival and resistance in evangelical America.

I

American evangelicals have long balanced fears for the decline of the "city of man" against expectations for the advance of the "city of God." This tension has not often been analyzed, either in the literature produced by born-again Protestants or in scholarly writing about them. But, throughout the history of the evangelical movement, these themes of failure and success have been unexpected fellow travelers.

American Protestants have always been interested in biblical prophecy. Since colonial times, the "doomsday theme has never been far from the center of American religious thought," which center has been a "fundamentalist evangelicalism with powerful millenarian strands."[8] This was evident in John Winthrop's description of a "city on a hill" (1630) as much as in Michael Wigglesworth's best-selling prophetic poem, *The Day of Doom: or, A Poetical Description of the Great and Last Judgment* (1662), and informed the jeremiads of the later seventeenth century as much as the euphoric accounts of revival in the mid-eighteenth century. Jonathan Edwards was not alone in believing that the Great Awakening (1735–43) signaled that the millennium was beginning on American soil. The eschatological narratives that competed for the attention of early New Englanders were standardized in the aftermath of this revival to consolidate around a structure that later theologians would identify as "postmillennialism." This reading of Scripture argued that revivals of religion would continue until Protestant Christianity had expanded around the world, with other end-times indicators including the destruction of Roman Catholic and Islamic powers, the conversion of the Jews and, sometimes, their restoration to the promised land, together with the final defeat of the Antichrist. This optimistic futurology did not promote passivity as to the accomplishment of these events. Instead, believers were actively to participate in evangelism and social reform in the confident expectation that God would use their labor to extend his kingdom.[9]

There were varieties within this paradigm. In the late eighteenth and nineteenth centuries, postmillennial ideas circulated on both sides of the Atlantic, and became a key marker of the confidence of the evangelical movement, even as these ideas began to evolve. Edwards's eschatological optimism, for example, was critical of that of his predecessors, and did not tend to apply divine law to social or political questions.[10] This new optimism was confirmed at the end of the eighteenth century, as American evangelicals embarked on an ambitious attempt to sacralize their newly independent republic, creating the "civil religion" that would embed evangelical language, if not the theology to which it referred, as elemental to the expression of American national identity.[11] This confidence in the future of American religion—and the "redeemer nation" that it described—was shattered during the Civil War. The struggle that cost more lives than all other American conflicts combined provided for the abolition of slavery at the same time as it destroyed expectations of the inevitable successes of the cultures that campaigned either for or against the "peculiar institution." The American Protestant mainstream was divided by the political issues at the center of Civil War polemic.[12] Darwinian ideas of natural selection challenged traditional readings of Genesis, even as advanced text critics, who were growing in influence within conservative denominations, questioned the integrity of biblical narratives. Liberals advanced their hopes for a social gospel, while conservatives grew pessimistic as to the impact of faith on the broader culture. Northern Protestants developed new kinds of eschatology to explain their new situation, emphasizing themes of decline, and these ideas took root south of the Mason-Dixon line, powerfully shaping the articulation of popular Protestantism.[13] In a series of prophetic conferences and publications, born-again leaders promoted their platform of essential doctrines, in an "invention of tradition" that exchanged the "form of sound words" (2 Timothy 1:13) recorded in ancient ecumenical creeds and reformation confessions and catechisms for a sequence of slogans that was advertised as expressing what was fundamental to the Christian faith.[14] These key doctrines were given classic expression in the pamphlet series that lent the new movement its name. A ten-volume set of *The Fundamentals* (1910–15) was provided by two wealthy businessmen to every minister, seminary professor, and Sunday School teacher that they could identify within the English-speaking world.[15] Early leaders of the fundamentalist movement advanced far beyond the reticence of these pamphlets, following the arguments of the other central text of the new movement, *The Scofield Reference Bible* (1909; second edition, 1917), that Christendom was in irreversible decline, that Christians would become increasingly marginalized within American culture, and that their hope was in an evacuation to heaven by means of the "rapture."[16] The publicity surrounding the Scopes trial (1925) confirmed how marginal were believers in the brash vitality of the "roaring twenties." The expectation of eschatological decline that was now widely shared by evangelicals was invoked to explain their reversal of fortunes. Postmillennial ideas had made sense of the world as the influence of evangelicals continued to expand, but premillennial ideas explained why their situation had been so suddenly and, apparently, irretrievably reversed. Evangelical preachers and writers made the case for premillennialism as they withdrew from public view to build the institutions and organizations that would help them survive in a hostile world.[17] By mid-century, these believers had found in Billy Graham and other media-friendly evangelists their representatives of choice. Graham's preaching invoked prophetic doom-saying, even as its upbeat style facilitated the production of media designed to appeal to the unchurched of the new youth culture. The strategy of mass communication simplified the outlines of dispensational prophecy—and much else besides—as the message was shaped by its medium. The rapture was described in popular forms as the target audience of the mediatized evangelists expanded to include the growing counterculture of the 1960s. And the most enduring of these popular formats was an unexpectedly successful book about the end of the world published by a forty-something "Jesus People" evangelist.

In 1970, in Westwood, California, Hal Lindsey opened a communal ministry in an old three-story frat house close to the UCLA campus.[18] The Jesus Christ Light and Power Company was established as a base from which Lindsey could expound the prophetic expectations he outlined in *The Late Great Planet Earth* (1970). This book was a simplified presentation of the dispensational premillennialism that Lindsey had been teaching his students, and it would go on to become the *New York Times* best-selling nonfiction work of the 1970s and an icon of the evangelical movement as it evolved to become a major political force in the 1980s and beyond.[19] *The Late Great Planet Earth* was an immediate sensation, bringing Lindsey the status of an evangelical "superstar."[20] Like a number of other key texts from the period, it presented the world as facing imminent disaster, but it framed its scenarios with detailed references to the Bible. Lindsey argued that the geopolitical crises of the Cold War would develop into a cataclysmic struggle in the Middle East, in which Russia would be "a Gog." The Antichrist would rise from Europe to be identified as the "future Fuehrer." Jesus People wordplay made sense of the rapture as the "ultimate trip."[21] Lindsey tempered his hippie hyperbole by acknowledging that he did not know "exactly when the world is going to end," and admitted that some plans for the future should be made. It was "important, terribly important," to elect "honest, intelligent men to positions of leadership," even though politicians could not "provide the answers to the basic and visceral questions of man."[22] Nevertheless, he continued, the prophetic events described in his book could take place "within forty years or so of 1948.... Many scholars who have studied Bible prophecy all their lives believe that this is so."[23] Politics were of limited importance, for there wasn't much time left for the "late great planet Earth."

Lindsey's book was an urgent and polemical text that was developed in opposition to an alternative set of eschatological ideas with roots that ran deep in American Protestant history. Lindsey developed his arguments in conscious opposition to the arguments of those Christians who still adhered to the older view that the preaching of the gospel would "root out the evil in the world, abolish godless rulers, and convert the world," bringing about the "Kingdom of God on earth." These Christians, he explained to an audience that could hardly make sense of their forebears' optimism, expected that the "institutional church" would reign on earth for one thousand years of "peace, equality, and righteousness," after which "Christ would return and time would end." Lindsey believed that these claims were bogus, and that they could be sustained only if their advocates abandoned the literal interpretation of Scripture. Fortunately, he reassured his readers, this unfounded utopianism had been "virtually wiped out" during the horrific events of World War I, which had destroyed all assumptions about the "inherent goodness of man." Five decades later, he concluded, "no self-respecting scholar who looks at world conditions and the accelerating decline of Christian influence" could be convinced by this naïve and old-fashioned postmillennialism.[24]

In making that claim, Lindsey might not have been paying attention to developments in his own back yard. Precisely at the moment when its more recent alternative was so markedly gaining in popularity, the postmillennial expectation for the success of the gospel in history was being repackaged and presented to new, and influential, audiences. As *The Late Great Planet Earth* began to circulate in the millions, and as Lindsey followed its publication with a sequence of other bestsellers, his house for Christian hippies attracted visitors who did not share his views. In the mid-1970s, the Jesus Christ Light and Power Company provided a forum for the very ideas that Lindsey had argued were extinct—ideas that would become a powerful challenge to his theory of eschatological decline.[25] For Lindsey had invited into his community the theologian who was responsible for a "single-handed revival of 'postmillennialism.'"[26]

II

Lindsey was promoting the theology of *The Late Great Planet Earth* even as his communal house for Christian hippies provided space for the articulation of the eschatological system that would do the most to challenge his ideas. The sixty or seventy students who were associated with the Jesus Christ Light and Power Company house had access to a library containing a broad range of literature, including works by Francis Schaeffer, who was moving to combine his dispensational premillennialism and evangelical Calvinism with an interest in politics that was much stronger than that of Lindsey, and a call for social action that would lead eventually to his arguing for civil disobedience.[27] Lecturers at the house could be similarly eclectic. One of the ministers who spoke at the Jesus Christ Light and Power Company was R. J. Rushdoony, who by the early 1970s had cultivated sufficient links among religious and political conservatives to warrant his reputation as an emerging culture warrior of note.

Rushdoony an activist who was "always aspiring to be the grand theorist."[28] While he addressed different kinds of audiences, and wrote regularly for a farming magazine, his published work could be unexpectedly demanding. His first book, *By What Standard?* (1959), had offered a subtle and discriminating analysis of the philosophy of the Dutch Reformed philosopher Cornelius Van Til.[29] Over the several decades following, Rushdoony applied this densely argued account of Christian epistemology to a wide range of social and political problems. He pushed his readers to recognize that noetic differences existed between those who were Christians and those who were not. Abandoning any notion of intellectual common ground, either for the purpose of religious debate or for agreement on social order, he pressed the antithesis between Christian and non-Christian provisions for knowledge and, consequently, political and social ideals. This vigorously philosophical approach to the defense and confirmation of the faith was entirely different from the almost tabloid populism of *The Late Great Planet Earth*. It inevitably raised questions—if only to ask why Christians should think about the biblical basis of social order if, as many apologetically oriented fundamentalists assumed, it was futile to "polish the brass on a sinking ship." But Rushdoony's solution to this question was also eschatological. He addressed the question explicitly in 1971, in the introduction he supplied for *An Eschatology of Victory*, by J. Marcellus Kik.[30] Rushdoony's introduction directly addressed *The Late Great Planet Earth*, challenging its author's account of the history of postmillennialism.[31] Christians should think about the biblical mandate for social order because, Rushdoony insisted, as the gospel advanced and societies were increasingly reformed, believers would be responsible for implementing it. His writing of resistance was based upon a distinctive new hope.

Rushdoony formalized his eschatological arguments around the same time as the publication of Lindsey's bestseller. His conclusions, presented in *Thy Kingdom Come: Studies in Daniel and Revelation* (1971), did not presuppose the "inherent goodness of man," as Lindsey had (inaccurately) argued had been typical of previous postmillennialists.[32] Instead, Rushdoony promoted the Calvinist doctrine of total depravity, the idea that sin affects every aspect of human personhood, a position that he used to sustain arguments that were deeply critical of American society and institutions, and even of democracy itself, which he described as "the great love of the failures and cowards of life."[33] He considered that the large and visually compelling charts that were increasingly used to teach dispensationalism encouraged Christians to "walk in full and open sight" rather than to "walk by faith."[34] Rushdoony was entirely dismissive of the eschatological piety he considered to be a "masochistic desire for self-atonement by means of suffering," and described the sensationalist premillennialism that was growing to dominate popular evangelical culture as promoting the "sorry tribulation-complex of a smug and self-satisfied church, surrounded by ease and luxury."[35] Dispensationalism was "practical denial of the Christian faith, a revival of the

Phariseeism which crucified Christ, and an offense to the Savior who came, not to establish a Jewish kingdom, but as the Lamb slain from the foundation of the world, come to give His life [as] a ransom for many."[36] The notion that Christians should not "polish brass on a sinking ship" was, he argued, "arrant paganism and radically at odds with Scripture," which always required ethically responsible action, and always criticized apocalyptically justified indolence.[37] Rushdoony's refutation of dispensationalism was swingeing and excoriating. Its advocates had entirely misunderstood the Christian future, he claimed, as well as their own responsibility to contribute to it. Their fascination with the politics of the Middle East was as irrelevant as their pessimism was unfounded. The prophecies of Revelation were "not a promise of defeat," but a "declaration of the sovereignty, lordship, and victory of Christ in history."[38] If the "whole of Scripture proclaims the certainty of God's victory in time and in eternity," then Christians should be working for a "world which has been brought under the discipline of the gospel and evangelized in every area."[39] In time, earthly powers would "collapse," the "saints" would "triumph," and a "Christian society" would be established in "every realm."[40] Rushdoony's program advocated for survival, resistance, and victory.

Rushdoony explained what this "Christian society" would look like in the first volume of his *magnum opus*, *The Institutes of Biblical Law* (1973). Rushdoony had expounded the content of the book "over a period of three years," he explained, "before a large number of groups—students, civil officials, businessmen, housewives, and a great variety of persons."[41] In almost 900 pages, he related each of the Ten Commandments to modern American life, creating an approach to social order that was quickly dubbed "theonomy." The work was never short of controversy, not least in its envisaging the end of the prison system by means including a massive extension of capital punishment, and in asking questions about the number of Jews who became victims of the Nazi regime, questions which have in turn led to not very clearly substantiated claims that Rushdoony was engaged in Holocaust denial, as we have already seen.[42]

In raising questions about the obligations of Old Testament law, or what its impact might be, Rushdoony was not writing into a social or political vacuum. In the same year as the publication of *The Institutes of Biblical Law*, the Supreme Court ruled that the right of women to have an abortion was guaranteed by the constitution. *Roe v. Wade* (1973) sent shockwaves through American evangelical culture, and, more than any other event to date, pushed born-again Protestants to recognize how much the world around them had changed, and to understand that they could no longer assume that their convictions were those of the cultural mainstream. Historians have argued that evangelicals were slow to realize the significance of the Supreme Court decision.[43] There was no collective agreement as to how best to respond. Organizations within the Southern Baptist Convention advocated in favor of liberalizing abortion legislation.[44] Billy Graham cautiously welcomed the *Roe v. Wade* decision.[45] A similar variety of opinion existed among Reformed theologians. John Frame, a conservative Reformed theologian, argued in the run-up to the Supreme Court decision that abortion could in some circumstances be permitted.[46] Rushdoony emphatically disagreed, and knew almost immediately how the challenge to traditional Christian ethics should be managed. "To restore abortion as a legal right is to restore judicial or parental murder," he concluded, insisting that the "penalty for even an accidental abortion is death," and complaining that "innocent victims are killed" while "capital punishment is withheld from their murderers."[47] These arguments were quite different from those of the emerging pro-life mainstream, around which evangelical leaders had slowly begun to gather.[48] Frame's views and Rushdoony's responses were discussed by believers on both sides of the Atlantic, as correspondence between Gary North and Iain H. Murray, a trustee of the British Reformed publisher Banner of Truth, suggests.[49] For in advance of this issue's mobilizing of the Religious Right, Rushdoony's "basic premise," Molly Worthen has explained, was that "life is not sacred." His premise was instead that "all life belongs to God, and only his will is sacred. To believe that life must be preserved at all times—even in violation of God's law—is to make a golden calf out of human life and commit idolatry."[50] This ethical claim made demands on eschatological systems. Much of Rushdoony's frustration with dispensationalism was driven by his perception that adherents of this eschatological system could not provide a reliable defense of biblical ethics as those ethics became subject to unprecedented challenge. He noted with disdain that a faculty member of one of the most prominent dispensational seminaries had published in *Christianity Today*, the flagship evangelical monthly magazine, an argument that abortion was in certain circumstances permitted in Old Testament law.[51] America was changing, but the evangelical movement, dominated by dispensationalism, with its dismissive attitude toward social action, was doing and could do nothing to resist the cultural revolution. And Lindsey, in circumstances that are now impossible to reconstruct, enabled Rushdoony to offer his critique of dispensationalism at the heart of his dispensational empire.[52]

And so, on the early morning of December 10, 1975, Rushdoony turned up at the Jesus Christ Light and Power house to speak for one hour on the subject of "Dominion man vs. disposable man."[53] Famously economical with his outputs, Rushdoony printed the text of his presentations in his ministry newsletter, the *Chalcedon Reports*, in December 1975 and January 1976.[54] From these notes, it appears that his discussion focused on the renunciation of objective meaning in politics and art, and argued that the trend toward subjectivity in modern painting highlighted a drift toward pragmatism in modern politics and the value it attached to human life. "Since Darwin, meaning is dead in the modern world," Rushdoony argued, and "all attempts to cope with the growing collapse of the modern age are futile, because there is nothing in humanism and the doctrine of evolution which makes possible a restoration of cosmic meaning. As a result, man becomes more lawless, anarchistic, and senseless as he accepts the modern world view's picture of himself." Retrieving Van Til's emphasis on Christian epistemology, he insisted that "there is not a meaningless nor a disposable fact in the universe. Everything has meaning, God's meaning, and the direction of all things is neither death nor meaninglessness, but the triumph of God's glorious plan and purpose."[55] Therefore, he concluded,

as the old pagan forms of humanism erode, the only possible form of civilization and culture is increasingly manifest: it can only be a Christian culture, one firmly rooted in the whole counsel of God and His law-word. If you are not working to reconstruct all things in terms of the word of God, you are headed for the graveyard of history and God's judgment.[56]

Consequently, he told the students, the Christian's duty was to "know and understand the word of permanence, God's word, and to apply its requirements of change to himself and the world, and to every area and aspect thereof." Rushdoony described this approach as "godly reconstruction."[57] And the outcome of that effort "cannot be in doubt. Dominion Man will prevail over Disposable Man."[58] Rushdoony's references to postmillennialism and theonomy were implicit, at least in the published version of his presentation, but his arguments were clear. Rushdoony was challenging ideas that were central to the ministry of one of the most influential writers among the Jesus People movement—and doing so in the communal home that Lindsey had established.[59] Despite the claims of his host, the author of *The Late Great Planet Earth*, and the decisions of the Supreme Court, Rushdoony insisted,

Christians should be working for victory, mobilizing around the issue of abortion, building resistance in the confident expectation of victory.

This turn toward postmillennialism was picked up in the same period by a number of Reformed authors on both sides of the Atlantic.[60] In the United Kingdom, Iain H. Murray published *The Puritan Hope: Revival and the Interpretation of Prophecy* (1971), which confirmed the historical valence of Rushdoony's postmillennial claims. Murray's book challenged pessimistic assumptions about the future of evangelical religion, and turned to the literature of the Reformed tradition to offer proof that earlier generations of Christians had expected and worked for the extension of the kingdom of God throughout the world. These claims were supported by a cottage industry of writers that developed to reflect upon and defend Christian Reconstruction, as Rushdoony's movement was increasingly being described, and its adherents quickly acquired the accoutrements of academic respectability. Gary North, who became Rushdoony's son-in-law, had grown up as a dispensationalist until attending Westminster Theological Seminary in 1964, where John Murray, a professor of systematic theology whose works the Banner of Truth had published, made persuasive arguments for a postmillennial reading of Romans 9–11 and for the continuity of Old Testament ethics.[61] Working closely with Rushdoony, and ever the entrepreneur, North established *The Journal of Christian Reconstruction* in 1974 to provide the discussion of eschatology and ethics with a solid scholarly base.[62] He admitted, in a 1976 issue on the theme of the millennium, that small numbers had been attracted to the postmillennial platform. But, he continued, "what kind of remnant are we? A permanent remnant, impotent culturally because the 'times' are against us? Or a temporary remnant, whose era is coming?"[63] His confidence was persuasive, and, for a while, with its burgeoning culture of print, the movement may have seemed larger than it was. Trans-Atlantic contacts continued. North published on postmillennial themes in Murray's *Banner of Truth* magazine, a key journal among British Calvinists, and included a review of Murray's historical study in *The Journal of Christian Reconstruction*.[64]

For a time, the British and American movements seemed to draw close to one another: Murray corresponded with North, and noted that he greatly appreciated some of Rushdoony's recent work.[65] But the Americans quickly became critical of the neo-Puritan revival on the other side of the Atlantic, which they believed to be insufficiently engaged in cultural reform. North appreciated the extent to which evangelical publishers had begun to market

Reformed writing from the sixteenth and seventeenth centuries, but was concerned that the British publishers' emphasis on theology and piety overlooked the interest in social and political renewal that their favorite early modern authors had also promoted.[66] "There are those who regard themselves as neo-Puritans who will resent the very idea that many . . . of those who called themselves Puritans in the seventeenth century believed that God's Old Testament law-order should be imposed in New Testament times," he observed.[67] North recognized that the future imagined by postmillennial theologians required the development of a Christian social theory. In this, he thought the Puritans a good model for American evangelicals. "There is no doubt that one's eschatological views will influence one's list of earthly priorities," he noted. "If, as one dispensationalist leader once remarked concerning this pre-rapture world, 'you can't [shouldn't] polish brass on a sinking ship,' then his listeners ought to conclude that passing out simple gospel tracts is of greater importance and urgency than developing a distinctly Christian philosophy, economics, or chemistry."[68] Almost all of the theologians involved in the debate about Christian Reconstruction expected a near-future crisis, but could not agree upon the kind of society to which that crisis would lead. "The brass polishers will get little help from the tract passers. . . . It makes a difference what men believe about eschatology."[69] But North could hardly have anticipated how a broader constituency could embrace elements of his program for social renewal without abandoning their expectation of social decline.

The evolution of evangelical eschatology in the later decades of the twentieth century is not simply an account of the growth of one system and the decline of another.[70] Postmillennial ideas did begin to circulate more widely, as did the new emphasis on Christian social theory, but these narratives prospered only insofar as they were distinguished from each other. The movement of Christian Reconstructionists, although always small in numbers, expanded during the late 1970s and early 1980s. It is impossible to know how far or with what influence its ideas may have circulated: Ingersoll recalls seeing in the 1980s Reconstructionist books on the shelves of Washington lobbyists, and the second-hand copy of Gary North's *The Sinai Strategy: Economics and the Ten Commandments* (1986) that I purchased in the late 1990s came from the archive of the Royal Bank of Scotland.[71] But that influence seemed quickly to decrease. By the early 1990s, Worthen has suggested, "no one outside a small circle of conservative evangelicals" was paying much attention to Rushdoony's ideas.[72] The movement's leading apologists "tempered" their conclusions "for popular appeal," without seeing the results for which they hoped. North's association with Y2K survivalism did little to build the reputation of the movement he represented, which, by 2008, Worthen has argued, was "largely dead."[73] But this analysis fails to reckon with the extent to which the Christian Reconstruction had already been born again. By the end of the 1990s, some very significant new audiences were consuming repackaged and rebranded Reconstructionist ideas. In a quiet and often organic way, the theonomists' program for survival and resistance was beginning all over again.

III

In the 1980s and 1990s, Reconstructionists found it easier to persuade born-again Protestants of their political than their eschatological convictions. Dispensational writers continued to argue for their own end-times system, taking advantage of the end of the Cold War and the beginning of new conflicts in the Middle East to appeal to evangelical readers by developing themes and formats that Lindsey had been among the first to investigate. But they were also tinkering with the structures and assumptions of his theology in sometimes foundational ways. As evangelical leaders became convinced that they did have cultural and political responsibilities, the advocates of pre- and postmillennial systems no longer felt the need to remain opposed. This new agreement upon the importance of political involvement was a key factor in the national political ambitions of evangelicals in the 1980s, including Pat Robertson's controversial presidential campaign, and the emergence of a sometimes nervous and hesitating evangelical left.[74] By the turn of the century, advocates of these eschatological systems were describing such similar ethical agendas that scholars could represent them, not entirely accurately, as supporters of a single political vision, described by its critics as a "far-right fantasy" that they identified as "dominionism."[75]

While critics were right to note the significance of these efforts at top-down reform, they did not often notice that advocates of the new social engagement were becoming increasingly skeptical of national politics and the hegemonic ambitions of the old Religious Right. In developing local programs to promote social change, these evangelical critics of the Religious Right were adopting a model of political disengagement that had been pioneered by Christian Reconstructionists, preferring bottom-up to top-down strategies for social change. While left-leaning evangelicals might have wished to dissociate themselves from the legacy of Rushdoony, they often retained his strategy of preferring the local—attempting, as Joel McDurmon, Gary North's son-in-law and until recently the president of American Vision, has put it, to "restore" America "one county at a time."[76] Providing an ethical emphasis for politically active premillennialists on the evangelical right, and a strategy of localism for those on the evangelical left, the sum of Christian Reconstruction may have become greater than its parts.

In the 1980s and 1990s, this coming together of politically active premillennialists and the small body of theonomic postmillennialists was made possible by shared concerns that the political short term would involve a period of tribulation. This expectation of imminent crisis became acute in the last years of the century. For many evangelicals, the impeachment of Bill Clinton (December 1998–February 1999) illustrated the declining condition of American morality—a point not lost on John W. Whitehead, a lawyer who had attended Rushdoony's presentations in the Jesus Christ Light and Power house before beginning the career in advocacy that included his representing Paula Jones, whose lawsuit for sexual harassment had driven the Senate's impeachment proceedings.[77] At the end of the 1990s, this crisis in American democracy and public morality occurred at the same time as a crisis in technology, as fears grew that a hardware glitch would cause havoc as computer systems rolled over into the twenty-first century. Hal Lindsey, who had once explained that he had "never taken to the hills with my possessions and loved ones to await Doomsday," witnessed some of his postmillennial critics do exactly that.[78] As the Y2K crisis loomed, Reconstructionists adopted the ideals and strategies that had been developed by paramilitary survivalists. Gary North frankly admitted that "history is coming to a head," and suggested that, following the pattern of the days of creation in Genesis 1, the six thousand years of human history were about to be followed by a seventh millennium of rest. He was unconcerned about the risks of date-setting: "If I turn out to be wrong, my embarrassment will be posthumous. I can live with that."[79] Despite having spent decades ridiculing Hal Lindsey's ambiguous prognostications, North capitalized on his own date-setting to do a little selling, offering his readers the chance to purchase a "Y2K preparation, protection, and survival kit," while recommending the area around Moscow, Idaho, possibly because of its proximity to a growing church community that shared elements of his religious and political outlook.[80] North's concerns about Y2K may have informed those of James Wesley Rawles, who moderated the forum on North's

Y2K website and defended his mentor from criticisms on another discussion board, and who appears to have relocated from California to Stites, Idaho, in the months before the expected disaster.[81] In the years that followed, this part of northern Idaho would become an important environment for the emergence of communities that balanced their expectations of short-term crisis against the certainty of long-term improvement in the reconstruction of a Christian America. Drawing upon these themes, Douglas Wilson, leader of a growing community of conservative Presbyterians in Moscow, Idaho, used a column in his magazine, *Credenda Agenda*, to set out a program for action.

By the late 1990s, Wilson had moved a considerable distance from his dispensational and charismatic background and environment.[82] The Christian reconstruction of Moscow that he promoted was, in some senses, a family project. In the 1970s, his father, Jim Wilson, a navy veteran with a Southern Baptist background and a bookshop ministry, had moved his family to Pullman, where he became pastor of a church. Drawing upon his training, Jim Wilson concluded that his role as an evangelist would be best advanced by working in a small but significant location in which his message could achieve maximum saturation, and he identified Moscow as that kind of "feasible" and "strategic" evangelistic objective.[83] In the late 1970s, a church was formed as a result of these missionary efforts, and Douglas Wilson became its leader.[84] In the 1980s, as Douglas Wilson became increasingly influenced by Reformed ideas, he and a number of colleagues began to work together on a magazine. First published in 1988, *Credenda Agenda* featured wry and often satirical articles that popularized elements of Rushdoony's political and eschatological vision while emphasizing the value of Reformed theology, life in community, and the importance of the liberal arts. The magazine was made available free of charge, and by the late 1990s had grown to establish an international subscription base of around 22,000.[85] One of its regular columns promoted postmillennial eschatology, along with the "preterist" reading of Revelation that understood the book to refer to the fall of Jerusalem in AD 70 and the consequent "end of the old covenant"—ideas that until that point had been most fully developed among evangelicals in books published by Gary North's Institute for Christian Economics.[86] Despite this intellectual debt to the theorists of Christian Reconstruction, issues of *Credenda Agenda* maintained a critical distance from the movement's leaders, often criticizing or making fun of North, who, Wilson observed, "has written much that is truly outstanding, along with other things that are, to use a theological phrase, 'more than a little odd.'"[87] Another contributor continued the criticism of

North's position in a book review: "Reading Gary North is like sitting behind an unusually witty drunk at a football game: you enjoy his wisecracks and even laugh at them, yet you feel embarrassed for the guy."[88] But this criticism of North might have been an example of the narcissism of small differences. This strategy reflected an effort on the part of the magazine's authors to maintain a critical distance from the broader Christian Reconstructionist project, precisely because their goals and presuppositions were in many ways so closely aligned with it. Wilson's ministry, in its commitment to the social application of biblical law and in its expectation of the global expansion of Protestant Christianity, was clearly influenced by ideas that first came together as a package in Christian Reconstruction, an intellectual debt that he has more recently recognized in including Rushdoony among the writers that have had "greatest impact," "in both content and style," upon his own work.[89] The reconstruction of Moscow was to develop on a broader cultural base than the program of the Christian Reconstructionists, but it shared the same kinds of goals. As its subscription base expanded, *Credenda Agenda* became a very considerable ideological and recruitment resource. In the late 1990s and early 2000s, the magazine served as a vital tool in building the Moscow brand. Its readers included an international community of fellow travelers, some of whom joined a network of related congregations that in 1998 came together as a new denomination, the Confederation of Reformed Evangelical Churches (CREC). In 1999, Wilson's congregation, Community Evangelical Fellowship, rebranded itself as Christ Church, to become a more formal, if liturgically eclectic, congregation of the CREC.[90]

But the reconstruction of Moscow was to involve much more than religious ideas. As his convictions developed, Wilson came to firm convictions about the kind of society he wished to re-create. "The medieval period is the closest thing we have to a maturing Christian culture," he explained in *Angels in the Architecture* (1998).[91] Recovering a holistic life in family, church, and community, he argued that "Christians need to start thinking more about plotting the rest of that story, preparing for the death of modernity over the next century."[92] Like North, Wilson combined this vision of the future with a conspiratorial view of national political life in the present. "The nation which we call the United States *has already been lost,*" he explained in 1998:[93]

> *Of course* our regime is a regime. *Of course* we live under a tyranny. *Of course* the American experiment is a sham and a farce. *Of course* our elections are rigged. *Of course* somebody needs to wake up.[94]

And, of course, by the late 1990s, Wilson could refer to plenty of evidence that federal agencies could, in fact, be corrupt: he was only slightly overstating when he suggested that "everyone in the country" knew why the deaths of American citizens at Ruby Ridge, in north Idaho (1992), and Waco, Texas (1993), had been "legal travesties."[95] But, he worried, these incidents were being used to justify concerns about small religious movements with unusual programs for action, just as other members of his growing congregation noted that the *New York Times* was connecting the emergence of the radical right to the growth of homeschooling.[96] As government perfidy became in their view more obvious, the call to strategic relocation became acute, and leaders of the Moscow congregation encouraged their readers to consider what, including migration, "can be done for preparation."[97] "A man must protect his family, and in the coming years a thinking man will be looking for a good hill to defend," Wilson considered in 1998; "families should begin congregating in communities where these duties are understood, and the men of those communities have every intention of fulfilling those duties."[98] And the need for preparation became paramount as the technological disaster of Y2K loomed at century's end.

Wilson offered advice for Y2K preparedness in an unusually long article in *Credenda Agenda* in the summer of 1998. After warning of "alarmists," and recognizing that "the hubbub about Y2K may turn out to be some mere sound and fury, signifying nothing," he explained the technical risks for household appliances, computer systems, the infrastructure of banking, and government agencies. "What will happen if the river of welfare checks, Social Security checks, food stamps . . . dries up? . . . Christians who think about what the biblical role of government should be will obviously take all this as good news," he considered, while realizing that the sudden contraction of government could result in "civil unrest, and possibly riots."[99] He advised his readers to pay off debts and to switch out of bank and retirement accounts into precious metals, which should be "buried behind the barn," and to have up to six months of food in storage, along with household and sanitary supplies, hand tools, and non-hybrid seeds.[100] He advised those members of his congregation who were employees of the local university to put in a place a contingency plan "in case of cutbacks or layoffs." Otherwise, Wilson was optimistic that life in the Pacific Northwest might be relatively undisturbed by the national calamity that he expected:

> The Palouse is a good place to be. We are a healthy distance from densely-
> populated areas where the dislocations, if they come, will be more severe.

The hunting and fishing are good in our area, the forests have a good supply of wood if we need it, a great deal of land is available for growing our own food . . . we have a community of saints committed to one another covenantally.[101]

So "do not start to think or act like a 'survivalist,' " he cautioned his readers: "do not do anything with fear in your heart."[102] Even as calamity approached, life in Moscow was to be a life of faith.

Wilson's caution contrasted with the advice that was being disseminated by others who were also advertising the benefits of a redoubt in the region around Moscow. In 1999, North was also promoting the town as "the best place to be when the uncertain New Year is ushered in."[103] But Wilson did not welcome this attention. He recognized that North's Y2K website provided "good information and links," but was very concerned by its "intemperate" language.[104] Hostile to the paramilitary style survivalism that had taken root in North's Presbyterian church in Tyler, Texas, writers in *Credenda Agenda* feared that Y2K concern was a strategy of the devil to create panic among Christians.[105] And so, as the moment of crisis approached, Wilson began to moderate his claims. At the beginning of 1999, he encouraged readers to be "ready for anything, including the possibility that Y2K does not represent the end of our civilization."[106] As spring turned into summer, he noticed that "key doomsayers are starting to hedge their bets. So prepare for anything, including the possibility that the whole thing will be a yawner."[107] And in the last issue of the year, as the crisis loomed, he and the other contributors to *Credenda Agenda* turned to comedy: "We are thinking of sponsoring an exciting conference on the Y2K threat, registration half off."[108]

And so, at the end of the 1990s, the essential elements of the ideology of religious migration to the Pacific Northwest were already in place, and its key protagonists had been identified. Rawles was drawing down North's pessimism about near future political, social, and technological conditions, while following his mentor's exhortations to move to a secure location. Wilson was issuing practical advice on survival and resistance to those who had already migrated into Idaho, while including this advice within the magazine that was then being distributed free of charge to an international subscription base of 22,000.[109] Neither Rawles nor Wilson was presenting himself as a Christian Reconstructionist, although several issues of *Credenda Agenda* around this period advertised Wilson's speaking at events alongside prominent Reconstructionist Kenneth Gentry, while writers within the community continued to refer to Rushdoony's work and provided an obituary upon his death in 2001.[110] The program for religious migration to the Redoubt came together around concerns about Y2K, but its appeal lasted long after the technological crisis had passed, as the relationship between the Moscow community and Christian Reconstruction became both more complex and overt.

There was no Y2K disaster, of course, but its sense of impending crisis was enduring. *Credenda Agenda* continued to argue for preterist postmillennialism as it offered a critique of evangelical commitments in American politics, popular eschatology, and social passivity. New Saint Andrews, the liberal arts college founded by members of Wilson's congregation in 1994, began to attract students from across the United States and, increasingly, beyond. Young people came to study, graduated, married, and continued to live in Moscow. As the community grew, its members established homes, families, and successful businesses, which in due course required the establishment of a second congregation and eventually, as the community's religious, educational, and social infrastructure supported further expansions in membership, an international denomination. Wilson and his faculty colleagues continued to defend postmillennialism within the classroom, and promoted it by means of the growing literature ministry associated with Canon Press, which they established to publish their work, as well as in the activities of cultural production that in time became associated with major publishers and leading public intellectuals. As the congregation grew, its members constituted an ever-increasing proportion of the town's population. The congregation declared their intention to make Moscow a Christian town, and their postmillennialism encouraged them to believe that their goal could be achieved. As their numbers grew, they became the fulfillment of their own prophetic hopes. The success of Christ Church, New Saint Andrews College, and Canon Press both depended upon and warranted the community's postmillennial hope.

IV

Moscow may now be America's most postmillennial town: measured between decades, the growth of the community associated with Christ Church and New Saint Andrews College has been explosive. The town's two explicitly postmillennial congregations now number just under 2,000 members and adherents, making up around 10 percent of the permanent local population.

An increasing number of commercial premises on Main Street are owned and operated by church members—including Moscow's only student-friendly bar, named after a prominent leader of the Protestant reformation, and the town's most important technology employer. This growth has been deliberate, and hard-won. The goal of this work is frequently restated: the brochure given to attendees at Christ Church services states that the ambition of the congregation is to "make Moscow a Christian town."[111] But this may be more complicated than it seems. Members of the congregation do not agree on what this means, and so cannot agree on when that goal can be said to have been achieved.

Even a congregation of postmillennialists may disagree about how much hope is warranted. During fieldwork, in summer 2015, one student informed us that the congregation's goal had been achieved: she thought of Moscow as a "picture of what you would like your home town to eventually be like." Others among her peers thought there was much more work to be done before the town could be said to be converted. One student was "not content" that only 10 percent of the townspeople were identified with the community's congregations: "We are wildly postmillennial . . . I'd call the town 'Christian' when it's 90 percent Christian . . . That's why I don't think Moscow is Christian yet." Others thought that Moscow had become so significant that it could become the ground zero of a new attack on American Christianity, an attack so vigorous that it would drive believers into emigration and, consequently, into global mission:

> I think there will come a breaking point of some kind, and it wouldn't surprise me if that breaking point came in Moscow, because of the work that we do, but here is what will happen, people will then leave Moscow . . . it would not surprise me at all if there was a great persecution of Christians in America in the next 50 years . . . but that doesn't change my postmillennial views, because then people will go to China.[112]

The community was growing with one eye on local critics, and with the other on the possibility of global expansion, planning strategies of survival in the confident hope of victory. If Moscow wasn't yet a Christian town, it certainly would be soon.

But the question remained of how that Christian influence upon the town might be measured. Despite this student's naïve ambition for global influence, her sense of the significance of "the work that we do," and the sometimes

panicking response of local liberals, the Christ Church community has made
very little impact on local politics. In the summer of 2015, local newspapers
described a struggle for control of the local farmer's co-op—members of the
church having stumbled into a controversy that was represented in the local
press as an attempt to gain raw political power.[113] But this appointment, like
every other step in the community's advance, was being fiercely contested
by local citizens, many of them associated with the Moscow-Pullman area's
two universities, who pointed to zoning irregularities and headlines about
the criminal activity of a tiny number of church members to justify what
they explained to us as an unofficial boycott of businesses that were owned
by "Kirkers." These critics were dismayed by what they perceived to be the
community's preference for crusading rhetoric, and worried about the reactionary emphases that informed some of Wilson's earlier writing, including
Southern Slavery as It Was (1996), a pamphlet that he coauthored with Steve
Wilkins, who was at the time on the board of the controversial League of
the South, which sought to defend the "peculiar institution," and which was
roundly condemned by a local professor of history, William L. Ramsey.[114]
The revision and expansion of this book, *Black and Tan* (2005), which Wilson
prepared on his own, sustains his revisionist account of the experience of
American slaves, but its explicit rejection of racism has not satisfied all of his
critics. It is not simply that small towns have long memories: Wilson's more
recent writing also gives his critics cause for alarm. For his rhetoric is triumphalist. Jesus Christ is "already the king of Idaho," Wilson has explained. "We
have the task of announcing to the remaining rebels in the hinterlands that
their capital city has already fallen, their rulers dethroned, and that resistance
is futile."[115] These themes resonated with the New Saint Andrews students
that I interviewed, some of whom described Moscow as the "Reformed
capital" of the United States of America, and the "Reformed Mecca" of the
world.[116] Some among their number were so happy to live in Moscow that
they struggled to think of living in any other situation. But others among
their number understood that the expansion of the kingdom inevitably involved their being willing to move. Throughout our fieldwork, we found the
community geared toward expansion, with high hopes of social and cultural
influence, and encouraged by Wilson's argument that "there is no wall of separation between the authority of Jesus Christ and the authority of the civil
magistrate."[117] The college community understood that this claim did not
represent a distinctive political agenda: as one faculty member put it in conversation, "we preach the Bible, and see what happens next."[118] But he could

already see what was likely to "happen next." The congregational infrastructure began with the foundation of Logos School, which provided Christian
education K–12, in the 1970s; and New Saint Andrews College, which was
founded in 1994, developed to provide a four-year high-quality liberal arts
education, as its graduates began to find their way onto graduate programs in
Ivy League and major European universities. As the community developed
a successful social infrastructure, others moved into Moscow to join the
congregation, to build new businesses, and so to complete the community's
virtuous circle of education, marriage, employment, and multigenerational
prosperity. Postmillennial theory made sense of this success. The community
had become the fulfillment of its most extravagant hopes.

The Moscow community grew in numbers as it grew in confidence. This
growth had been made possible by the expectation of growth. In several of
our conversations, Wilson emphasized that postmillennialism didn't bring
any new ethical responsibilities, but gave its adherents the confidence of success: "it's easier to play when you are on the winning team."[119] For all that
the Moscow community is geared toward short-term conflict, its emphasis
is on victory. Students at New Saint Andrews College have little time for the
programs for retreat outlined in Rod Dreher's *The Benedict Option*. Instead,
as they watch their denomination expand around the world, to include at the
time of writing almost eighty congregations, they want to play a part in this
great sweep of conquest, either by raising a godly family on the Palouse, or
committing to church plants across the United States or far beyond. The confidence of the Moscow community is distinctive. The north Idaho kinists, for
all that they share Wilson's postmillennial confidence, are much less confident of success, and are much closer, in terms of social critique, to the premillennial theory that they criticize. Rawles is much less confident still. Rejecting
postmillennial theory in favor of historic premillennialism, his fiction and
online articles encourage his readers to prepare for paramilitary action
during a coming tribulation. It is eschatology that distinguishes the migrants'
response to the "end of white Christian America," and which suggests possibilities beyond the withdrawal that would be represented in adopting a
"Benedict option." While the prescriptions for the ideal society vary, these
groups are promoting renewal beyond strategies for resistance and survival.
In Moscow, and in homeschooling families across the nation, evangelical political disengagement may be less a signal of surrender than a sign of hope, a
reminder of growing confidence that America can be restored, "one county
at a time," as McDurmon puts it, achieving ever closer approximations to

the ideal godly society, until Jesus comes again. For, Wilson has explained, the second coming will be the "culmination of what is happening right here, right now." In more ways than one, perhaps, the community in Moscow is a window into America's future.[120]

V

American evangelicals have long been motivated by their hopes and fears about the near and longer-term future. Since the late nineteenth century they have largely adopted expectations of increasing conflict in the Middle East, an "any-moment rapture," followed by a seven-year period of tribulation and the rise of the Antichrist, the standard elements of the narrative that have been most famously outlined in Lindsey's *The Late Great Planet Earth*, and, more recently, in the Left Behind novels.[121] This dispensational premillennialism has traditionally discouraged social or political involvement, imagining, as one of its critics has put it, that "the world is God's Vietnam, and the return of Christ consists of the few lucky ones helicoptered off a roof during the fall of Saigon."[122] This criticism may be misplaced—for advocates of the system continued to engage in public politics throughout the early and mid-twentieth century, long before the evangelical political renaissance of the 1970s.[123] But this political renaissance was made possible by a recasting of the tension between eschatology and social ethics. Since the 1980s, an increasing number of evangelicals have come to combine their pessimism about the future of Christianity with social and political activity intended for its improvement—in effect, fighting against the prophetic fulfillments that they expect—while others have abandoned the tension and have embraced varieties of postmillennialism which provide a clearer rationale for virtuous action in the present. This ideological shift has precipitated a theological crisis among dispensationalists, with prominent voices within the movement proposing a radical restructuring of premillennial expectations, and a more general move toward elaborating an eschatological system that makes sense of this working for the common good.[124] These believers continue to be compelled by hope and fear of the near future, but are now more likely than an older generation of premillennialists to expect that the social crisis that they believe to be imminent will be followed by an evangelical renaissance, a future in which believers will enjoy growing levels of influence in a society that increasingly conforms to their ideals. But other believers are moving away from the tensions of this socially committed premillennialism to adopt a prophetic narrative that makes better sense of the work they want to do, believing, as Wilson has put it, that this world, "the one we live in now, will be put to rights, before the Second Coming, before the end of all things. The only enemy not destroyed through the advance of the gospel will be death itself (1 Cor. 15:26)—and even that enemy will be in confused retreat (Is. 65:20)."[125] This revival and reification of postmillennialism highlighted the continuing fragmentation of the American evangelical movement in the dark days of late Christendom, a fragmentation that reveals believers' deep disillusionment with the political and cultural futures advocated by those public figures who are often assumed to be their political leaders. By rejecting political solutions and national aspirations, these radical voices are challenging—and may yet eclipse—the influence of those evangelical leaders who have done most to facilitate the political re-engagement of their fellow believers.

Postmillennialists need to plan for the renewal of culture, but they do not need to plan for revolution. Unlike amillennialists, who, North has argued, believe that "history is inherently ambiguous," postmillennialists believe that history advances with predictable effects.[126] "Men who are confident concerning the future, in time and on earth, can plan for a very long run," North has observed—for "centuries, if necessary."[127] With this confidence in the future, "God's people . . . should have faith in both time and continuity," working for and expecting a situation in which "every person" is "worshipping weekly in a local congregation of some Trinitarian denomination," in which those citizens who choose to remain part of a nation the majority of whose voters had agreed to adopt biblical law should become the subjects of compulsory baptism.[128] North's coercive ambitions illustrate why it is appropriate for him to write about "God's invading kingdom."[129] North's work to promote preparedness brought together the key themes of survival and resistance while identifying the future leaders of that eclectic movement, among them James Wesley Rawles, who acknowledged North in the preface to his first survivalist novel, *Patriots*, and who described North as "my mentor" in his bestselling Penguin preparedness manual, *How to Survive the End of the World as We Know It* (2009).[130] For all their differences, in strategy and objective, the small group of kinists in Coeur d'Alene, the community of several thousand church members in Moscow, and the tens of thousands around the world who read Rawles's novels or website are all participants in a larger movement away from dispensational despair. For all of their diversity, these strategies of survival and resistance are being driven by a new hope that sees on the other side of a short-term tribulation the reconstruction of America.

3

Government

We need to think like Christians and not like People for the American Way.[1]

To say that someone is a conservative does not tell us what he is interested in conserving.[2]

Driven by new hope, those born-again Protestants who expect to contribute to the long-term reconstruction of the United States of America agree that this renewal will have significant implications for government. Over the last two decades, this radical rethinking of "the American way" has developed with sometimes startling results, not least in the Pacific Northwest. In June 2015, Candlelight Christian Fellowship, a large and prosperous evangelical congregation in Coeur d'Alene, Idaho, was the venue for a conference on the topic of politics, reform, and what organizers described as "righteous resistance."[3] Sponsored by the International Coalition of Abolitionist Societies, the event focused on the extent to which Christians should campaign against abortion using extra-judicial or even illegal means. As the conference title suggested, presenters pressed home the dichotomy between divine and human law, emphasizing that they were not "anti-government," but "pro-God"; that Christians ought to "obey God rather than men"; and that those Christians who did obey God were, consequently, "never disobedient."[4] One speaker, Chet Gallagher, had been a police officer in Las Vegas, when, in 1989, he attended an anti-abortion protest to read out a speech explaining why, having sworn to protect human life, he would not enforce the law by arresting the protestors—an action that cost him his job.[5] Other speakers were prepared to go beyond this example of civil disobedience. Matthew J. Trewhella, a pastor from Milwaukee, Wisconsin, defended the doctrine of the "lesser magistrate," a political theory that was developed during the Protestant Reformation and that identifies the conditions within

Survival and Resistance in Evangelical America. Crawford Gribben, Oxford University Press (2021). © Oxford University Press. DOI: 10.1093/oso/9780199370221.003.0004

which citizens may, with biblical justification, take up arms to resist the government. The effect of his arguments, as one attendee approvingly noted, was to prove that Christians could legitimately disobey "any government which runs afoul of God's law."[6] Conference organizers were clear that they were not encouraging Christians to take up arms—but they were certainly encouraging the rebirth of a controversial theology of resistance to government in a region with a long history of subversive violence.

This conference's defense of the doctrine of the lesser magistrate—however nuanced in presentation and contextualized in terms of historical scholarship—may justify one of the most enduring worries in recent writing on this revival of conservative religion. Concern about a power grab by American evangelicals—a democratically facilitated *coup d'état*—was revitalized by the election of President Donald Trump in 2016. Within the first month of his inauguration, and as the new administration began to refer to "alternative facts," classic works of dystopian fiction shot to the top of bestseller lists. Publishers rushed to supply demand, printing 75,000 copies of George Orwell's *1984* (1948) and 100,000 copies of Margaret Atwood's *The Handmaid's Tale* (1985), with the latter being adapted into a very successful television series in spring 2017, the success of which was followed by *The Testaments* (2019).[7] Atwood's sequence of novels describes a near-future society in which a major terrorist incident has justified the suspension of the American Constitution and the establishment of competing theocratic republics, and in which Old Testament societal norms, including the use of concubines, have been reinstated. Atwood's depiction of the Republic of Gilead played on the concerns of many progressives that feminist gains were being threatened by the Religious Right, and their fear of what might happen if some evangelical leaders were to push their arguments about God and government to their logical conclusion.[8] Those concerns have not diminished. Since the election of President Trump, *The Handmaid's Tale* has been widely received as a tract for the times, a fact underscored by the success of *The Testaments*.

The critique of religious politics that provided Atwood's narrative foundation has been advanced by commentators in a sequence of exposés. From outside the movement, Chris Hedges's *American Fascists* (2006) epitomized the hyperbole of the growing number of these revelations of the dangers of conservative faith. Hedges argued, as his subtitle put it, that the Religious Right was engaged in a "war on America." Reprinting as a preface Umberto Eco's extended description of fascism, Hedges described his subjects' culture of despair, cult of masculinity, war on truth, and fascination with apocalyptic violence, lumping together a diverse range of individuals, institutions, and communities in a vast, right-wing conspiracy that included the controllers of "at least six national television networks . . . virtually all of the nation's more than 2,000 religious radio stations," and "denominations such as the Southern Baptist Convention."[9] Religious fascists, he argued, shared "obsessions with conspiracy theories, magic, sexual repression, paranoia and death," an "infatuation with apocalyptic violence and military force," relationships with "shadowy paramilitary groups, such as Christian Identity," and a common intellectual source. For the movement's "most important book" was, as Atwood might have feared, a massive exposition of the Ten Commandments—*The Institutes of Biblical Law* by R. J. Rushdoony.[10] Echoing the narrative structure of *The Handmaid's Tale*, Hedges argued that Rushdoony's adherents were plotting a revolution. Members of the Religious Right were already "taking over the machinery of U.S. state and religious institutions" while waiting for a "fiscal, social or political crisis, a moment of upheaval in the form of an economic meltdown or another terrorist strike on American soil, to move to reconfigure the political system" by drawing upon "public clamor for drastic new national security measures."[11] Nothing less than regime change was the intended result of the evangelical program of political action. "What is happening in America is revolutionary," Hedges explained. "A group of religious utopians, with the sympathy and support of tens of millions of Americans, are slowly dismantling democratic institutions to establish a religious tyranny."[12] The description was not overloaded, for Rushdoony's *Institutes*, the movement's ur-text, he continued, encoded a "radical Calvinism" that shared "many prominent features with classical fascist movements" and dallied with Holocaust denial.[13] And at the core of this "American fascism" was an ideology that Hedges identified as "dominionism."[14] His rhetoric was urgent and alarming, if also tendentious, hysterical, and sometimes badly mistaken. But his conclusions were confirmed by a source within the evangelical movement. Randall Balmer's *Thy Kingdom Come* (2006) lamented the ways in which the religious community to which he belonged had betrayed American democracy, and identified the pernicious influence of Reconstructionism at the heart of the enterprise of the Religious Right—an attempt by those who had become "infatuated with Rushdoony's ideas" to "deconstruct democracy."[15] Hedges and Balmer agreed that the political positions of the Religious Right aimed at the radical reform of American structures of government, and worried that some believers were prepared to advance their cause using extra-judicial means. These were points that were made explicit at the conference in Coeur d'Alene.

His rapprochement with Balmer notwithstanding, Hedges's analysis was in many other ways wide of the mark. Perhaps he mistook the subjects of his analysis by looking for their ideological consistency—this suppression of difference being a common technique in the manufacture of conspiracy theory. For one of the most significant features of the "dominionist movement" that Hedges describes is its lack of consistency. The "movement" is much more varied than he imagines. While they may use similar language, fully developed Christian Reconstructionists, politically engaged Southern Baptists, and racist paramilitaries work with incompatible values, distinctive aims, and competing strategies toward quite different kinds of political change, only a tiny proportion of which could be described as "revolutionary." Hedges's "movement" contains activists working for top-down political change, a category that would include those with fairly conventional political instincts who supported presidential campaigns from that of Pat Robertson (1988) to that of Ted Cruz (2016), as well as institutions such as the recently founded Patrick Henry College, in Purcellville, Virginia, which had close links to the White House during the George W. Bush era.[16] His "movement" also contains those working for reform from the bottom up, a less conventional group that includes reactionary conservatives, libertarians, Christian Reconstructionists, and even some self-identified anarchists. To complicate things further, these movements for top-down and bottom-up reform include individuals who adopt political positions that might otherwise be considered to be mutually contradictory: North combines theonomy with libertarian economics; Rawles argues both that "the foundational morality of the civilized world is best summarized in the Ten Commandments" while also insisting that "governments tend to expand their power to the point that they do harm."[17] Further from the center of this "movement," other believers are opting for more extreme agendas for governmental change. Some are relocating to areas including the American Redoubt, while a smaller number have embraced full-blown secessionist movements, such as Christian Exodus, taking practical steps to set up communal or regional polities in which to consolidate their demographic and to legislate for their political ideals. Across the various communities that might be misunderstood as representing a "dominionist movement," gun rights or political violence are being defended only by a tiny handful of believers, and then almost always for the purposes of self-defense. Like the evangelical cultures upon which it depends, therefore, the "dominionist movement" that Hedges assembles contains multiple and contradictory agendas for societal or governmental change. For, as Hedges notes, the cultures that exist within this movement may make radical proposals for the renewal of political life, but they do not generally expect the revolutionary changes they anticipate to be achieved by revolutionary means.

This chapter will survey a variety of these evangelical responses to recent trends in American government. It will argue that the large pan-denominational and politically pragmatic religious coalitions that dominated an earlier phase of evangelical political engagement have fractured, and have given way to a much more vigorous, variegated, and entrepreneurial evangelical political landscape. The Moral Majority, which was "never in fact the majority it claimed to be," has been replaced by a large variety of smaller interest groups, who clamor to advance competing agendas.[18] In this new landscape, the hope for social and moral transformation that was once widely shared across evangelical political movements has given way to a fear that believers have been betrayed by their national political leaders, that they have lost the big political battles, and that they are being pushed toward—and perhaps beyond—conventional cultural margins and into involuntary cultural exile. These believers understand that they have lost the cultural high-ground, or, to change metaphors, that the Overton window has been firmly shut behind them, so that their cultural preferences no longer make sense within the public square. These believers are not sure how best to respond to their sense of marginalization, but many among their number are returning to and developing the arguments of earlier Reconstructionists. This chapter will explore the complexity of political thinking among those born-again Protestants who embrace their marginal status in order to propose strategies of survival, resistance, and reconstruction in evangelical America.

I

American evangelicals spent the central part of the twentieth century wondering how they lost political influence and whether that influence could ever be regained.[19] After the debacle of the Scopes trial, conservative Protestants withdrew from public engagement, building new institutions and identifying the spokespersons through whom they might reconstruct their damaged reputation and begin to make more credible interventions in modern American life.[20] Historians have often described this period of withdrawal as pietistic, sometimes pacific, and generally politically passive. In fact, as

Matthew Avery Sutton has recently demonstrated, evangelical leaders continued to make significant interventions in public life through the middle of the century, even if the seed they scattered was falling on stony ground, and failing to bear fruit.[21] But larger changes were afoot. The renewal of conservative Protestantism was made possible by the forces of social change that attracted skilled workers "from the Bible Belt to the Sun Belt," as Darren Dochuk has put it: by the end of the 1960s, the population of Southerners who had relocated to California exceeded the total population of Arkansas.[22] This demographic shift was accompanied by significant theological reinvention of the region's revitalized religious communities. Sensing the limits of reactionary fundamentalism, with its anti-intellectual veneer, born-again Protestants developed new emphases in their presentation of the gospel and promoted engagement with the religious mainstream in a raft of new publications, including *Christianity Today*, and new institutions, including Fuller Theological Seminary, which, like a number of other key organizations, was based in California, and headlining preachers, principally Billy Graham.[23]

These "neo-evangelicals" grew in confidence and expertise through the 1950s and 1960s, during the period in which American conservatism was being reconfigured, and with the help of some unlikely allies.[24] Inspired by F. A. Hayek's *The road to serfdom* (1944), facilitated by such organizations as the William Volker Charities Fund, and arguing for the overreach of federal government while dodging as best they could any association with racial politics and the failure of the Barry Goldwater campaign (1964), a small but well-connected group of academics and businessmen created a conservative "counter-intelligentsia" whose responsibility it would be to work for the shrinking of federal government, a "fifth column movement . . . the likes of which no nation has ever seen."[25] While some in the new movement could be deeply critical of traditional Christian ethics, for example using the parable of the Good Samaritan to undercut obligations to charity, others looked to Scripture for patterns of social renewal, while finding biblical reasons to support the broader claim that "democracy was inimical to economic liberty."[26] The organizations funding these religious and irreligious libertarians were working for a "right-wing political movement determined to undo the modern democratic state," Nancy MacLean has argued, and agreed that change should be driven by reform rather than revolution, following the advice of the libertarian economist James M. Buchanan that "in the boring fine print . . . transformations can be achieved by increments that few will notice, because most people have no patience for minutiae."[27] As a multidisciplinary thinker capable of working from a consistent set of religious and political first principles, Rushdoony was welcomed into this movement, where as a consequence of his brief period of employment with the Volker Fund in the early 1960s he found the financial support that launched his rapidly expanding ministry: a report on his activities in 1965 and early 1966 noted his speaking in locations as far apart as Houston, Los Angeles, Seattle, and on the campus of Reformed Theological Seminary in Jackson, Mississippi.[28] Even at this early stage, his writing combined references to theonomy with references to liberty. "Liberty rapidly declines when biblical Christianity declines," he observed in *The mythology of science* (1967). "Where men are not ruled by God, they are ruled by tyrants."[29] The financial and organizational context of Rushdoony's early work is illuminating, as Michael J. McVicar has noted: Christian Reconstruction, for all of its emphasis upon the social application of divine law, was a creature of the mid-century libertarian revolution.

As conservative Protestants slowly emerged into public view, the influences of Christian Reconstruction remained hidden in the background. Hal Lindsey's *The Late Great Planet Earth* provided the re-energized evangelical movement with its first modern bestseller. Lindsey's prognostications had sold millions of copies by 1976, the year in which both candidates in the presidential election described themselves as "born-again": American media rushed to explain the phenomenon, and *Newsweek* heralded "the year of the evangelical." The Jimmy Carter and Gerald Ford campaigns illustrated the cultural visibility of popular Protestantism while suggesting something of its inherent ideological weakness. Carter, a Southern Baptist, and Ford, an Episcopalian, had markedly different politics. Despite his well-advertised religiosity, evangelical voters discovered that Carter was not the kind of president they had hoped to elect, not least because of his support for *Roe v. Wade*, the issue around which evangelical culture warriors slowly but inevitably began to coalesce.[30] Disappointed by their options within the political mainstream, evangelical leaders entered the political arena in earnest, and centered their campaigning strategy around Rushdoony's emphatic denunciation of abortion.[31] James Dobson founded Focus on the Family (1977) and the Family Research Council (1981) to support traditional views of gender roles and family life. In 1979, Jerry Falwell established the Moral Majority to raise support for campaigns for conservative social causes and, ultimately, Republican candidates. Ronald Reagan was the earliest beneficiary of his largesse, beating Carter in the 1980 presidential election in a landslide to set about the administrative and financial reforms that created his "morning in America," campaigning in support of school prayer, drawing upon evangelical prophetic rhetoric in his escalation of the Cold War while pursuing "peace through strength," and leading the political realignment that facilitated the re-energizing of conservativism. And his success pointed to the extraordinary impact that was being made by the program of Christian Reconstruction: *Newsweek* responded to his inauguration by identifying Rushdoony's think-tank, the Chalcedon Foundation, as the most important intellectual center within the Religious Right.[32] But Reagan reneged on his supporters' hopes. The new president's most doctrinaire evangelical supporters were disappointed by his performance in office. By 1982, the "Reagan revolution" had stalled, and conservatives had split into three factions. The Republican Right refused to cut entitlements, but pressed on with tax cuts, with the effect that national debt tripled during the Reagan administration. A small group turned toward social democracy, arguing that economic revolution was impractical in a context in which governments were chosen by majorities, and that taxation policy should be realistic about this fact. Only the libertarians, pursuing occasional links with the Christian Right, and fortified by Rushdoony's arguments, pressed on with their goal of the massive reduction of federal government.[33]

With the failure of the "Reagan revolution," conservatism began its long reconfiguration, and some evangelicals took up increasingly defensive positions. John W. Whitehead established the Rutherford Institute (1982) as a more conservative version of the American Civil Liberties Union (ACLU), convening a group of trustees that included Rushdoony and radical culture warrior Franky Schaeffer before moving away from the "central tenets of reconstructionist thought," the aspirations of which he would later dismiss as utopian.[34] Other activists continued to covet the big political prizes. In 1988, Pat Robertson, a successful evangelical broadcaster and educational entrepreneur, competed to become the Republican Party's presidential nominee, to advance upon Reagan's conservative revolution by pushing public policy in the direction of Old Testament law. His campaign was short-lived, but it created the networks and infrastructure that coalesced in the Christian Coalition, which Robertson established in 1989 to consolidate and expand evangelical political interventions.

The establishment of these and similar evangelical ministries and campaign organizations was a powerful signal of the entrepreneurial imperative within popular Protestantism and of its inevitable internal market. The new organizations tended to agree on the significance of the same moral issues, but offered diversified routes by which these issues would attract national attention, and differed on the extent to which their moral views should be advanced by tactics of coercion. The widely publicized scandals besetting major televangelists were not replicated among the new lobbying organizations, but they did not help the public image of the evangelical movement in the 1980s. In the 1990s, and beyond, Presidents Bill Clinton and George W. Bush, both self-identified evangelicals, did little to build confidence in American institutions among those born-again Protestants who combined a high view of elected office with the libertarian ideals of a small state. But it was the election of Barack Obama in 2008 that confirmed to many believers that American society was heading in the wrong direction. Obama's surging popularity in opinion polls illustrated the sudden confidence of the Left, and the international acclaim that resulted in his being nominated for the Nobel Peace Prize within eleven days of his taking up office was almost messianic.[35] The Obama phenomenon provided evangelicals with an ideal foil—the "invaluable tactical advantage of appearing under siege by a powerful enemy."[36] The United States of America was lurching to the left, many believers feared, and resistance and survival became the order of the day.

II

Even as they represented themselves as being pushed to the margins, evangelicals developed a powerful counter-narrative about the possibility of long-term change. This quiet confidence was not based on new strategies for political intervention, for believers shared a widespread and long-standing skepticism about the viability and appropriateness of national reform. After all, born-again Protestants had been pursuing radical political options long before the "year of the evangelical" and the religious renaissance of the 1970s, some of which, in the context of the Cold War, could have appeared to be distinctly anti-patriotic. Like their irreligious libertarian cousins, these believers could be excoriating on the subject of American democracy. While other evangelicals toyed with reforming policy, Rushdoony and many of those whom he had influenced objected to the democratic system itself.[37] In 1962, in a foreword to a volume in the series that he edited for Presbyterian & Reformed Publishing, he complained that the "modern state . . . views family, church, school and every aspect of society as members and phases of its corporate life and subject to its general government." Like governments behind the Iron Curtain, he continued, the American state "claims prior or ultimate jurisdiction over every sphere, and steadily encroaches on their activity."[38] One year later, he argued that the "doctrine of universal human rights ends in the mutual cancellation of rights in either social anarchy or the surrender of rights to the mass man, to the state. Democracy always perishes from an overdose of democracy. Standards perish before majority rule."[39] The United States of America might be locked in global conflict with the Communists, he argued, but its democratic political system meant that the eclipse of Christian social values was, ultimately, inevitable.

This rewriting of the character of American government was consolidated in *A Theological Interpretation of American History* (1964) by C. Gregg Singer, who had been a professor of history in several leading evangelical liberal arts colleges.[40] Unlike other conservatives, Singer dismissed the idea that America had been founded as a Christian nation: "The reference to God in the Declaration of Independence, and the apparent submission to his will, should not blind us to the tragic misuse of biblical ideas to convey Deistic principles for the realization of a society which would be essentially humanistic and anti-supernaturalistic in character," he declared.[41] Singer recognized that many evangelicals would not accept this claim, fearing that it would concede ground to "those who, in our own day, wish to carry this process of secularization to even further excesses than occurred in the early days of the Republic," and he understood that his argument about the American founding would "come as a sad shock to many Americans and to many Christians if they were to recognize the true nature of the democratic philosophy which they so often, and so erroneously, identify with the Christian way of life."[42] Nevertheless, he continued, the "American Revolution in its basic philosophy was not Christian, and the democratic way of life which arose from it was not, and is not, Christian, but was, and is, a Deistic and secularized caricature of the evangelical point of view."[43] Singer linked the democratization of politics to the "democratization of theology," and explained that "modern political liberalism, with its economic and social overtones, stems from a theological liberalism which either seriously modifies, or totally rejects, Christian orthodoxy."[44] Christianity was incompatible with liberal democracy.

It need hardly be said that the interpretation of American history that Singer's work proposed was deeply reactionary. His rejection of the welfare state would have echoed with many of his most conservative contemporaries, but only the most advanced libertarians would have agreed with his critique of democracy, and not many of these would have shared his entire rejection of economic individualism.[45] Building on the well-established Southern Conservative tradition, Singer developed a reading of the Civil War that identified political orthodoxy with the institutions of the Confederate states, and linked campaigns for abolition to northern theological heresy. In his view, the Civil War was defensive: "the South seceded from the Federal Union in order to save the Constitution."[46] But that defense had failed. At the end of the nineteenth century, as the country evolved from republican to democratic government, the "older American concept, that law was rooted and grounded in the very nature of things as an expression of the will of God," gave way to the conclusion that "law should meet the needs of man."[47] By the mid-twentieth century, the new view was in the ascendant, and political thinking had become humanistic and pragmatic. There was no longer any place for Christian principles in national life. Singer worried that, after the Second World War, "the voice of Christianity at large" had been "stilled to an alarming degree in national circles."[48] And the consequence of this drive toward democracy and irreligion could be seen in the societal changes that had rocked the South. Singer listed "compulsory de-segregation" among the "liberal and even radical" policies of those who were determined to destroy what remained of the antebellum world.[49] He described the Supreme Court decision to declare as unconstitutional the segregation of public schools as being of "doubtful legality," and, he hoped, of "only temporary legal authority."[50] Faithful Christians were called to conflict, Singer believed, for the "logical and almost necessary outcome of the rejection of biblical insistence on the sovereignty of God" is the "final negation of freedom in the name of democracy."[51] These positions were certainly distinctive, but Singer's argument identified the themes that would resonate through neo-Confederatism, radical libertarianism, and the theological-political theory of Christian Reconstruction, as, under Rushdoony, its political and social program began to emerge.[52]

Singer was associated with this controversial new movement.[53] *A Theological Interpretation of American History* was published by Craig Press, an independent publishing venture established by the director of the Presbyterian & Reformed Publishing Company, with Rushdoony's editorial advice.[54] In that circle, Singer's ideas were very much in the air. Rushdoony repeated some of his arguments in *The Politics of Guilt and Pity* (1970), which appeared under the same imprint. This book set out Rushdoony's concern about the nature of the American political system—and his consolidating convictions about what ought to replace it. Avoiding any discussion of race relations, he argued that "the freedom of the individual in a democracy is only a transitional freedom, existing briefly as the source of law moves from God to the state. It is impossible for the individual to maintain his liberty very long in a democracy, because it is delegated . . . to the general will of the democratic mass as it expresses itself in the state."[55] He contrasted the "foundation of classical, liberal political thought," which he identified as "natural law and the authority of the autonomous reason of man," with the "foundation of orthodox Christian political theory," that is, the "divine decree and the authority of the infallible Scripture."[56] Being "divorced from God" in its philosophical foundations, the state is "divorced from responsibility: it is not a law unto itself, a power seeking more power. . . . Democracy is thus totalitarian," he concluded.[57] One year later, in *The One and the Many: Studies in the Philosophy of Order and Ultimacy* (1971), Rushdoony continued his critique of the American democratic system by outlining how Trinitarian theology could address the question of the location of political and religious authority, offering an extensive and detailed version of the program of reform that he had been building for the previous decade and that he would publish in *The Institutes of Biblical Law* (1973).[58] This was, by any account, a radical view of American history and politics that challenged the patriotic narratives at the heart of evangelical identity in the run-up to *Newsweek*'s "year of the evangelical" (1976), but it began to develop a following. *Christianity Today*, the "flagship magazine of evangelicalism and the most reliable bell-weather of evangelical sentiments," hailed the *Institutes* as its "book of the year."[59] Others were nuanced in their appreciation. Reviewing the work for the *Westminster Theological Journal*, Reformed theologian John Frame described the *Institutes* as "a big book, with great strengths and great weaknesses." Frame could not help but be impressed by the author: "Rushdoony is one of the most important Christian social critics alive today . . . the extent of Rushdoony's reading is astonishing." His arguments, Frame admitted, "have a *prima facie* cogency about them which ought to be taken seriously by his critics." It was not enough for the critics of Christian Reconstruction to reject its idealization of a society that "executes homosexuals, forbids hybridization and transplants" and "legislates against sexual intercourse during menstruation." For Frame recognized that, with their valency within Reformed theological tradition, Rushdoony's arguments could not easily be dismissed: "if indeed we object to these laws as such, then we are questioning the wisdom of God, and that is sin." Therefore, Frame continued, "even if a theological argument is forthcoming to refute Rushdoony's general thesis about the civil law, we must seriously ask ourselves what better law can be found, what wiser proposals can be made for the complex and difficult business of governing a nation."[60] It was not enough for Reformed theologians merely to criticize Rushdoony's arguments. It was time to put up—or shut up.

But the Reconstructionists continued to work. Also in 1973, Greg Bahnsen defended his ThM thesis at Westminster Theological Seminary, Philadelphia, on the subject of theonomy and biblical ethics, and prepared for doctoral studies at the University of Southern California. One year later, Rushdoony's son-in-law, Gary North, with a UCLA history PhD, established *The Journal of Christian Reconstruction*, which he continued to edit until 1981.[61] By the mid-1970s, Rushdoony's ideas were circulating and being developed among a cadre of closely connected, creative, and often entrepreneurial disciples.

Some evangelicals provided a receptive audience for the new ideas. In January 1984, Robert Tilton, a televangelist with broad appeal among Pentecostals and charismatics, invited a panel of Reconstructionists to address a conference of around one thousand "word of faith" pastors and their wives, an event that led to other opportunities to publicize within this rather unlikely constituency of supporters the obligations of Old Testament law.[62] These break-through moments allowed some Reconstructionists to become triumphalist, even as their previously stolidly theological publications began to reflect the strong supernaturalism of their new allies. In the months after this meeting with the Pentecostals, North assumed that the "intellectual battle is very nearly won by the theonomists," and argued that "if the establishment theologians remain silent for another eight years, the theonomists will have captured the minds of the next generation."[63] The network he was building was certainly unconventional: he admitted that many Presbyterians were "disturbed" by the "growing alliance between charismatics and Reconstructionists." And there is some evidence that North's new friends were influencing his thinking as much as vice versa: the Presbyterian congregation with which he was associated in Tyler, Texas, began to practice prayer for healing, with results that North regarded as nothing short of miraculous.[64]

Whatever the impact of these short-term wins, the final victory of Christian Reconstruction remained elusive. From within the evangelical mainstream, critics rose to Frame's challenge, publishing critiques of Christian Reconstruction that, Greg Bahnsen later complained, were "misleading and misconceived," and which in his opinion too often resorted to defamation.[65] Reconstructionist writers struggled to find an audience as Reformed evangelicals identified their belief system as a cuckoo in the confessional nest. Bahnsen's *Theonomy in Christian Ethics* (1977), a manifesto of the movement's key political and juridical ideas, was reportedly banned from at least one Reformed seminary bookstore.[66] It made little difference that theonomic ideals were shared by many of the early modern theologians and key confessional texts that had provided the Reformed tradition with its intellectual foundations in seventeenth-century England. It was simply no longer politic to hold these views in evangelical America. By the end of the decade, it seemed, Rushdoony's followers had enjoyed their fifteen minutes of fame.

The movement's critics picked up speed. In February 1987, only fourteen years after the magazine hailed Rushdoony's *Institutes* as its book of the year, *Christianity Today*, the closet thing in evangelicalism to a journal of record, published a cover-story exposé of the theonomist movement. This bad publicity, in such a prominent title, marked a sea-change in understandings of the movement.[67] Bigger names began to pile on pressure. H. Wayne House and Thomas Ice, two popular advocates of dispensationalism, published *Dominion Theology: Blessing or Curse?* (1988).[68] One year later, Hal Lindsey, the godfather of popular dispensationalism, warned his readers of a "rapidly expanding new movement . . . that is subtly introducing the same old errors that eventually but inevitably led to centuries of atrocities against the Jews and culminated with the Holocaust of the Third Reich." *The Road to Holocaust* (1989) attacked "one of the most serious doctrinal errors about which the New Testament warns," pursuing *ad hominem* arguments against its theorists, while offering a prescription for evangelical political action that sounded almost identical to that of the Reconstructionists, while making a telling, perhaps polemically fatal, admission in recognizing that "Biblical Law should serve as a pattern for civil law."[69] It is not clear that he fully understood the movement he was condemning. The controversy reached across the Atlantic. In 1987, on a visit to England, Rushdoony was entertained at 10 Downing Street, where he met Brian Griffiths, the chief policy advisor to Margaret Thatcher; Griffith had been reading Rushdoony's work for twenty years and regarded himself as his "son" in the faith, Rushdoony confided to his journal.[70] (In 1979, Griffiths had taught some seminary classes in Regent College, Vancouver, which were attended by the young Douglas Wilson.[71]) The guardians of British orthodoxy might not have realized how close were

these theonomist ideas to centers of real political power—for they could only
see their theological danger. Peter Masters, an influential English fundamentalist, published *World Dominion: The High Ambition of Reconstructionism*
(1990) to warn British readers against this creature of the American culture
wars, following which the General Assembly of the Free Church of Scotland,
the most important conservative denomination within the United Kingdom,
responded to a presentation by Bahnsen in one of its Glasgow congregations
by attempting to ban theonomists from holding any ecclesiastical office.[72]

It may have been the tenor of these responses—with the recognition of
the dangers of guilt by association—that encouraged the production of a
more intelligent response from within the Reformed community out of
which the movement of Christian Reconstruction had emerged. The faculty of Westminster Theological Seminary, Philadelphia, and Westminster
Seminary California produced a collection of essays, *Theonomy: A Reformed
Critique* (1990), which recognized that over the preceding decade "this
school of thought has produced a vast amount of literature, influenced the
Christian-school movement, affected many churches, and stimulated some
previously quietistic evangelicals to political activity," while appealing to a
growing body of born-again Protestants, from Calvinists to charismatics.[73]
This volume's criticisms of Reconstruction were sustained. Its publication
provoked a response, the titular wordplay of which was typical of its editor.
Theonomy: An Informed Response (1991), edited by North, noted the significance of the Westminster intervention: in the history of the seminary,
he observed, faculty members had only three times before collaborated on
a shared volume, and always to defend doctrines that were central to the
Christian faith.[74] But it is possible that some of the Westminster contributors
may have grown in appreciation for the movement they had worked together
to critique. In a monograph published in the same year, Vern Poythress,
who had contributed a chapter on mathematics to a volume edited by North
in 1979, described Bahnsen and North as "friends" who had helped him
to "love God's law," and he apologized for "any way in which I may have
underestimated the insights of their positions in the past or even in the present book," even as he recognized that "theonomists have a deep concern for
healing the hurts of modern society, including especially the elimination of
the tyrannical use of state power."[75] Bahnsen found this kind of qualified approval from fair-weather friends as frustrating as outright condemnation. He
complained that the "desperation to keep the Christian public from contact
with hearing or considering the theonomic point of view makes one think

we are dealing with pornography, rather than stodgy, age-old Puritan theology."[76] With some influence among charismatics but with a very mixed reception among the Reformed, Christian Reconstruction could not break into
the evangelical mainstream.

Disappointed by this failure to reconfigure the broader evangelical movement, a small number of Reconstructionists retreated into intentional communities in which to experiment with new kinds of social identity. One
of the earliest and most important of these communities was formed in
Tyler, Texas, in 1979, where Gary North and other theonomists developed
a new and more churchly style of Christian Reconstruction.[77] Westminster
Presbyterian Church, the congregation around which this community
gathered, provided a center for North's expanding publishing enterprise,
but became, at least in the minds of its critics, associated with preparations
for disaster that some fellow travelers found unusual. The Tyler community established its difference from Rushdoony's vision of Christian reform,
and a well-publicized breakdown in relationships within Rushdoony's extended family led to denunciations of survivalism in *The Journal of Christian
Reconstruction* and to North describing his father-in-law as a racist who had
backslid from his earlier Calvinist convictions.[78] This bad blood was not
thicker than water, and the Tyler community began to disperse. The new
communities into which some theonomists gathered and the organizations
that others began to form served to expose the divisions that existed within
the movement. Gary DeMar, who became the director of American Vision,
argued that America had been founded as a Christian nation—a position
with which Singer had disagreed.[79] Bahnsen argued that the Old Testament
food laws were now irrelevant—a position with which Rushdoony disagreed.
And North argued that Christian education should have no place for classical learning—a claim that was rejected by an outsider to this ideological
cadre who would nevertheless build the most significant theonomic center of
education, as conservative Calvinists from across the United States migrated
to north Idaho, to participate in the new community that had recently been
established in a quiet, liberal college town.

This community, gathering in Moscow, Idaho, was led by Douglas Wilson.
In the early 1980s, Wilson had moved from charismatic spirituality and dispensational theology to the Calvinist reformation through "a small hill of
Rushdoony's books," eventually coming to embrace his distinctive system
of "postmillennial, Calvinistic, Presbyterian, Van Tilian, theonomic, and reformed thought."[80] He shared his enthusiasm for Reconstructionist authors

with others in the new community, repackaging Rushdoony's philosophically orientated theonomy and postmillennialism with a much stronger emphasis on evangelism and cultural engagement.[81] He was routinely concerned with politics. His political theory drew on the literature of classical liberalism "in a thoroughly jumbled way," with Augustine, Anselm, King Alfred, John Calvin, John Knox, Thomas Jefferson, Edmund Burke, Robert E. Lee, T. S. Eliot, C. S. Lewis, J. R. R. Tolkien, G. K. Chesterton, Russell Kirk, and Rushdoony being among the writers he valued most.[82] Wilson maintained a radically libertarian view of government, which was modified by his theonomic instincts. He was not persuaded by the American political system: what "we call . . . democracy . . . Solomon called . . . foolishness."[83] Neither did he fall back on typically conservative arguments for "law and order": "there should be no war on drugs, and drugs should not be illegal . . . a man will search in vain for any hint that God wants civil penalties attached to drug use, per se."[84] Nor did he feel any great compulsion to back red or blue in the American electoral competition:

> One faction wants to drive toward the cliff of God's judgment at sixty miles an hour, while the loyal opposition wants to slow down to forty. Hardworking and soft-thinking Christians bust a gut to get the latter group into power. And then, when they do assume control, they compromise with the ousted group and settle on a moderate and well-respected speed of fifty-eight. But the Bible prohibits establishing a ruler—whether a ruler or judge—who does not fear God.[85]

With sentiments like these, it was hardly surprising that the Moscow community became known to its friends and enemies as a "hotbed of Christian Reconstructionism," even as it distanced itself from some of the movement's most prominent authors, and qualified the movement's arguments in witty journalism that drew upon a broad and complex discursive field.[86] Wilson emphasized that his eclectic influences did not combine in a manifesto: "We have no political agenda, but we most certainly have an agenda for politics."[87] His vision was to achieve revolutionary ends without using revolutionary means—and perhaps, he hoped, without using politics at all. He was not so much interested in "Reconstruction 2.0" as "Reconstruction 0.5," Wilson explained to me in an interview. After all, "if a modern State were to embrace biblical law, the result would probably look more like the absence of a State than an Islamic tyranny or the 'family values' of the Christian Right (which of the two is more frightening?)."[88]

Wilson's arguments against American systems of government and its political culture rested upon traditional Reformed arguments that the state should recognize its responsibility to God. Like Bahnsen, he insisted that "the idea of a secular state, one which divorces its authority and standards from religious considerations about God and His will, is completely alien to Biblical revelation," while recognizing that "true Christian obedience to the law of God will take us beyond a concern for ourselves to a concern for the obedience of those around us."[89] Nevertheless, he would also have agreed with Bahnsen, Christians were not to advocate the "forcible 'imposition' of God's law on an unwilling society," but to preach unbelieving individuals into voluntary submission to Scripture, allowing the political consequences of religious ideas to take care of themselves.[90] Politics, as a means to coerce an unwilling general public, was a short-cut to nowhere. The social reform that Wilson imagined would not be a consequence of political action, but of evangelism on a massive scale. The fact was, he explained, that the "severe problems this nation has do not admit of a political or cultural solution," and that the key to the transformation of America was the gospel.[91] "Why would we use the grimy little god of politics to try to usher in what Jesus Christ has already purchased on the cross with His own blood?"[92] And so, in the 1980s, as evangelicals elsewhere linked up with the consolidating Religious Right, the Moscow community stepped out of the binary of the American political mainstream to argue against the supporters of both parties that "politics is no savior."[93] This stepping away from the political binary was a movement out of the tradition of evangelical activism, the "most disturbing feature" of which, according to one member of the community, was their "trust in princes," as the history of the Moral Majority would prove.[94] The strategy of evangelical political action was simply misplaced, Wilson insisted: "Any serious attempts at cultural reform, based upon 'traditional values,' which precede a reformation and revival in the church, should be considered by Christians as worthless."[95] In its methods and in its goals, Wilson argued, the Religious Right was not sufficiently Christian. The divisions within Christian Reconstruction made believers look for solutions elsewhere. In Moscow, Idaho, it was time for something new.

III

Wilson's "agenda for politics" emphasized prayer, evangelism, and faithful Christian living, avoided the occasionally racist and less often avoided the anti-democratic themes of some earlier Reconstructionist writers, and developed in creative ways the responsibility of the state to govern according to divine law.[96] Wilson, who recognized that "Christians are in far greater danger of being seduced by the right than by the left," offered a conservative vision that was deeply distrustful of conservative politics.[97] He was especially concerned by the radicalization of the religious right and the consequent possibility of violence—perhaps because he had already seen an example of how quickly and with what disastrous consequences this kind of radicalization could occur, as we will later see. In north Idaho, as elsewhere in evangelical America, these kinds of anti-government sentiments were certainly in the air. Another member of the community recognized that the "palpable anti-government movement" that was organizing in the mid-1990s was "not hard to understand. Those who rule over us subject us to confiscatory taxation, turn our wealth over to the wicked for the advocacy and practice of every sort of evil, and impose criminal penalties for all kinds of innocuous behaviors."[98] Nevertheless, Wilson argued, "those on the 'traditional values' side of the conflict are consistently outmaneuvered because they refuse to go back to first principles. They do not see that unless Christ is acknowledged as Lord in the public square . . . then every manner of rebellion and disobedience must be tolerated there."[99] Political change depended on social change, which depended upon individual change, which could only be wrought by means of conversion—and that depended upon evangelism rather than political action.

Nevertheless, as the Moscow community grew in numbers, it developed a distinctive political philosophy, which was outlined in multiple issues of its magazine, *Credenda Agenda*, and in other printed materials.[100] The foundational assumption of this theory was that the state was under obligation to God. Greg Dickison, himself a lawyer, drew upon rich seams in the Reformed tradition to argue that the magistrate should be regarded as

> God's minister of wrath upon the evildoer, and his power is manifested in bearing the sword. He is also God's minister of good to the righteous (Rom. 13:4). He does not just punish; he praises as well (1 Pet. 2:14). The magistrate, by God's grace when sought by His saints, keeps the peace. It is not a secular peace, kept so we can live our mundane material lives. The magistrate keeps the peace so the gospel can spread, and the great commission be fulfilled (1 Tim. 2:1–8).[101]

And so, despite its numerical significance in north Idaho, the community did not expect to realize these objectives by throwing itself into political campaigns. They had no reason to do so, given their conviction, as Dickison had argued, that "simply electing evangelical Christians to office won't change anything (especially if they are going to morph into generic conservative, Republican, family-values Judeo-Christians). . . . Institutions, even institutions filled with Christians, cannot produce a Christian culture."[102] The evangelization of the Palouse would eventually achieve a legislative impact, the community's leaders argued, but that would come as a consequence of faithful Christian living rather than as a consequence of successful political efforts.

As the community's foundation of a liberal arts college suggested, its vision of faithful Christian living involved the production of the distinctly Christian culture without which, it believed, a Christian legal framework could not be sustained. Wilson recognized that "our adversaries are fighting on behalf of a certain culture which they have successfully established [in] art, music, architecture, philosophers, and more. We Christians are fighting for a Christian culture which no longer exists." A great deal of preparatory work had to precede any effort to engage in the political sphere. "Before we can enlist in the culture war, we have to have a culture. And that culture must be Christian."[103] Or, as Douglas Jones put it, without a Christian cultural hegemony, "talk of Christian politics only terrifies our non-Christian neighbors," and a victory for Christian ethics achieved by any form of coercion, including the ballot box, "would be like painting smiley faces on Egyptian tombs."[104] "Politics is not our savior," Dickison continued, "but politics will be saved."[105]

Pursuing the salvation of politics, in the absence of that cultural hegemony, and with such a strong emphasis upon evangelism, there was no reason for Christians to become involved in political campaigns. Although "I should care a great deal who leads this country," Nathan D. Wilson considered, "I couldn't care less whether Bush or Gore were in office, and I don't intend to lift a finger in support of either of them."[106] The debate among born-again Protestants about whether to support the candidate who was the lesser of two evils—which debate was perennial until evangelicals swallowed hard and swung in to secure the election of Donald Trump in 2016—was not something in which he wished to intervene. "Every election these issues are discussed. Christians argue whether or not voting for an unbeliever is acceptable, whether voting for a little evil instead of a medium or bigger evil is in itself evil. . . . The sooner Christians stop attempting to back a winner, and begin to back righteous men regardless of their odds, then we will suddenly realize that their odds are shortening."[107] The Moscow Christians were not lining up behind national candidates, therefore, and neither were they intending to intervene in local elections. There was too much to do before political activity in pursuit of any kind of Christian government could be viable. Prayer, evangelism, and the building of a Christian culture had to come first.

Evangelism had to be a priority because activity that was merely political could not deal with the fundamental problem besetting American society—the problem of divine judgment. The political engagement of the Religious Right had tended to assume that spiritual problems could be solved by political means. The Moscow Christians disagreed. Their analysis of the failure of this approach became apparent in the issue of *Credenda Agenda* that commemorated the 9/11 attacks. Entitled "God Struck America: Land That We Love," this issue described the "day of infamy" and what it represented. Stepping away from the patriotism around which evangelicals gathered in the aftermath of the attacks, the editors insisted that the tragedy had been deserved—that it was the judgment of a just God upon a people who had begun to "drink from the cup of God's wrath." After all, Wilson continued, "that same week contained another infamy, far worse in nature" than the terrorist attacks, despite their thousands of victims, and "far more damaging in that it was not recognized."[108] His reference was to the Day of Prayer and Remembrance that was held in the National Cathedral on September 14, 2001, when a multi-faith service of commemoration for the three thousand victims of the attacks was conducted by Billy Graham and other religious leaders. Wilson feared that this multi-faith service only compounded the national sin that had warranted the earlier outpouring of God's judgment. His response was excoriating:

> We are the reason the nation is under this judgment. The judgments have been building up over the course of the last generation—abortion on demand does not just bring judgment, such abortion is a judgment. God has struck us with a frenzy, and we kill our children, calling it freedom of choice. Sodomy is the same kind of thing—the Bible describes it as the wrath of God revealed from heaven, and God gives men up. When God does this, it is a display of His wrath, and it results in gay-pride marches in broad daylight.[109]

In other words, what happened on 9/11 was God's judgment for America's sins. God "controlled, directed, predestined, for His own wise and holy purposes, this attack on us."[110] Whatever the 9/11 attacks suggested about attitudes among Muslims in the Middle East, they proved above all that "God hates America."[111] And that was why the Moscow community saw political activity as a waste of time. God had to change the soul of the nation before its laws could be transformed.

For the same reason that politics was a waste of time, the Moscow community also dismissed any effort to impose godly rule by force. Godly government could not be established by means of separatism or secession. This was an important point to make, as, in the early 2000s, communities of kinists emerged in north Idaho, and used the internet to connect with similar groups elsewhere. Racial separatism had to be taken off the agenda. Of course, the subject of race did occasionally feature in Canon Press publications. In 2002, Wilson recognized that "the peoples of European descent are steadily committing sexual suicide. In 1960, we were one fourth of the world. In 2000, we were one sixth. In 2050, we will be one tenth, and we will be the oldest tenth."[112] But he made no effort to argue that white Christians should make any attempt to resist this demographic change. While some local kinists identified Wilson as a half-hearted fellow traveler, a theme that recurred in conversations during fieldwork and that has been picked up by some of his critics, especially in connection with his views on American slavery, his published work has been consistently critical of the radical right and of its racial politics. From the late 1990s into the first decade of the 2000s, the leaders of the Moscow community directly challenged racialist ideology. Wilson dismissed as "skinists" the racial separatists that were growing in number in northern Idaho.[113] And in *Black and tan*, a meditation on the values of the Old South that channeled Singer's *A Theological Interpretation of American History*, Wilson reported that his work had "infuriated" white separatists.[114] Ironically, this volume also infuriated those elsewhere on the political spectrum who rejected the book's revisionist account of the conditions of American slavery, and who dismissed its arguments as racist. But the editors of *Credenda Agenda* forthrightly rejected these kinds of claims. "We call upon every Christian who risks being called a racist bigot (and what good Christian today doesn't run such a risk?) to behave in such a way that makes all such accusations ludicrous as soon as they are made."[115] From Wilson's point of view, at least, there was no inconsistency between valorizing the society of the Old South, with its peculiar institution of slavery, and combatting racism on the Palouse, in the name of godly government.

And, if separatism was off the agenda, so too was any recourse to redemptive violence. It was important for Wilson to insist upon this point. After all, one of the readers of *Credenda Agenda* was already serving time on death row after his murder of an abortion doctor and his bodyguard. Wilson's correspondence with Paul Jennings Hill was published in the magazine in 1996.[116] In his letter to the murderer, Wilson recognized that revolution would be a constant temptation for the religious right, as it considered whether to attempt to impose by political or militaristic force what could only be achieved through salvation and organic social change. But Wilson condemned Hill's brand of revolutionary politics in unequivocal terms, not least because, as he later explained, "change is reformational and never revolutionary."[117] For "*rebel* is a word that should never fit a Christian," another community member insisted. "When we disobey one authority, we must always be able to appeal to a higher authority to which we are in submission, whether that authority be a higher magistrate, a court, a constitution, or the Bible." On this basis, he continued, believers should pay taxes "to avoid giving unnecessary offense. . . . Paul wanted a peaceful environment in which the gospel could flourish (1 Tim. 2:1–2)."[118] Sometimes the Christian's responsibility was to suffer, and "sometimes," Douglas Wilson suggested, "direct action is necessary."[119] His son confirmed the point: "Christians should be willing to get violent with the establishment," but only if "victory is possible" and "if it would be a sin" not to do so. "In our position today, we can't win; nor are the tyrannies extreme enough to cause sin in us if we submit to them," he continued. "We must bide our time and pick our battles."[120]

This sense of the need for Christian endurance within a hostile culture dominated conversations during my fieldwork at New Saint Andrews. "We are in the midst of a setback," one group of students explained in the summer of 2015. "This has been a really hard year in America. Consider the Obergefell decision [to require all states to legalize same-sex marriages], which was the Supreme Court . . . overstepping their bounds. The second setback was . . . the atrocities of abortion that came to light with [allegations of selling body parts made against] Planned Parenthood. . . . It's been a hard year."[121] But the community was mobilizing, with large numbers of members of the Christ Church and Trinity Reformed congregations joining in an anti-abortion protest of around five hundred individuals on the Moscow-Pullman highway.[122] Even though the protest was well attended, one recent graduate complained that people within the Moscow community displayed an "apathetic cynicism" toward politics.[123] His peers were not sure of how best to respond at a national level to the threat to Christian values. "Obama was the natural outcome of where we have been going," one explained, but, in the summer of 2015, none of the group of half-a-dozen former students was expecting to vote for Donald Trump.[124] He did not embody the values that they wanted to promote, and they were not prepared to support the candidate who was the lesser of two evils. They were not sure who to support instead. And these students struggled to explain whether they saw themselves as theonomists. Some were concerned that they were being perceived as radicals who were "planning a coup."[125] The reality was quite the opposite, they explained: "we're going to have a hard time fixing anything if we focus on the national level, the federal level." "God tends to work with the people that aren't out there grasping for power," one student continued: "God tends to work through smaller things."[126] There was still too much to do. The conditions were still not right for effective Christian political engagement.

Of course, the gospel parable to which this student alluded made the point that mustard seeds can grow into very large trees. And if the thought leaders of this community were not clear about its short-term political obligations, they were explicit about their expectations of governmental change in the longer term. They insisted that righteous government, when finally established, would not be involved in "forcing people to become Christians." But it would compel citizens to "outwardly conform to a Christian standard," and enact laws that would "protect . . . the Christian religion."[127] In developing this argument, Dickison gestured toward libertarian ideals at the same time as he invoked the traditional Reformed doctrine of a confessional state: "a righteous government would not be nearly as busy as ours."[128] Nevertheless, if the means were not revolutionary, the end of this program of action certainly was, and this description of the end-game of Christian Reconstruction resonated with the political impulses of mid-century libertarians. "The fulfilment of the Great Commission . . . requires the establishment of a global Christendom," the *Credenda Agenda* editors insisted, and that victory requires "the necessary exclusion of secular democracy."[129] Wilson saw his work contributing to the realization of a "network of nations bound together by a formal, public, civic acknowledgement of the lordship of Jesus Christ and the fundamental truth of the Apostles' Creed."[130] "Secularism is a spent force," he continued, and "traditional values can't fight sin."[131] And this is why "Christian ministers must proclaim the crown rights of King Jesus everywhere, and over everything."[132] What this will achieve would be a "baptized civilization," in which the practice of non-Christian religion would be permissible only within private homes.[133] And in his most recent writing Wilson has no qualms about describing his goal as "theocracy."[134]

It is hardly surprising that these kinds of sentiments, openly circulating in a left-leaning college town as reflecting opinion within its largest and most influential congregations, should have provoked consternation and fear. The Moscow-Pullman media has regularly featured stories—and complaints—about the community that was promoting a revisionist view of Southern slavery while quietly consolidating its plans for a monolithic religious state.[135] The Moscow Christians have not always been sure how best to respond to this kind of local criticism. Some of their number have dismissed these claims as "editorial smears," but others have welcomed "the blessing of being scary. Throughout Scripture, it's a good thing when God's people terrify the wicked."[136] For critics of this expanding and increasingly powerful community are worried about the changing character of their town. To be fair, that is often the effect of schemes for global conquest.

IV

The critics' fear may spread, for the ideas that the Moscow community have articulated are being advanced in new contexts and across the United States. Wilson's critique of American modernity and the dangers of its liberal democratic culture is widely shared—as are the solutions he proposes. One of the most important recent introductions to Christian Reconstruction has been prepared by Gary North's son-in-law, the former director of American Vision, a think tank based in Atlanta, Georgia. Joel McDurmon's *Restoring America One County at a Time* (2012) set out a very practical program for action. Setting aside any explicit discussion of millennial theory, his argument counseled patience and multigenerational preparation for a very long game. Like Wilson, McDurmon was concerned by the duplicity and pragmatism of the Religious Right. "Between 1980 and now . . . Christians essentially have been used by conservative politicians while making very little if any political progress" toward realizing the goals of godly government.[137] In their quest for power, politicians have made promises to conservative evangelicals that they have been unable or unwilling to keep. Their duplicity has been driven by the short-term considerations of a demanding electoral cycle. But, McDurmon emphasized, "you will not take back America overnight no matter how you go about it, and anyone—especially a politician—who promises you that you can is lying to get your vote."[138] In fact, a conservative who believed in an organic social community would not want to "take back America overnight": "societies are simply not designed for abrupt structural changes. Instead, we need to turn the boat slowly."[139] America's problems were simply too entrenched for anyone to "magically transform the nation."[140] Counseling patience, McDurmon proposed a ten-step program to limit the power of the state, with objectives that included the expansion of private education, the abolition of Social Security, states' rights, the decentralization of taxation, the imposition of a flat rate of income tax of less than 10 percent, the cessation of fractional reserve banking, the use of private courts, including informal arbitration, and the abolition of a permanent standing army, which would prevent the development of an aggressive foreign policy and the "sin of militarism."[141] And—of course—he hoped for an end to abortion: "perhaps the most important and powerful issue for Christians that can be addressed by state power is the abomination protected under *Roe v. Wade*."[142]

But McDurmon's writing steps away from the simplistic denunciations of the termination of pregnancy to ask bigger questions of what it means to be pro-life. In this, as in other policy areas, his book counsels the wisdom of small gains rather than a revolutionary "great leap forward":

> the strategy of a "once-for-all" reversal of *Roe* has been ineffective for almost forty years now. That is not to say it's an impossibility. But had the already spent time and money been focused on local solutions instead, we might very likely see life more properly protected in a vast array of states today, with the forces of infanticide pushed to the blue fringes of the nation. Those who will accept only a single, national solution to abortion are saying that, if they cannot outlaw abortion *everywhere*, then they don't want it outlawed *anywhere*.[143]

The best way to secure an end to abortion, in other words, was to defend states' rights, to adopt a gradualist approach that would see abortion banned in one state—say, Georgia, where, in 2019, severe restrictions on access to abortion were signed into law, only to be contested and blocked in court—in the hope that other states will follow suit. To be pro-life is therefore to be in favor of local over national government, and to pursue strategies of change that work from the bottom up—the very antithesis of revolution.[144] And to be pro-life, McDurmon argues, is also to become much more skeptical about the value of American military power. "Too many Christians who decry the government-protected slaughter of children in the womb are way too tolerant of government-mandated slaughter of kids at nineteen or twenty, not to mention the slaughter of thousands of civilian bystanders. A consistent pro-life view will avoid this terrible oversight."[145] Once again, strategies of reconstruction would run counter to patriotic narratives: "we have to stop applauding everything the military does as if it were automatically the gleam of national greatness, quit praising all soldiers all the time as sacrosanct individuals, and quit forbidding any criticism of the military as if it were the holy of holies."[146]

While McDurmon casts a critical eye on the military, other theonomists are becoming more positive about the potential for the righteous use of arms. Wilson was clear about his rejection of the political violence pursued by Paul Jennings Hill, but others are prepared to consider the radical solutions that he proposed, though they have differed in identifying the circumstances in which that resort to arms would become permitted. One of the speakers at the "righteous resistance" conference in Coeur d'Alene prepared a short book that outlined his version of this doctrine of resistance. Matthew J. Trewhella's *The Doctrine of the Lesser Magistrates: A Proper Resistance to Tyranny and a Repudiation of Unlimited Obedience to Civil Government* (2013) advanced a forthright account of the believer's rights and responsibilities during a period of national decline, which he connected to the "population control industry" that provided access to abortion.[147] He believed that an urgent response was necessary. The federal government "has trampled our Constitution, assaults our person, liberty, and property, and impugns the law of God. Americans are now nearly a completely conquered people."[148] But there was a mechanism in Reformed theology through which the government's attack on the Constitution could be curtailed, he believed. In the sixteenth century, Reformed theorists had argued that "lesser magistrates" were properly equipped to interpose in tensions between rulers and those they ruled, "often without the shedding of blood."[149] Importing this idea into American modernity, Trewhella argued that modern-day "lesser magistrates," including sheriffs and other locally elected officials, should "oppose any laws that subvert existing law or divine law, to "refuse and resist any laws that subvert the Constitution."[150] There were strict limits upon that kind of intervention. The lesser magistrate is "only justified in defying the higher authority when the higher authority clearly contravenes the law of God . . . or makes a law or policy which violates the Constitution."[151] But sometimes the shedding of blood could not be avoided, he added: "there comes a time when men must cross swords."[152] For, "if Congress and the President continue to walk

down this dark road of rebellion and anarchy, the military may someday
have to rise up and interpose, as they have a long and prestigious history of
doing."[153] Realizing how surprising this claim would be to many of his evangelical readers, Trewhella lamented the political impotence of the modern
American church: "America's present day pulpits need to repent of their idolatrous views regarding the State. . . . Thankfully, America's founders established three well-known 'boxes' by which we can preserve liberty and resist
tyranny. These are—the ballot box, the jury box, and the cartridge box."[154]
This doctrine of the lesser magistrate was—almost—a call for a coup.

Other theonomist writers made more explicit their expectation of a
second civil war. Gordan Runyan, pastor of a small congregation based in
Tucumcari, New Mexico, published *Resistance to Tyrants: Romans 13 and
the Christian Duty to Oppose Wicked Rulers* (2012) to reflect his concerns
about big government, which, in its expansive interventions, "has become
the closest thing to a Messiah for many in our day: and those who worship it
pray to it constantly to come and make all things new."[155] "Nationalism . . . is
idolatrous," he observed.[156] For Runyan, godly government was always limited. "God has ordained the institution of civil government. He has also given
it its only legitimate marching orders, a narrow and simple mission: to do His
will, by serving Him in the prosecution of His own rules of righteousness,
against all wrongdoers."[157] The prescriptions for government in Scripture
said "nothing . . . about the State becoming the educator, or the banker, or the
doctor, or the charitable outlet, or the babysitter, or the consumer advocate
of the people. A ruler who takes one of these duties to himself has become
a ruler who has abandoned his God-given mission."[158] Godly government
would strictly limit its role: "protect the good guys from the bad guys. Just
do that, and we'll all be happy."[159] The problem with the American government, of course, was that it did both much less and much more than was necessary. Only an unjust government would imprison a farmer for collecting
rainwater on his farm while protecting the abortion of around 3000 babies
each day, or "about a million and a half each year."[160] The "list of offenses that
are being perpetrated on the American public at this hour . . . is incontro-
vertible evidence of a government in full rebellion against God. It is not good
government making mistakes. It is tyrannical and wicked. For me, the line is
crossed."[161] In overstepping the boundaries of godly rule, the government's
"claim to power is usurpation."[162] Runyan encouraged his readers to

understand that "submitting to and serving" the "tyrants" of American government is an "act of treason against the King of kings."[163] Referencing Wilson alongside Rushdoony, he insisted that "armed resistance [is] our last option," but only if there is a genuine possibility of victory.[164] " 'Jesus is Lord' is not politically neutral"; however, it has become a theological cliché. But, Runyan continued, "rulers in rebellion toward God hear it as a threat. It is right for them to hear it as a threat because it is."[165]

Perhaps James Wesley Rawles offers the most striking—and most widely circulated—discussion of the possibility of political violence. His writing does not offer the same kind of critiques of American government, partly because, as he explained to me in 2013, "all politics are local," and with "readers in dozens of countries . . . it would be foolish for me to dwell too much on American politics."[166] Nevertheless, Rawles's writing is driven by a consistent political vision. Describing himself as a Christian libertarian, he explained that "if people simply recognize the Ten Commandments and the spirit in which they are given, and they recognize the right of life and property for others, and they uphold contracts . . . you can live in a pretty peaceful, tranquil society, with no great need of government, because people are essentially self-governed."[167] But this liberty would be possibly only for the redeemed:

> I believe in individual liberty in a Christian context, and that is if people are saved through the blood of Christ I believe that by the Holy Spirit they will be constrained to live in a righteous way. That should be the only constraint they live under . . . I believe in absolutely minimalist government. If people are going to be governed by anything it should be by the elders of their local church.[168]

Nevertheless, as his blogging and fictional writing shows, Rawles expects the current difficulties within American government to precipitate ever greater crises. Even self-government may need to be defended, and Rawles took time to outline in his survival manuals the weapons required for self-defense and in his fiction the tactics of defense. Survival and resistance had to come before reconstruction. Believers needed to consider the ethics of bearing arms—after all, as one blogger names himself, invoking a notorious Old Testament assassin, "Ehud would." But "would," the latter-day theonomists remember, is not "should."

V

Pushed to the cultural margins, evangelicals who have drawn upon Rushdoony's legacy have been forced to think seriously about the condition of American government, and what the proper response to its over-reach should be. These critics agree that government should be limited, and that its contracting legislative base should depend upon Old Testament law. They also agree that the current political system does not offer the means by which this change might have been made. When the nation is under divine judgment, any effort to pursue a Christian society by means of politics will necessarily fail. The followers of Rushdoony divide over what should happen next. Where their numbers are strongest, in the communities that have gathered in north Idaho, theonomists engage in culture and have developed an ambitious program of church planting and evangelism. The very considerable size and well-developed infrastructure of this community directs its energies into relatively normal behaviors. Where similar kinds of believers feel more isolated, or are less well organized as communities, they may turn toward more radical prescriptions to prevent the advance of the modernity that they interpret as rebellion against God. This may explain why the thousands of these believers who live around Moscow assume cultural and economic agendas for dominion, while their fellow travelers from smaller groups, in locations as close as Coeur d'Alene, find themselves considering what might be the circumstances that would warrant Christian involvement in political violence.

Yet this turn toward radical action is in many ways ironic. Even as these believers bunker down in the expectation of greater tribulation, the ideas about government that inform their views of ethics are finding a wider and more important audience. In the run-up to the 2016 election, a number of Rushdoony's proposals for biblical government were taken up by candidates for the Republican Party's presidential nomination, and were defended in national televised debates. Ben Carson advocated a flat tax of 10 percent on the basis that the state could not demand more than God.[169] Ted Cruz built his policies around the "seven mountains" version of dominion theology that circulates among charismatics.[170] And Donald Trump echoed Rushdoony when he proposed that women who had abortions should be punished—a policy position he almost immediately retracted when he realized how far he had advanced beyond the views of even the most aggressive pro-life organizations.[171] The president is no more likely to be a close reader of Rushdoony than are the Christians whose views he had thought to represent. And yet it is those who most share his enthusiasm for retribution against those who terminate their pregnancies who might also want to radically curb almost every other aspect of his power. "It is," as the editors of *Credenda Agenda* put it in a different context, "the only way we can see to stop Donald Trump."[172] The crisis in government at the "end of white Christian America" demands survival and resistance before any effort at reconstruction.

4

Education

Education in the modern age is a Messianic and Utopian movement born of the Enlightenment hope of regenerating man in and through his autonomous reason.[1]

We surrendered our children to be educated by men and women who did not fear God, and we thought there would be no serious consequences. But there were.[2]

Not many high school graduates have ever managed to memorize "huge portions of the Bible" while also having read "nearly all of the classics, the writings from the Scottish Enlightenment, and the Founding Fathers."[3] But Megan and Malorie LaCroix, two of the principal characters in Rawles's *Liberators*, had benefited from exactly that kind of education. Born into a family that was radically skeptical of the public school system and the values it promoted, the sisters had been educated at home, where their mother had instilled in them the virtues of hard work and the perils of American modernity. As adults, recognizing that the threat to their way of life was more immediate than ever before, they wished to pass on to the children in their care the knowledge and the religious and political perspectives that they had gained. As their culture crumbled around them, their home education became a first step in the war to save America.

While these characters are fictional, this kind of religious and political home education has grown rapidly in popularity in recent years, and might represent the aspect of evangelical resistance to American modernity that is most widely distributed and so most obvious to the general public. Of course, this growing interest in and support for home and private Christian schools stands in contrast to the traditional strategy of the Religious Right, which has long attempted to exercise control over the public schools. In the last few years, that influence has grown in very considerable ways. Katherine Stewart, author of *The Good*

Survival and Resistance in Evangelical America. Crawford Gribben, Oxford University Press (2021). © Oxford University Press. DOI: 10.1093/oso/9780199370221.003.0005

News Club: The Christian Right's stealth assault on America's children (2012), worried that there was now "more religious activity in American public schools than there has been for the past 100 years," and suggested that the Good News Clubs that operate in many of these public schools represent a "industrial-scale evangelical conversion machine."[4] Four years later, she was even more alarmed. Writing in the *New York Times* in December 2016, Stewart noted that President Trump's first pick for Secretary of Education had been Jerry Falwell, Jr., president of the fundamentalist Liberty University, and that his second pick, Betsy DeVos, who was installed as the eleventh education secretary in 2017, understood the religious control of public education as contributing to the expansion of God's kingdom.[5] Unexpectedly, perhaps, Reconstructionists would share many of Stewart's concerns, and would support her argument that explicitly Christian teaching has no place in public schools. At precisely the moment when their influence in public schools may be at its height, conservative evangelicals continue to push for an end to the system.

Whether it is being pursued in private schools or in private homes, Christian education is now very widely supported. Since the 1960s, and especially since 1993, when home education was legalized in the last of the states in which it had been forbidden, a growing number of American evangelicals have withdrawn their children from "government schools," seeking alternative provision either in private Christian day schools or in parentally provided education within the home.[6] At the time of writing, over two million American children are being home educated, and in the last few years, the number of children involved in home education has grown at a rate around twelve times that of the number of students entering public schools.[7] Devolving control to the level of the family, home education permits eccentricity as well as distraction, tolerating poor pedagogy while enabling precious achievement.[8] Extraordinary feats of memorization are not uncommon. Homeschooled children won the National Geographic Bee on five occasions between 1998 and 2007.[9] One researcher met a twelve-year-old who had memorized more than ten thousand words of biblical passages, an achievement similar to the memorization of "huge portions of the Bible" by the characters in Rawles's novel.[10] As the sector has expanded, there has developed a huge and almost bewildering array of resources to provide distinctively Christian curricula. Many of these private or home schools have chosen to use materials with values that compare to those of the LaCroix sisters. In the late 1970s, the "Accelerated Christian Education" (ACE) curriculum, which required students to memorize passages from the American Constitution and the Declaration of Independence, was being used by around 1,500 private schools and was being promoted among Christian Reconstructionists.[11] The ACE curriculum remains popular among evangelical homeschoolers, although it has often been criticized for its inflexible, "drill-and-kill pedagogy," as well as for promoting a "paranoid and conspiratorial fundamentalist world view."[12] But, as the sector has expanded, a wide variety of providers have emerged to offer educational packages through a variety of media that are more clearly attuned to theonomist goals, while other providers that are not part of this movement reflect within their materials the perspectives on family, church, and society that Reconstructionist writers promote. In her survey of this culture, Molly Worthen argued that while "explicit references to Rushdoony are few, today's Christian homeschooling literature is rife with Rushdoonyian language . . . about the absence of neutral ground between Christians and non-Christians, the governing role of parents, and the inherent religiosity of all education."[13] Drawing from Rushdoony's early condemnation of the public school system, and the "intellectual schizophrenia" that he believed it represented, those parents who provide their children with an "epistemologically self-conscious" education from kindergarten to college may have great expectations as to what their efforts might achieve. In home schools, private schools, and in several recently established, prominent, and influential liberal arts colleges, these children are being drilled in varieties of Reformed theology and armed with conservative political perspectives. Being prepared to resist and survive American modernity, the graduates of this movement for Christian education are enlisting in "God's emerging army."[14]

As the number of participants suggests, home education has become a very big business.[15] In 2009, Robert Kunzman noted, the market for homeschool curricula was worth almost one billion dollars per annum.[16] Mainstream publishers have begun to take an interest in the subject, with Norton selling *The Well-Trained Mind: A Guide to Classical Education in the Home* (1999, 2004), by Jessie Wise and her daughter Susan Wise Bauer, a vocal critic of conservative strains within the movement, and Palgrave Macmillan selling Leigh A. Bortins's *The Core: Teaching Your Child the Foundations of Classical Education* (2010).[17] It is telling that these crossover books privilege the classical tradition. The most recent report from the National Center for Education Statistics, collating data collected in 2012, suggests that almost all homeschooled children are white (80 percent), that many of them live in rural areas (40 percent), and that hardly any of them can be classified as poor (11 percent). Homeschooling families report high levels of religious observance: almost two-thirds of their number acknowledged that their motivation to withdraw their children from public or private schools had been driven by religious or moral concerns.[18] Investigators into this culture have observed that home education remains an attractive option for religious fundamentalists from many different backgrounds, and that the numbers of religious believers involved in home education increased after the practice was legalized across all fifty states in 1993.[19] In many parts of the United States, home-educating parents are not subject to onerous levels of external scrutiny or public accountability, and the states that have fewest restrictions on the content or delivery of home education tend to be those with the largest evangelical populations.[20] Around one-quarter of states "don't even require parents to notify anyone" if they decide to educate their children at home— and so the number of children involved in this form of alternative education is almost certainly vastly under-reported (and hence it is impossible to establish what "typical" learning outcomes might be).[21] But research into the character and outcomes of these pedagogical schemes overturns many of the expectations of their critics. For all that the decision to homeschool is represented in popular culture as a negligent social choice—prompting the familiar query, "what about socialization?"—the most recent ethnographic survey of homeschooling parents indicates that their intention is to be "ultra-responsible."[22] It is a serious decision: home education often comes with significant financial cost.[23]

There may be other costs, too. Journalists and other commentators worry about the meaning and purpose of this removal of children from the public education system and their introduction into private academies and home schools. Some critics of this movement fear the worst. Stewart linked the principal theorists of this homeschooling culture to the growth of Christian nationalism—which she suggests might represent the emergence of an American fascism. The removal of children from public schools represents a rejection of the "values of inclusivity and diversity," she argues, explaining that the leaders of this movement are intent on "destroying the system of public education."[24] Nor is Stewart's militaristic language merely metaphorical. Scholars have carefully considered the content and impact of ACE and similar kinds of curricula, and some, like Randall Balmer, worry that home education will "diminish the possibilities" for the creation of a common and pluralistic American culture, while contributing to a "ghetto mentality" among born-again Protestants.[25] Of course, the same argument could be made against the radically secular homeschooling that is portrayed in *Captain Fantastic* (dir. Matt Ross, 2016), and of the experience of Mormon homeschooling that is the subject of Tara Westover's memoir, *Educated* (2018), both of which illustrate the popularity of home education in the Pacific Northwest as well as the loss, isolation, and hyper-achievement to which it can lead. It is true that home education decentralizes decision-making about curriculum content to families, and consequently permits the inculcation of some very conservative views. Nor does home education necessarily provide the checks and balances against dangerous levels of introversion or political radicalization: mainstream media outlets are paying attention to the Christian homeschool background of the suspects in a number of recent mass murders.[26] But educational researchers suggest that there is no inevitable link between home education and any form of cultural ghettoization. Some evidence from the late 1990s suggested that homeschooling families were more involved in civic activities than were their public school peers, while more recent research indicates that Christian home education may promote greater tolerance for religious and political diversity.[27] The quality of other outcomes is mixed—and Robert Kunzman is right to caution against the "distortion" by homeschool advocacy groups of some of the relevant educational research.[28] But this tendency to embrace pluralism reflects the wider direction of travel in the political engagement of American evangelicals, which is to recognize their new minority status and to argue within it using rights-based narratives that assume a liberal political order.[29]

Nevertheless, in this as in other areas of evangelical life, a small number of evangelicals are resisting the tendency of their fellow believers to understand their future as a vigorous but always defensive minority within an increasingly diverse society. Across the United States, but especially in north Idaho, an increasing number of believers are turning to several varieties of Christian education to dispute the minoritarian and subcultural assumptions of those believers who have conceded to liberal expectations, and to educate a generation of the faithful that will work to reclaim and eventually control the cultural mainstream. The influence of conservative religion on the public school system has never been greater, but in home schools, private schools, and liberal arts colleges, education has become a vital weapon in strategies of survival and resistance in evangelical America.

I

The modern Christian education movement emerged out of widespread dissatisfaction among born-again Protestants with the system of public schooling. For several centuries, public education had been promoted in order to create a common culture from the "melting pot" created by immigration to America. Horace Mann (1796–1859) was one of many educational reformers who traveled extensively to promote the "common schools that would raise the masses up to the level of the middle-class Protestant consensus"—even as he had his wife teach their own children at home.[30] These progressive assumptions about education and the creation of a common public good were codified in state legislation, so that several states, including Washington (1912), Ohio (1927), and New Hampshire (1929), declared any system of home education to be illegal.[31] Even in states that cautiously permitted it, home education was widely regarded with suspicion.

At states created a monopoly for their public schooling systems, there was little reason for evangelicals to be concerned. In the late nineteenth and early twentieth centuries, born-again Protestants tended to support public education, as the social and religious values that it promoted generally accorded with their own. But the impact of secularization, which coincided with the collapsing credibility of conservative Protestantism in the 1930s and 1940s, and the social changes associated with the "twilight of the American Enlightenment" in the 1950s, pushed many believers to reconsider their relationship to the educational mainstream.[32] By the 1960s, reactionaries and revolutionaries found common cause in worries about mass society, as evangelical concerns about the state of public education were being echoed on the countercultural left. This movement for educational reform was influenced by theorists and practitioners with multiple and contradictory perspectives, from those influenced by A. S. Neill's anti-authoritarian Summerhill school to those who preferred John Holt's method of "unschooling."[33] But these educational reformers were joined by some surprising fellow travelers. During that decade of experimentation, radicals at both ends of the political spectrum engaged in homeschooling as an "act, even a movement, of self-conscious political protest against government."[34] Enabled by suburbanization, which provided families with the aspiration for privacy and the physical space that homeschooling required, and by the "American cult of the child," as Milton Gaither has argued, homeschooling increased in popularity as the "countercultural sensibility became the American sensibility," and anti-institutionalism became a norm in the social mainstream.[35]

The counterculture of the 1960s provided a rather unlikely context for the emergence of a distinctively Christian educational movement. The latter movement, as it expanded after the 1960s, was driven by the conservative social and political mores of its leaders, and by their fear that traditional Christian values were increasingly under threat. A number of historians have suggested that the evangelical movement toward alternative education was driven by resistance to the integration of the public school system, in the aftermath of *Brown v. Board of Education* (1954). Randall Balmer, for example, has argued that it was the forcible integration of public schools that drove white Southern evangelicals to consider alternatives to public education, and Julie J. Ingersoll, who had close family ties to some Reconstructionist education providers before leaving the community and writing a book about her experiences within it, found confirmation that a small minority of the earliest Christian schools had indeed been set up in response to compulsory integration.[36] Reconstructionist leaders were certainly concerned about the implications of schemes for racial balancing. The politics of segregation influenced early Reconstructionist writing, as we have already noticed, and provided a structural motif in Singer's theological interpretation of American history. Rushdoony understood the significance of the issue, and opposed the schemes for integration that multi-racial classrooms represented, not for reasons to do with racial supremacy but because he denied that the state should be able to wield the power by which this integration would be either imposed or prevented: he rejected "both legal segregation and integration, believing that both involve an infringement on the individual's freedom of association."[37] This nuance was not widely shared, and theonomist publications did not often represent resistance to the integration of public schools via laissez faire principles. Sometimes the negativity toward *Brown v. Board of Education* was overt. In 1977, for example, *The Journal of Christian Reconstruction* published a review of an academic monograph that was critical of the Supreme Court decision.[38] Some Reconstructionist writers were worried by this resistance to integration. Robert Thoburn, who established Fairfax Christian School, in Fairfax, Virginia, in 1961, and who contributed *The Children Trap: Biblical Principles for Education* (1986) to Gary North's "Biblical Blueprint" series, expressed his frustration that "outraged white parents" considered their "commitment to blood lines (race)" as more important than any other factor in the environment in which their children were educated.[39] But he was also critical of the decision of the Internal Revenue Service in 1978 to impose racial quotas on private schools, which quotas, he believed, targeted Christian institutions, and he was still critical of the practice of busing students across town to create racial balance in public schools when he wrote a book on Christian education in 1986.[40] While several historians have argued that the Christian school movement took off in reaction to *Brown v. Board of Education*, others, including Milton Gaither, have remembered that correlation is not causation, and have disputed this link between racism and religious education.[41] After all, opposition to the consequences of *Brown v. Board of Education* cannot explain everything about the growth of the Christian education movement in and after the 1960s, especially as the focus among theonomists turned from promoting private schools to promoting faith-based tuition at home. In the 1960s, home education was illegal in almost all states, but concerned believers nevertheless began to withdraw their children from the public education system, often finding themselves in serious trouble as a consequence. Harried by the courts, these pioneers in alternative education found a champion in the most important of the leaders of Christian Reconstruction.

Rushdoony's interest in Christian home education was long-standing. His earliest work, including *Intellectual Schizophrenia* (1961), a book that was based upon lectures that he delivered to the Christian Teachers Association of the Northwest in October 1959, and which was published with the financial help of the William Volker Charities Fund, argued that Christian parents should provide for their children an education that was philosophically consistent with their core theological beliefs. His later work, *The Messianic Character of American Education* (1963), argued that the education that was being provided by the state was of a similarly religious character.[42] In the 1970s and early 1980s, Rushdoony traveled extensively to provide expert witness in trials of homeschooling parents, testifying in twenty-three court cases between 1980 and 1988, and his contribution to *Leeper et al. v. Arlington ISD et al.*, in 1987, helped achieve the "watershed ruling" against the Texas Education Authority that represented the triumph of home education in one of the states in which opposition to the practice had been strongest.[43] Rushdoony's legal arguments developed themes that he had outlined in his earliest philosophical and theological writings, insisting that if education were inherently religious, then the prohibition of home education violated the constitutional freedoms of American citizens. Time after time, his arguments were effective, and the results of successive trials provided parents with new arguments, new rights, and new pedagogical opportunities for Christian home education. These efforts were of enormous significance: Milton Gaither, the principal historian of home education in America, has described Rushdoony as "one of the most important early U.S. homeschooling leaders."[44]

Rushdoony articulated his arguments clearly and consistently. *Intellectual Schizophrenia* was a closely argued rationale for Christian education. Despite its being written during the difficult last years of Rushdoony's first marriage, *Intellectual Schizophrenia* insisted upon the responsibility of families. Its premise was simple—that education was inherently religious, and therefore that the task of education was within the remit of the family, and not that of the government. His account of public education was—literally—damning. Referring to T. S. Eliot and C. S. Lewis, as well as to the eccentric Plymouth Brethren writer G. H. Lang, Rushdoony set about an excoriating review of modern educational theory and practice.[45] Condemning Lockean assumptions of a *tabula rasa*—the assumption that education could form children without reference to tradition—he insisted that modern education involved a "war against the past," an "unceasing war of attrition on all cultures and brooks no terms, demanding unconditional surrender for purposes of annihilation."[46] Modern education, he continued, is "statist education, and the state is made the all-embracing institution of which all other institutions are but facets."[47] But the state was sick, and its schools and the philosophy that lay behind it were "decisive and important aspects of a now faltering and waning culture."[48] In many ways, Rushdoony's analysis of the philosophical contradictions of the public school system anticipated as criticisms the observations that would become central to critical theory: he may have realized before many postmodernists that a "statist school . . . has no concept of truth to offer."[49] But Christians had a solution to this truthlessness. "Knowing Christ we know all things," he continued; in Reformed theology "we have the fundamental principle of interpretation."[50] Therefore Christians should not work for the acceptance of their pedagogy within a pluralistic educational system. Instead, believers should "attack the fundamental statist concept, separating all education, including parochial, private, and Christian schools, as well as 'public' schools, from the state and from state financial aid in any form," for "education must be truly free."[51] The "fundamental task of Christian education," he insisted, was to erect the "standard of Jesus Christ . . . in every field of life."[52] This was certainly going to be a challenge. "At present," he admitted, "nothing seems more unlikely" than the reconstruction of Christian education.[53] His goals were ambitious. Merely to reform the public school system would never create the kind of education for which he argued: "Let the dead . . . bury the dead; the living have work to do."[54] *Intellectual Schizophrenia* was a call for radical action.

Rushdoony's follow-up title, *The Messianic Character of American Education* (1963), provided a fairly dense series of "studies in the history of the philosophy of education," as its subtitle put it. With his work dedicated to his second wife, Dorothy, whom he had married in the previous year, Rushdoony's argument was that American education had become a vehicle to advance the democratic ideals and egalitarian political culture of which he had already expressed disapproval. He understood that the "attainment of pure democracy" was to be achieved, among other avenues, through "total social integration" in public schools. Dissenting from these ultra-democratic ends and the means by which they would be promoted, he believed that "Southerners" were "clearly wrong in resisting integration of white and Negro pupils."[55] But his argument was not that integration was either a good or a bad thing. Rushdoony wanted neither the social integration that multi-racial classrooms represented, nor the compulsion of the state by which this integration would be either imposed or prevented. "As a matter of record," he added in a footnote, "this writer would like to make clear his opposition to both legal segregation and integration, believing that both involve an infringement on the individual's freedom of association."[56] His concern was not to worry about race, but to resist the power of the state in educational affairs.

Rushdoony advanced his argument about educational practice from the philosophical principles that he had learned from Van Til and that he had outlined in his first book.[57] "For the consistent Calvinist," Rushdoony argued, "one common principle prevails in regard to reason, revelation, science, all knowledge, namely, that God, as Creator, is also the only interpreter of creation."[58] Rushdoony's primary claim was that all education was religious in character. This did not mean that the church should provide education for the children in its care. Instead, he insisted, the "emancipation of education from ecclesiastical control" had actually been a "major advance in liberal education." The passing of control of education from the church to the state did not represent progress, for the "truly liberal or free education" that he imagined would be free from the control of both.[59] This was not going to be easy. The power of the state was, in Rushdoony's view, almost ubiquitous, and the public school system had become its servant: "the state has become the saving institution, and the function of the school has been to proclaim a new gospel of salvation."[60] He described the public school system as the "true established church of these United States, dedicated to a catholic faith which is no longer semi-Christian moralism but social morality and social democracy."[61] His solution was for education to be privatized, on the basis that only privately funded schools could guarantee the "academic freedom" of their pupils and teachers.[62] As schools privatized, they would come under the authority of the families whose children they taught. Rushdoony hailed the "independent school movement," which, at the time of writing, he reported, represented the "sixteen percent of school children" who were "not in state schools."[63] After a long sequence of pen portraits of leading educational theorists, *The Messianic Character of American Education* set out a program for renewal. Rushdoony argued that the classical education that was often associated with reactionary pedagogy had to be reformed. Throughout history, "a liberal education has been ostensibly education for freedom and the mark of a free man. But what constitutes a *free* man? And what is the *ground* of his freedom?"[64] Education involved political and religious formation, he argued in *The Mythology of Science* (1967): "the evolutionary educator seeks to remake man in the image of his planned society; the Christian education must respect the image of God in man and can only seek to conform the student to the requirements of . . . Jesus Christ."[65] His answer to these questions was not reactionary, as if a restoration of classical education would finally address the problem. The promotion of classical education, he insisted, represented a "nullification of the victories of Augustine, Anselm and Calvin."[66] For a truly Christian education had to work from biblical premises, and had to engage with the literature of pagan antiquity only on the most critical terms. In rejecting the control of schools by church or state, in calling for a free market in education, and in rejecting the classical curriculum, Rushdoony's argument for educational reform was anything but traditionalist.

The state of education became a major theme in Reconstructionist writing in the late 1970s and 1980s. In 1977, Gary North devoted an issue of *The Journal of Christian Reconstruction* to this theme. In his editorial, North echoed his father-in-law's analysis of the problem of American education both in terms of its outcomes and its place in popular culture: "by every known academic measurement, government-subsidized, secular, compulsory education is a massive failure and getting worse . . . the public school system of this nation is America's only established church. Men have faith in it." But, he recognized, the campaign to provide alternatives had begun to take off. "Christian education is one of the few areas of American life where Christians are devising true alternatives to the secular institutions of our time." Despite their "lack of capital, their lack of experience, and their lack of printed materials for classroom use," Christian parents were "meeting the secular experts head-on, and coming out victors." North worried that the children of "millions of Christian parents" were still attending public schools as a consequence of their parents' "intellectual schizophrenia" and "misguided sense of evangelism." Fifteen years after Rushdoony recognized that "nothing seems more unlikely" than the reconstruction of Christian education, North reported that the numbers involved in the Christian education movement were still "pitifully tiny," representing such a small market that publishers could not find sufficient demand for new products.[67] Nevertheless, the movement was growing, he believed, as reaction to "forced integration, busing, violence, declining standards, student apathy, drugs on campus, and all the other blights which are basic to government education."[68] North's analysis added an economic aspect to the Reconstructionist argument. Christians should not attempt to take over the public school system, or to enforce the teaching of subjects such as creation science within it. North recognized that his arguments ran counter to those of many evangelicals, who approved of what was effectively "socialist" education as long as they could control it. But North wanted to respect the rights of non-Christian parents, too: "we do not believe in using force to extort money out of the pockets of one group, or even one man, in order to subsidize the schools that teach doctrines which the taxpaying individual despises."[69] Nevertheless, he continued, "if we can just get the Christians to stop taking State subsidies, stop lobbying for more subsidies, and start building *totally* independent educational institutions, we can get on with the task of Christian education. We must get our hands out of our neighbors' wallets."[70] Christian parents were wrong to prefer public education because it was cheaper than private alternatives. Their car bumper stickers might as well be "Jesus saves (on tuition)."[71]

This issue of *The Journal of Christian Reconstruction* was also one of the first Reconstructionist publications to draw attention to "The Lost Tools of Learning" (1947), a landmark essay on pedagogical theory by Dorothy L. Sayers, the English crime writer and cultural theorist. Sayers's lecture was a statement on educational method, the title of which would recur in works by other theonomist writers. One contributor to the journal argued that these principles of classical education would help in the "rebuilding of a Christian society and state," as faithful educators labored in the "ruins of our present civilization with the realization that God has ably equipped them to rebuild America and the world for the glory of God."[72] While opinion among theonomists varied as to the credibility of a formation in the classics, this kind of language would resonate in later discussions of the state of American education and the responsibility of reconstructed Christians to rebuild it. Sayers's vision became central to theonomists' retrieval of the classics.

This theme of rebuilding America was central to this project as it developed. The call for the reconstruction of education was a call for radical action. In 1982, North argued that every public school should be closed: "Refund the taxes to the tax-payers. Let the taxpayers seek out their own schools for their children, at their expense (or from privately financed scholarships or other donations). No more fraud. No more institutions built on the myth of neutrality."[73] This "myth"—the liberal or relativist assumption that different perspectives should be entertained within the same classroom—echoed with American principles of pluralism and religious freedom. The reformation of education required the undermining of American ideals, North explained. "As a *tactic* for a short-run defense of the independent Christian school movement, the appeal to religious liberty is legitimate," he argued, for that appeal would allow the Christian educator to "buy himself and his movement some time, some organizational freedom, and some power."[74] But this appeal to the ideal of religious liberty was a tactic, not a strategy, he explained:

> So let us be blunt about it: we must use the doctrine of religious liberty to gain independence for Christian schools until we train up a generation of people who know that there is no religious neutrality, no neutral law, no neutral education, and no neutral civil government. Then they will get busy in constructing a Bible-based social, political, and religious order which finally denies the religious liberty of the enemies of God. Murder, abortion, and pornography will be illegal. God's law will be enforced. It will take time. A minority religion cannot do this. Theocracy must flow from the hearts of a majority of citizens.[75]

And, North continued, the reconstruction of education would be central to the realization of this goal. The situation was exactly as some of its critics had feared. The Christian education that was being advocated by Reconstructionists did indeed reject the "values of inclusivity and diversity," and had indeed "set its sights on destroying the system of public education,"

en route to the end of liberal democracy itself.[76] This was the ambitious objective of "God's emerging army."[77]

II

However well-reasoned, North's aspirations would have been considered extreme by almost all of the participants in the movement for Christian education as it expanded through the 1980s. The numbers involved in home
education surged through that decade, a growth made possible by the very
traditional gendering of parental responsibility within conservative evangelicalism, which encouraged mothers to find their identity as homemakers,
and which gendered the experience of home education in ways not always
consistent with the Reconstructionist emphasis upon the responsibility of fathers.[78] By the end of the 1980s, an estimated 300,000 American children
were being educated at home.[79] Organizations were formed to defend their
rights, including the Home School Legal Defense Association (HSLDA),
which was founded in 1983, and the Rutherford Institute, which was led by
John W. Whitehead, and guided by a board, of which Rushdoony was an
early member.[80] But Rushdoony was not content to be an armchair theorist of educational reform. During the late 1970s and early 1980s, he spent a
great deal of time as an expert witness in court cases related to home education, which remained illegal in many states. By the 1980s, his early and quite
uncharacteristic pessimism about the short-term prospects of Christian
education had been overturned. In 1982 a special issue of *The Journal of
Christian Reconstruction*, which by then had come under the oversight of a
new editor, Douglas F. Kelly, reported on the movement's very considerable
achievements.[81] "There are now viable Christian alternatives to most of the
humanistically controlled institutions of the secular state," Kelly reported.
"Nowhere is this more true than in the field of education. Possibly as much
as one-fourth of all school age pupils under the 9th grade are now in private
and Christian schools; this number is growing literally every day."[82] If this
rate of growth were to continue, he projected, the "majority of all American
children will be in Christian schools" by the end of the twentieth century.[83]
And, he added, in a statement that would complicate but not eradicate
assumptions of the movement's racist character, many of the most exciting
initiatives in Christian education were being led by "black people on their
own under the impetus of a vision given them by the Lord and by the needs

of the times. There is a tremendous Christian school movement among black Christians."[84] Kelly referred to Rushdoony's expectation that the "black youths who are being trained in Christian schools and in churches that have recaptured the strong biblical wholeness of fundamental Bible preaching together with obedient life and compassionate outreach may well constitute the most effective Christian—and national—leadership in America by the turn of the century."[85] Kelly also recognized that the movement was being endorsed by Catholic and charismatic Christians, as well as among the Reformed, and he welcomed the "strong grassroots ecumenism of faith and service" that this trend represented. Working together, Calvinists, Catholics, and charismatics were "building effective Christian schools . . . reaching out in works of mercy to the needy . . . beginning to clean corrupt politicians out of office. They are doing together what none of them could do alone," and, he concluded, "this is of God."[86]

North, who had stepped down from *The Journal of Christian Reconstruction* as his relationship with Rushdoony deteriorated, had transferred his editorial entrepreneurialism into a new journal, *Christianity and Civilization*, which appeared in several issues in the early 1980s and which promoted some of the most aggressive strategies of survival and resistance in the print culture of Christian Reconstruction. His intentions were made explicit in the titles of each themed issue. The third issue, published in 1983, considered "The Tactics of Christian Resistance."[87] Despite the raciness of this title, North insisted, resistance to broader cultural norms was simply the everyday responsibility of every Christian. "Christian resisters are not to undergo a secret system of initiation, the hallmark of occult conspiracies. Christian resisters are not to adopt any and all resistance measures, irrespective of the morality of these acts. The Bible, a public document, provides the foundation of ethics, including the ethics of resistance."[88] In contrast to Kelly, whose article in *The Journal of Christian Reconstruction* in the previous year had highlighted what "black people" can achieve "on their own," North invited his readers to model their resistance to injustice upon that of a "Negro lady living in Montgomery, Alabama in late 1956 [who] had a hard day at work, and . . . just boarded a bus to go home."[89] North's suggestion that Rosa Parks might become a model of Christian resistance to broader cultural norms cuts away at assumptions that theonomy was necessarily linked to white supremacy. But it also worked to indicate the kind of resistance that North had in mind. The arguments of the theonomists did not support a " 'Christian' bloody revolution," he insisted. Violence was always going to be a possibility, he feared, but it could never be legitimate: "sporadic acts of violence committed by tiny, strategically un-skilled, and socially impotent terrorist groups that call themselves Christian" will never "build anything more lasting than a 'hit squad.'" Any turn to reli-gious violence would be fruitless: "sporadic terrorism does not reconstruct a civilization."[90] It would be a theme to which North would return in his published correspondence with Paul Jennings Hill, *Lone Gunners for Jesus* (1994). Violence offered a short-term response to the problems that could only be addressed through the long-term reformation that would be enabled by Christian formation in the home, church, and school.

To clarify his perspective, North published in his "Biblical Blueprints" se-ries the most detailed statement on Christian education to emerge from the theonomist movement. This book was written by Robert Thoburn, who had been working as a teacher in a private school when his adventures in alter-native education began. His concern, initially, was to educate his own chil-dren, who were approaching an age appropriate for kindergarten. Leaving his job, he began a new school in the basement of a house, with thirty-two students registering at the beginning of its first full academic year.[91] Later prominent in theonomist circles, Thoburn, an Orthodox Presbyterian Church minister, published *The Children Trap: Biblical Principles for Education* (1986) as a statement on the means and ends of Christian ed-ucation. "I am not going to write another book bashing the public school system. Nor am I interested in reforming the public schools. That is a waste of time," he admitted. Instead, he continued, "I decided long ago that it is better to light one little candle than to curse the darkness."[92] Thoburn's ar-gument drew upon libertarian economics: "when we send the children to the government school, we are accepting tax-financed welfare . . . we are stealing from our neighbors."[93] And so, he concluded, "getting the state out of education at every level is the only way to achieve God-honoring edu-cation."[94] He could not understand why "millions of Christians . . . vote for politicians who enact laws that compel Christian families to send their chil-dren into unsafe, drug-infested, humanist-dominated, anti-Christian sink holes (public schools)."[95] And so he pleaded for the separation of the state from the church, from the family, and from the school, and encouraged churches to pressure members to withdraw their children from the "gov-ernment schools."[96] North's introduction to *The Children Trap* underscored several of Thoburn's points. Philosophically, he insisted, the "legal founda-tion" of the public school system is the "myth of neutrality."[97] Like Thoburn, he highlighted the "power implicitly held by Christians," and suggested that "if every Baptist family in the American South would refuse to put its children into the public schools this year, the whole public school system would collapse overnight."[98] But he also recognized that these millions of Christian parents were not likely to follow his advice: "Christians want their education, but they want it cheap. So it has cost them everything, just as it cost Eve."[99] But perhaps he underestimated his fellow believers. Perhaps the postmillennialists had not been optimistic enough. By the end of the 1990s, fifteen years after the appearance of Thoburn's book, the number of American children involved in home education had risen past one million.[100] American education was changing.

III

The evidence of this change in American education could be found in some very remote places. Moscow, Idaho, could not be further away from the centers of American power. Unlike Patrick Henry College, which was established in Purcellville, Virginia, only fifty miles from Washington, DC, in an effort to encourage its students to become involved in lobbying and in work experience on the Hill, the Moscow community that had gathered around the ministry of Douglas Wilson had built its educational infrastructure in an organic way, as its numbers grew, and, as we have seen, with no agenda to promote short-term political change.[101] In the 1970s, as the community was being established, the idea of distinctively Christian education was rather new. Wilson himself had received a public school education—in integrated schools—from infancy until his Masters qualification.[102] Nevertheless, as the congregation grew, a number of families developed a shared concern about the prospect of sending their children into the area's public schools. In the late 1970s, there was no "adequate alternative" to the public school system in Moscow.[103] Toward the end of the decade, Wilson and two "like-minded parents" met regularly to discuss the problem and to pray and plan for a solution. Months later, Logos School opened in a rented church basement with an enrollment in the high teens.[104] There was no great strategy, or even any well-developed theory, behind their decision, Wilson later admitted: "at the time we were not trying to join any movement; we were simply trying to be good parents."[105] And in the absence of viable models for homeschooling, in the late 1970s, the Moscow parents could think only of establishing a Christian school.[106]

When they founded Logos School, Wilson and his partner parents had no idea that they were part of a larger movement of Christian education, this being years before his first encounter with Rushdoony's work. But the school's enrollment expanded as the congregation was shaped by Wilson's increasingly Reformed theological perspectives. In 1987, the school purchased and renovated an old ice rink, and constructed a one-acre playground. Enrollment continued to expand. By 1990, around two hundred children attended Logos, and the school average for the SRA Achievement tests was 85 percent.[107] The relationship between the church and school was never uncontested. Not everyone within the congregation found the vision to be compelling, while others outside the congregation did. In 1991, Wilson reported that around five percent of children within the congregation still attended public schools, while some of the children attending Logos School came from non-Christian homes.[108] The challenge facing the teachers was in knowing how to draw parents into the life of the school in a way that its publicly funded counterparts did not expect. "At Logos, we have many parents who take their responsibility for educating their children very seriously indeed," Wilson noted. "But sadly, we also have parents who give us nothing more than their children and the tuition money."[109] Providing lessons was not enough. The purpose of Logos School was to contribute to the formation of Christian character and the reconstruction of Moscow.

Despite these overtly Christian goals, the teachers in Logos School developed a curriculum that reflected their interest in classical education. These principles they found in Dorothy Sayers's lecture on "The Lost Tools of Learning" (1947), a manifesto that had been reprinted in the *National Review* in the early 1970s, and in *The Journal of Christian Reconstruction* in 1977, which became so central to their vision that it was published as a pamphlet by Canon Press (1990) and included as an appendix in Wilson's *Recovering the Lost Tools of Learning: An Approach to Distinctively Christian Education* (1991).[110] Wilson had developed this latter text after discovering *Turning Point: A Christian Worldview Declaration* (1987), by Marvin Olasky and Herbert Schlossberg, which he understood to represent a more cautious theonomist vision, and which encouraged him to approach the volume's publisher with a view to writing a related text on education.[111] *Recovering the Lost Tools of Learning* took the principles upon which Logos School operated and presented them as a norm to the wider evangelical world. With the aim of promoting a "classical and Christ-centered education," Logos teachers wanted to encourage among their students an "awareness of, and gratitude for, the heritage of Western civilization."[112] The Logos School curriculum was built around Sayers's vision for classical education, but it also drew freely upon the perspectives of poets such as John Milton and T. S. Eliot.[113] Wilson admitted that the influence of C. S. Lewis had been pervasive in his appreciation of culture: "I have come to love certain things simply because of Lewis's love for them."[114] This emphasis upon classical education rejected the criticisms of the culture of pagan antiquity that had been leveled by Rushdoony and occasionally by North. But Wilson also depended upon Reconstructionist writers as he developed his educational theory. His footnotes cited *The Journal of Christian Reconstruction* special issue on education and drew upon work by Bahnsen and Rushdoony, whose *The Messianic Character of American Education* was included in the dozen or so titles of his select bibliography.[115] The influence of Wilson's reading in Rushdoony was clear. "Education is a completely religious endeavor," Wilson argued, and so "it is a myth that education can be nonreligious."[116] For in education, as in any other sphere of life, there is "no such thing as neutrality."[117]

This application of Val Til's philosophical ideas drove Wilson to conclusions that any Reconstructionist would have found familiar. He appealed for an end to the public school system and for a free market in education.[118] Like North, he was cautious about proposals for school vouchers, believing on the one hand that they would improve competition and hence quality within the education sector, while also recognizing that those private and Christian schools that accepted the vouchers would put themselves under external supervision and control.[119] He insisted that public schools should not consider themselves as the transmitters of some kind of mainstream Christian culture, a mistake that was based upon the "myth of neutrality." So, while the issue of school prayer had driven conservative politics since the 1960s, he argued that Christians should reject teacher-led prayers in public schools, arguing that unless these prayers were offered by Christian teachers and with distinctly Christian content they would represent no more than a gesture toward the "God of the Lowest Common Denominator."[120] He insisted that the children of Christian families should be taught by Christian teachers. "One of the great ironies among modern evangelicals is the fact that many have higher and stricter standards for their children's baby-sitters than they do for their children's teachers."[121] And, he insisted, the movement in Christian education had to move beyond the reactionary motivations that had driven its earlier phase. It was not enough to wish to set up an alternative to failing standards, educational or otherwise. Christian education had to advance on a positively stated and robustly consistent biblical worldview.[122] And he was sure that the movement would do so. For, like the Reconstructionists, Wilson was energized by hope. In a nod toward the postmillennial theory that he shared, but did not explicitly mention, Wilson outlined his expectation for the growth of Christian education as the gospel spread throughout the world.[123]

The Moscow community grew their educational projects through promotional vehicles such as *Credenda Agenda*. From time to time, the magazine included testimonials from families who had relocated to Moscow from locations elsewhere in the Pacific Northwest in order to enroll their children in Logos School.[124] But other sympathetic parents could not make that kind of transition, and could not find a suitable local alternative. And so, just as the wider Reconstructionist movement swung from its support of Christian private schools to home education, so the Moscow community began to provide resources for the many families who shared their cultural and theological vision, and who wished to pass that on to their children without moving from their home. In 2001, Wesley Callihan, Douglas Jones, and Douglas Wilson coauthored *Classical Education and the Homeschool*, which was much more positive about home education than had been Wilson's *Recovering the Lost Tools of Learning*. In a pamphlet that was strikingly non-polemical in tone, the authors insisted that their opposition to the public school system was not based upon its often poor outcomes. The authors spelled out the main themes and presuppositions of classical Christian education, drawing freely upon Rushdoony in order to make their case.[125] And the project has been successful. The Association for Classical Christian Schools, established in Moscow in 1994, has grown to include within its membership several hundred schools across the United States, with around 1,300 individuals gathering in its 2019 annual conference to listen to an address from Republican senator Ben Sasse.[126] And yet, while Wilson and his colleagues continued to find inspiration in Rushdoony's writings, they sought to establish a critical distance from the wider theonomist movement. In 1995, for example, Wilson responded to North's criticism of classical Christian education by describing his hostile review as "pure North—well-written, entertaining, incisive, and seventy-five percent correct."[127] And he has sought to maintain that critical distance. Wilson's approach to education is bigger than that of the Reconstructionists—but it meets all of their goals.

For the Moscow community has succeeded where early communities of theonomists failed. Back in the 1960s, Rushdoony had argued that

Christians and other conservatives should "get back to the countryside and start homeschooling . . . living off the land, breeding, and getting back to the basics of American society."[128] Yet, for all that he contributed to the legalization of homeschooling, and enabled the extraordinary growth of educational alternatives, Rushdoony was never able to realize his ambition of establishing a full-fledged Christian college, from which he might disseminate the Christian Reconstruction movement.[129] From around 1993, Chalcedon publications had run advertisements for Christ College, a very recently established four-year college that offered a BA in Christian Thought and described itself as "the ONLY Reformed AND Reconstructionist undergraduate residential college in America for Calvinism and Christendom."[130] Liberal only in its enthusiasm for capitalization, the new institution certainly had good claims to the Reconstructionist title, with some teaching provided by Greg Bahnsen, and other classes presented by some of his former seminary students, including Ken Gentry and Gary DeMar.[131] Its proprietorial effort to monopolize the theonomist brand was helped by Rushdoony's increasingly polemical attitude to the classical turn in Christian education. This "revival of 'classical' education in supposedly Christian schools" was "horrifying," he argued in 2000, and was undermining everything for which the program of Christian Reconstruction had fought: "Socrates and Plato . . . were homosexuals. Plato's *Republic* was a blueprint for a dictatorship more extreme than those of Stalin and Hitler. . . . If you do not separate yourself from classicism, you will, in time, separate yourself from Christ."[132] But his arguments may not have been persuasive: it was Christ College that folded, around a decade after its founding, while a new institution, which combined theonomist and classical ideals, rose to take its place.

Like the formation of Logos School, the Moscow community's liberal arts college emerged in an entirely organic way. As Wilson's children approached the end of their secondary schooling, he began to plan for the next level of their studies. From 1994, *Credenda Agenda* began to feature advertisements for the new institution, which was named New Saint Andrews College. Early advertisements for the college acknowledged its start-up status: "we have no campus (yet), and our small meeting-building has no ivy or residential dormitories . . . and we are legally forbidden in the State of Idaho to grant degrees without compromising our program."[133] These advertisements pushed for the value of classical education, observing that "Saint Augustine . . . was not a computer science major." But local business contacts were key to the college's success.[134] Its purpose was not merely to educate, but to form students in a sustainable faith community, as a result of which many graduates have chosen to remain in the area.[135]

This situation in a viable faith community has provided the college with significant institutional stamina. Its history was surveyed in a short recruitment video that was made to celebrate the twenty-first anniversary of its founding. *Sword and Shovel* (dir. anon., 2016) was a short film that was packed with messages not only about the history of the college but also about its vision. Drawing upon accounts of the rebuilding of Jerusalem in the Old Testament books of Ezra and Nehemiah, the narrator described the project of the college as being that of "rebuilding the walls of Christendom . . . in the ruins of the West." Like the followers of Nehemiah, who worked with a trowel in one hand and a sword in the other, faculty and staff worked with a book in one hand and a "weapon . . . in the other." But the film represented the project of survival and resistance as contributing to significant reconstruction. The film portrayed the college community as building a great cathedral, as a town, then a city, began to form around it. "In the ruins we live," the narrative voice continued, "we film, and we write, and we read, and we laugh, and play rugby with pumpkins"—the latter reference nodding toward a rather peculiar New Saint Andrews sporting tradition. Drawing upon the postmillennial theory that underlay the faculty's instruction, the film represented the project of survival and resistance as contributing to the virtuous cycle by means of which the Moscow community continued to grow. The film depicted the reality that students came to Moscow to study, and stayed to marry, raise a family, find work, and participate in the life of the church. Wilson had long been clear that his project was intentionally multigenerational: "When a man and a woman marry, they should think of it (normally) as settling down. And they should hope and pray and labor to settle down in a place where their children can also marry—and settle down."[136] And from the evidence of the students and recent graduates that I met, this is exactly how the community is growing.

New Saints Andrews College offers a single four-year undergraduate curriculum, that leans heavily on the classical tradition. This is, of course, an imitation of the Great Books programs that are features of other conservative colleges, but it also represents a deliberate historical sense: "We must read, but there is too much to read. Consequently, if we want our reading to be cultural communication, and not just entertainment, we should take care that our reading is canonical," two faculty members had explained in the late 1990s.[137] As might be expected, therefore, the core reading list of the

New Saint Andrews curriculum depends upon extensive interaction with the pagan and Christian writers of antiquity, with some of the principal writers of the Protestant reformation, and with little else besides. In theology, students read Anselm, Athanasius, Augustine's *City of God* and *Confessions*, Irenaeus's *Against Heresies*, Luther's *Bondage of the Will*, and Calvin's *Institutes of the Christian Religion*. In science, students read Euclid's *Elements*, Newton's *Principia*, and Darwin's *Origin of Species*. In studying politics, students read Plato's *Republic*, Aristotle's *Ethics and Politics*, Cicero's *Republic* and *Laws*, Aquinas's "Treatise on Law" and *On Kingship*, Machiavelli's *The Prince*, Hobbes's *Leviathan*, Locke's *Second Treatise on Government*, Rousseau's *Discourses*, and Marx's *Communist Manifesto*. In history, they read Herodotus, Plutarch, Thucydides, and Bede's *Ecclesiastical History*. The poetry they read includes Homer's *Iliad* and *Odyssey*, Virgil's *Aeneid*, *Beowulf*, Dante's *Divine Comedy*, Spenser's *Faerie Queene*, and Milton's *Paradise Lost*. They read drama by Aeschylus, Aristophanes, Euripides, Sophocles, and Shakespeare, and fiction by Bunyan, Defoe, Austen, Dickens, Dostoevsky, and Faulkner. They learn about art and architecture from Vitruvius, and philosophy from Aristotle, Aquinas, Boethius, Descartes, and Nietzsche. To develop skills in communication, they study Plato, Aristotle, Cicero, Quintilian, Plutarch, and Montaigne. Whatever its negligence of modern literature, this curriculum can hardly be considered to be narrowly focused, and it is hardly surprising that its graduates enter programs in elite European universities and the Ivy League. For what matters, of course, is not just the content of the books that New Saint Andrews students read, but also the perspective from which and the rigor with which those books are taught. And the quality is impressive. At the time of writing, the dozen or so faculty members include two with Oxford doctorates, and one author of a book that was published by Oxford University Press.[138]

Christian Reconstruction has contributed to the fundamental reorientation of American education. For twenty years, Rushdoony flew across America to defend the rights of homeschooling parents. Now the eleventh secretary for education shares his approval of godly education, and sees the public schools as an effective delivery mechanism. But many Christians disagree with her approach. Rod Dreher describes the classical Christian school movement as "one of the most important pieces of the Benedict Option movement," and calls upon believers to withdraw their children from a deteriorating public school system.[139] The heirs of Rushdoony agree. Across

America, Christian educators do their best to survive and resist. In Moscow, they have begun to reconstruct.

IV

The extraordinary growth of homeschooling since the 1970s testifies to the very considerable cultural power of Christian Reconstruction. Rushdoony's efforts have paid off. With two million American children now being home educated, and many more in private Christian schools, the hegemony of the public school system has been broken. And, as critics allege, there is evidence that the content of much of this Christian education is designed to weaken the expansion of the state. These libertarian arguments are sometimes explicit. After all, popular homeschool resourcing organizations continue to provide Reconstructionist material. Gary North's principles are encoded in the Ron Paul Curriculum, while Sonlight has promoted Rushdoony's *Institutes* as part of its course on civics.[140] Molly Worthen is right to observe that Christian homeschooling literature is "rife with Rushdoonyian language."[141] For the movement for Christian education has succeeded where the first generation of Reconstructionists could not, and its influence is most obvious in the educational project that has been most successful and that enjoys the widest cultural reach. It is in the area of education that the ambition and achievement of the Moscow community have born most fruit—and those achievements are without parallel anywhere else within the theonomist world. For in the short and longer terms, education is central to survival, resistance, and the reconstruction of evangelical America.

5

Media

Publishing is warfare; and all reading is reading for keeps.[1]

Moscow may seem better in print than it actually is.[2]

The New Saint Andrews student who showed us around the Canon Press warehouse expected us to be impressed—and we were. She was pointing to a large printing machine, which, in the summer of 2015, was the most advanced model in use anywhere in the United States, and was maintained by an engineer who had to travel from the other side of the Atlantic. The community to which this publishing enterprise was central had been formed around a coterie of writers, whose distinctive arguments had come to prominence in a self-published magazine of theology and cultural criticism, *Credenda Agenda* (est. 1988), and whose status and influence, thirty years later, had grown to warrant their working with major publishers, such as Random House and HarperCollins, and prominent writing partners, such as the late Christopher Hitchens. But, even as some of its members achieved impressive success, the community continued to operate its own press, publishing books across multiple genres, and its new machine could print and bind these works in any quantity and in many formats. The machine represented the technical self-sufficiency that had sustained this community, and its writers, as it had expanded in size and influence over three decades.

Back in the 1980s, Douglas Wilson's decision to continue his ministry in Moscow had been made possible by his access to emerging technologies in desktop publishing.[3] *Credenda Agenda*, the magazine that advertised the Moscow theology and cultural view, was an in-house production, which moved slowly from the photocopied pages of the earliest issues toward a more professional and eventually glossy magazine format, which was funded entirely by donations, and was published only when content and capital could warrant it. The magazine's unique combination of Reformed theology,

Survival and Resistance in Evangelical America. Crawford Gribben, Oxford University Press (2021). © Oxford University Press. DOI: 10.1093/oso/9780199370221.003.0006

postmillennialism, theonomy, cultural criticism, and satirical bite attracted a growing readership, and by the end of the 1990s, when issues were appearing every second month, they were being printed in runs of 22,000 copies, distributed internationally and at no cost to readers.[4] The growth of *Credenda Agenda* represented a significant challenge for the editorial team. In the early 2000s, the editors abandoned print publication to post new issues on the internet, before changes in technology, such as the short runs made possible by the new printing machine, meant that they no longer had to worry about warehousing or managing an off-site inventory. The magazine sold some very old ideas and some very new books—but most of all it sold the community that was gathering around Wilson's ministry, advertising opportunities to move into north Idaho and emphasizing the educational and ecclesiastical opportunities of which migrants could take advantage.[5] As Benedict Anderson has noted of other contexts, the print capital of the Moscow community was central to its creation of a real as well as an "imagined community."[6]

As the growth of the community and the success of some of its authors indicate, this media strategy has certainly been successful. It has also been extremely ambitious. In the Canon Press warehouse, stacked high on long sets of industrial shelving, were handbooks on classical and Anglo-Saxon languages, works of poetry and fiction, theological, biblical, and legal studies, and an extensive range of materials for home educators. Almost all of these titles had been written by authors within the Moscow community, and almost all had a serious intellectual tone, as if the editors at Canon Press had consciously decided to resist the "democratization of American Christianity" by sanctifying the middle- and high-brow.[7] For the elevation of taste was strategic. As the New Saint Andrews curriculum suggests, the community's leaders recognized the need to move beyond the production of the evangelical equivalents of popular fiction and popular music to create a viable Christian counterculture with a distinct sense of historical values. Cultural production, and other media work, had become an essential component of the Moscow community's mission. "Our adversaries are fighting on behalf of a certain culture which they have successfully established on the ground," Wilson observed in *Credenda Agenda*. "They have their art, music, architecture, philosophers, and more." Christians were "fighting" for a "culture which no longer exists," and so, he believed, they had to produce new and self-consciously Christian media before they could meaningfully intervene in the "culture war." The Moscow community was demonstrating its ambitions to resist and replace the decadence of American modernity by developing high-minded cultural products in a broad range of genres, alongside the capacity to publish them. The nation's most advanced printing machine was a symbol of how the tools of American modernity could be used to challenge its presuppositions, and a symbol of how Christians could fight for a "culture which no longer exists" by becoming the accidental leaders of technological change within the publishing industry.[8] This was a broadly conceived and ambitious attempt at reconstruction. In Moscow, necessity was the mother of invention—and publishing, the contributors to *Credenda Agenda* believed, "is warfare."[9]

Like the religious migration to Moscow, and the promotion of theonomy more generally, the broader migration to the Redoubt has been made possible by the inventive use of media. Entrepreneurial writers, including pastors, homesteaders, and survivalists, have created and then supplied an audience by means of paper and electronic publications that have encouraged individuals, families, and entire congregations to travel to Idaho while allowing others, who still live outside the Redoubt, to participate in its life. Some leaders within the Redoubt are concerned that too much may be promised in this culture of persuasion—that the imagination of community may in fact be too powerful. Indeed, the variety of materials that are produced and sold within the Moscow community—and which offer advice on subjects as diverse as marriage, poetry, and economics—may lead some readers to believe that life within the community has been more fully reconstructed than is actually the case. The elders of Christ Church, for example, have encouraged potential migrants to "realize that no one out here walks on water. For many of you, your knowledge of our area has been gleaned from our publications, and under such circumstances it is sometimes possible to find yourself with a set of unrealistic expectations. Moscow may seem better in print than it actually is."[10] Media may advertise strategies of survival and resistance, even as it exaggerates their impact.

Building on recent work on the renaissance of evangelical media since the mid-1990s, this chapter will argue that print and online publications have become central tools for the promotion by theonomist writers of migration to north Idaho and for broader programs of reconstruction. While some researchers have described theonomist cultures as "notoriously secretive," this chapter finds that some of the most successful exponents of this package of religious, cultural, and political ideas are innovating, attracting followers, and are only too happy to advertise the fact.[11] While some of my interviewees, such as the kinists, were cautious about publicity and worried about its longer term effects, others were only too happy to show and tell. For it is in their creative use of media that the north Idaho theonomists are developing their most effective tools for recruitment. The migration movement has been a media phenomenon. In novels, preparedness manuals, and on the internet, a series of pastors, preppers, and polemicists have established an "imagined community" in which those who have relocated and those who may yet relocate into the Redoubt can share strategies of survival and resistance. But blogs, novels, and other media products identify links between Redoubt communities that, in reality, may not exist. The ready availability of these media products allows readers to fashion a consumptive bricolage, an individual and virtual experience of migration that confirms their religious and political predilections, inventing social networks that have yet to be established on the ground. These patterns of consumption may overlook the thematic or strategic variations in the media of the Redoubt—the emphasis within the Moscow community on family life, cultural engagement, and organic reconstruction, or the paramilitary preferences of the preparedness and survivalist websites. These consumptive patterns resist more ambitious attempts to fashion and then defend a broader culture, and point instead to the inevitable process of democratization in a marketplace of religious and political ideas, identifying the tensions in building a popular movement without resorting to popular tastes—an aesthetic restatement of their arguments against democracy.

With a developing audience and a range of cultural products, the media of migration has grown exponentially. In the 1990s, calls for intentional relocation to the Pacific Northwest were being made by the racist groups who had identified the region as a bastion of white Americanism—and whose stock, after terrorist outrages, security infiltration, and bad publicity, was on the decline—as well as by members of Wilson's Moscow congregation, who recognized its potential as a location for a reconstructed Christian community. Over thirty years later, the racist groups have suffered serious decline, while the Moscow community continues to grow, benefiting from its status within the broader culture of the Redoubt. This status is ironic, for, as my interviews identified, many of the congregants in Moscow are unaware of the almost talismanic regard in which their community is held by others among the migrants: the cultures of the Redoubt depend upon the Moscow community far more than vice versa. For the project of relocation, at which the Moscow community is the center, is being supported by a broader network of sometimes associated media. Potential migrants listen to advice provided on internet radio stations and read guidance on popular websites, while preparedness manuals and novels outline strategies for paramilitary resistance, and the broader culture of survival and self-sufficiency is shaped by self-published fiction as well as the novels and nonfiction books that have been placed with premier publishing houses, among which several titles have become *New York Times* bestsellers, benefiting from the trend that has seen "virtually every major multinational media conglomerate" promote their evangelical credentials.[12] Across these media, the cultural products of the Redoubt encode similar kinds of themes, highlighting the religious and political assumptions around which the migration movement has been predicated.

Of course, for evangelicals, this leveraging of media influence is nothing new. American evangelicalism has long been driven by a tendency toward populism and media experimentation.[13] The democratization of born-again religion has been marked in its cultural products, and in their sometimes extraordinary audience reach. The sheer success of these products can sometimes contradict their frequent claims about the marginal status of believers—as in the success of the Left Behind series, the 65 million sales of which rather belied its argument that Christians were being pushed to the cultural margins as the last days approached.[14] And the paradox of popularity may create similar problems for the literature of the Redoubt, as "evangelical markets" are cultivated in order to generate "evangelical publics."[15] Surveying this media culture, and the productions of the Moscow community that is at its center, this chapter will describe a well-resourced and increasingly influential conservative cultural movement that is preparing for survival, resistance, and the possibility that, as materiel for "God's emerging army," pens may be mightier than swords.[16]

I

The prominence of these themes of survival and resistance in recent evangelical writing is indicative of the movement's recent cultural and political turn—but they also resonate through this movement's literary history, as well as the writing of the American West, and especially in the writing of the American Redoubt. The characters in Rawles's novels are not unique in considering how best to evade and reconstruct modernity, nor in doing so by relocating—and relocating to—an American frontier.

Protestants with interests in the dissemination of their distinctive religious ideas have had long-standing interests in the mass communication of the gospel. John Bunyan's *Pilgrim's Progress* (1678) was one of several popular spiritual allegories to be published in the later seventeenth century, though it had to defend its choice of medium as being suitable for the edification of its readers. In the eighteenth and nineteenth centuries, Bunyan's allegory became a staple of evangelical piety even as it circulated through an expanding missionary culture into contents in which its religiously and politically demotic values could be sometimes radically reworked.[17] As this missionary interest in *Pilgrim's Progress* suggests, the identification of the most fruitful methods of evangelism was deeply pragmatic, and it is no surprise that this pragmatism eventually overcame the long-standing suspicion of fictional writing in conservative Protestant cultures. And while evangelicals generally looked down upon the possibilities of fictional writing, the origins of children's literature may be found in edifying writing for children.[18] Paradoxically, one of the earliest examples of conversionist fiction appeared within one of the most conservative and reactionary of Victorian religious movements. While members of the Open Brethren continued to repudiate the charms of literary fiction, it was an Exclusive Brethren writer who, in 1879, published the earliest known fictional account of the rapture.[19] And the audience for this kind of writing continued to grow. Over two hundred years after the appearance of *Pilgrim's Progress*, Charles Monroe Sheldon's *In His Steps* (1896) dwelt on ethical themes and posed the question, "What would Jesus do?"—and in the process, with sales of over 50 million copies, became one of the best-selling novels of all time.[20]

Of course, the real question, as Erin A. Smith has observed, may be, *What would Jesus read?*[21] For a number of evangelical publishers, at the end of the nineteenth century, the answer was clearly popular fiction. Ralph Connor, the pseudonym of a Presbyterian clergyman named Charles William Gordon, was the author of cowboy novels that combined Protestant piety with frontier courage to make him one of the most popular Canadian novelists of the early twentieth century.[22] His earliest novel, *Black Rock: A Tale of the Selkirks* (1898), outlined the themes of piety, temperance, responsibility, social improvement, and beneficent providence that would dominate his work.[23] His second novel, *The Sky Pilot: A Tale of the Foothills* (1899), sold over one million copies, and consolidated his position as an advocate of an ethically keen, if theologically ambiguous, "social gospel."[24] Connor's heroes embodied the qualities of courage, self-reliance, and heroic individualism that had been outlined in Frederick Jackson Turner's influential thesis on "the significance of the frontier in American history" (1893), in which "perennial rebirth, this fluidity of American life, this expansion westward with its new opportunities, its continuous touch with the simplicity of primitive society, furnish the forces dominating American character."[25] The frontier provided the touchstone of authentic American values and shaped the collective character by which the continent was won. The frontier was a "military training school, keeping alive the power of resistance to aggression, and developing the stalwart and rugged qualities of the frontiersman."[26] If Connor emphasized a rugged individualism, more communal values were advanced by Lucy Maud Montgomery, the wife of a Presbyterian minister, whose enduringly popular novels, including *Anne of Green Gables* (1908) and its sequels, romanticized the virtues of the small towns of the remote Prince Edward Island. But, whatever its sales success, the heroism and domesticity of this evangelical literary culture looked somewhat shabby in the aftermath of the Scopes trial (1925), when H. L. Mencken's witty and acerbic reportage defined the enduring relationship between science and religion, even as his representation of hillbilly religion was extrapolated to characterize conservative Protestantism at large.[27] Realizing that they had lost control of their representation, believers created their own media subcultures, in which to express new forms of identity, as part of their program of reinvention. Some of these cultural products achieved significant purchase within the American mainstream, a signal, perhaps, of the conservatism that, in mid-century, was still residual within wider society.[28] Ironically, one example of the crossover potential of evangelical media signaled that a biblically based science might not be as marginal as the popular response to the Scopes trial had appeared to suggest. In 1945, Dr. Irwin A. Moon, a California preacher, combined forces with the Moody Bible Institute to establish the Moody Institute of Science.[29] The new organization began to produce a series of "sermons from science," documentary films in which Moon moved from experimental demonstration to a presentation of the gospel. These films were extraordinarily popular. In 1947 and 1948, three of these "sermons from science" attracted an audience of 2.5 million, and by the mid-1950s, with reduced religious content, they had become fixtures within 389 school systems across 46 states.[30] Schools continued to present the Moody Institute of Science films until 1962, when the Supreme Court decision on school prayer stymied this combination of faith and empirical method, and the Moody Science Institute reverted to its primary audience within churches.[31]

In the mid-twentieth century, evangelical media culture expanded to reflect the changing emphases and strategies of the reinvention of born-again Protestantism.[32] In the 1940s, as Joel Carpenter has noticed, the evangelical renaissance was made possible by the development of new leaders, such as the Chicagoland youth evangelist Billy Graham, the foundation of new institutions, such as Fuller Theological Seminary, and the emergence of new publications, such as *Christianity Today*, alongside an entrepreneurial use of the existing media outlets. While many of these innovations reflected the vision and determination of individuals, often supported by voluntary ministry organizations, these individuals participated in an often small and close-knit movement: *Christianity Today* was founded by Billy Graham's father-in-law, for example, and the founder of Fuller Theological Seminary was a popular radio evangelist. Without any effort at coordination, the leaders of the new evangelical movement developed a media strategy that provided popular content through the medium of interdenominational newspapers, ministry newsletters, and radio, as well as more demanding or scholarly content in publications such as *Christianity Today* and the *Westminster Theological Journal*. These fora did not encourage the production of Christian fiction writing, which had largely but not completely overcome the suspicions by which it had earlier been attended. A. W. Tozer gave voice to the concerns of many conservative evangelicals when he argued that "Christian fiction" was a contradiction in terms, but his was an increasingly isolated voice.[33] The populist impulse that was advanced as evangelistic concern nevertheless pushed for the communication of the gospel in accessible genres.

It was in the emerging counterculture of the late 1960s that evangelical media was born again. Christian bookshops were established to sell "Jesus People" the Bibles, books, musical recordings, cards, and clothing that would provide Christian hippies with their distinctive material culture.[34] These popular culture artifacts were not always of especially high quality, and some of the participants in the new "contemporary Christian music" industry began to complain about the commodification of their faith.[35] But the demands of media capitalism seemed to be irresistible. In the 1970s and 1980s, Erin A. Smith has suggested, there developed an "evangelical culture of letters"—a literary culture that saved religious publishing.[36]

For, in the early 1970s, religious book publishing was collapsing. As mainstream denominations continued to decline in size and significance, their traditional publishers declined with them. In 1971, *Christian Century*, the magazine of the religious mainstream, declared the sector to be in crisis. But in the same period, evangelical publishing had begun to boom. "Evangelical publishing was burgeoning during the 1970s and early 1980s," and its growth was encouraged by "disenchanted youth, economic recession, unrest in the Middle East, distrust of social institutions, and an evangelical revival."[37] Mainstream publishers turned to evangelical authors and religious paperbacks in order to shore up their bottom line. Their strategy worked. With "low cost . . . low returns . . . long life . . . evangelical books took the risk out of bookselling."[38] The sector began to grow: sales of religious books expanded by over 112 percent between 1972 and 1977.[39] The sector began to innovate: Moody Press began selling fiction for adult readers in the 1970s.[40] And the sector began to adapt: while some participants in this new media, such as Hal Lindsey, Keith Green, and Larry Norman, managed to retain their credibility by publishing books and songs that set out their views with little self-censorship, other writers and musicians presented their work with greater regard for mainstream acceptability, and so toned down the most distinctive elements of their message. But titles with a more emphatic theological message continued to do well. Evangelical publishing became a "multimillion dollar business."[41] Hal Lindsey's *The Late Great Planet Earth* (1970) was turned into a film with narration by Orson Welles (1977). In the 1980s, the new evangelical publishers enjoyed their first taste of crossover success. Frank Peretti's *This Present Darkness* (1986), which sold 1.9 million copies, and *Piercing the Darkness* (1989), which sold 1.3 million copies, remained at the top of the Christian bestseller lists for over a year, and were among the first evangelical novels to be marketed to men.[42] But the emphatic claims of these novels were unusual. At the tail end of the "Reagan revolution," and during the period of evangelical media dominance, the overtly faith-based commitments that Peretti's novels represented gave way to the much more muted and more broadly ecumenical religiosity of Focus on the Family's *McGee and Me* (1989–95) and *VeggieTales* (1993–present). The Christian Booksellers Association, which, Douglas Wilson has averred, "never met a wind of doctrine it didn't like," screened out novels with references to alcohol or luck on behalf of its almost two thousand member shops while permitting enormous theological variety.[43] The price of influence in the cultural mainstream appeared to be theological ambiguity and a focus on ethics, most often drawn from Old Testament narratives, instead of any specifically Christian theological reference, and a focus on the gospel as preached by Billy Graham.[44] The success of moralistic and therapeutic products in American popular culture spoke volumes about the character of the so-called religious revival of the previous two decades.[45]

This situation began to change in the later 1990s, as new kinds of evangelical cultural products began to find a mainstream market without reducing their theological content or opting merely for moral instruction. This change became evident with the success of the first installments of the Left Behind series, an expanding sequence of novels detailing life after the rapture, the combined sales of which amounted to over 65 million copies—and counting. For all that it appeared to narrate a familiar prophetic scheme, however, *Left Behind* (1995) and its sequels made a significant change to how evangelicals might consider their situation in society, and in that sense its success was ironic. Dispensational eschatology had primed believers to expect continuing marginalization in a culture that would become increasingly hostile to their faith. But the series attracted a readership that amounted to around 10 percent of the American population, and generated merchandise that included a controversial video game and several cinematic releases, the most recent of which starred Nicholas Cage (dir. Vic Armstrong, 2014). The novel series that did the most to popularize evangelical expectations of marginalization actually worked to highlight the extent to which these ideas had become part of the cultural mainstream.

In making this demonstration, the Left Behind series showed the capacity of evangelical media culture, without calling attention to the irony that this extraordinary degree of market success was generated by novels that assumed the relentless marginalization of the faith they described.[46] The series made an impact on popular culture—even an episode of *The Simpsons* wondered what it might mean to be "left below" after the removal of true believers in the rapture.[47] But this often ironic reception of these cultural artifacts only proved, as Amy Frykholm observed, that readers who were not born-again Protestants could consume evangelical products "against the grain."[48] This may explain why the extraordinary success of the Left Behind series encouraged other Christian authors to consider aiming for crossover appeal, while also suggesting to secular novelists the narrative possibilities of the dispensational prophetic scheme: Liz Jensen's *The Rapture* (2009) took the structures of popular dispensationalism quite seriously, and wondered about the latent dangers of evangelical religion, while in Tom Perrotta's *The Leftovers* (2011) the event of the rapture is left unexplained as a background to a society that almost immediately returns to its obsession with sexual politics. But the Left Behind series also opened up the cultural mainstream for other evangelical texts, including William P. Young's *The Shack* (2007), an initially self-published title, the unorthodox depiction of the Trinity in which did nothing to prevent its sales of over ten million copies.[49] Meanwhile evangelicals continued to appropriate others. Walden Media released new film versions of classic children's stories of C. S. Lewis, *The Lion, the Witch, and the Wardrobe* (dir. Andrew Adamson, 2005), *Prince Caspian* (dir. Andrew Adamson, 2008) and *The Voyage of the Dawn Treader* (dir. Michael Apted, 2010). At the end and in the aftermath of the George W. Bush era, evangelical publishers could capitalize upon the increasing profile of evangelical apocalyptic theories in the culture at large and, as their books and films generated impressive profits and market share, meaningfully intervene in debates about the relationship between the "center" and "margins" of the culture.

A distinctively evangelical space was beginning to develop in mainstream media—though whether this represented the cultivation of evangelical consumers or the cynical commercial exploitation of evangelical norms is a question that is as yet unresolved. The ambiguity of the evangelical presence in mainstream media was made obvious in responses to the Learning Channel's *19 Kids and Counting* (2008–15). This long-standing series provided a mainstream platform for a concept of family that has been related to the Quiverfull movement, and in turn to Christian Reconstruction to which critics sometimes related it.[50] The Duggar family, which continued to expand over the course of the series, embodied many of the values, if not the complete theological system, that had driven the theonomy movement. Operating a home business, with strict patriarchal mores, the Duggar family campaigned against the expansion of LBGT rights before an abuse scandal involving one of the sons cost them the show and a related income of an estimated $25 million per annum.[51] Whether their series was designed for the purposes of edification or exhibition, it was very big business. Yet the hyperconservatism of the Duggar family was not typical of the most successful evangelical interventions in mainstream media. Whether in the Left Behind series, or in *19 kids and counting*, evangelical media has made some very conservative cultural claims, encoding its individualism and other values in the stories prepared by its favorite authors.[52] Their novels are the stories they "tell to themselves and about themselves," and the literary culture of which they are a part provides "powerful examples" of the way in which their culture "thinks about itself."[53] As their growing market share suggested, born-again Protestants like to find themselves in the cultural products they consume.

At least, most of them like to do so. But the movement that might have exercised the most influence upon evangelical politics was strangely reluctant to engage in this broader literary culture. Christian Reconstructionist writers were prolific—even relentless—in their literary production. From the mid-1960s, Rushdoony's extraordinary self-discipline enabled his publication of a massive volume of printed materials—sermons that were turned into chapters, chapters that were turned into books, and books that were turned into a movement. Gary North was even more prolific, as if determined to swamp by sheer volume of words any criticisms of the movement he led. His books regularly highlighted the rapid speed at which they had been composed—and the famous anecdote of his rushing into print (in less than three months) David Chilton's response to *Rich Christians in an Age of Hunger* (1978) for the occasion of a debate with its author, Ronald J. Sider, was not atypical of his almost compulsive attitude to polemic and publication.[54] Theonomist literary culture was almost entirely entrepreneurial. With hardly any exceptions, its writers stepped away from working with the major evangelical publishers to have small Reconstructionist presses distribute their work. Working with a small number of recognizable publishers was a good way for the movement to build its brand, for authors within the movement to clearly delineate their party boundaries, and for everyone concerned in promoting the movement to reassure readers that the materials they consumed had been screened by trusted leaders. From the 1970s, Reconstructionist writers produced newsletters, pamphlets, magazines, academic journals, and closely reasoned books—presenting their theological analysis and cultural polemic in multiple formats. But—unless we count lectures that they distributed on cassettes—they did not develop multiple genres or move away from didactic prose. Reconstructionist writers produced legal studies, biblical commentary, as well as political, historical, and cultural reviews. But they hardly ever turned to genres such as poetry or fiction. Their work restated a core set of ideas without considering their imaginative potential.

There were, of course, some exceptions to this rule. The most widely circulating novel to be written by Christian Reconstructionists may have been written by Michael S. Hyatt and George Grant, who had contributed *In the Shadow of Plenty: Biblical Principles for Welfare and Poverty* (1986) and *The Changing of the Guard: Biblical Principles for Political Action* (1987) to North's "Biblical Blueprints" series.[55] This novel, *Y2K: The Day the World Shut Down* (1998), was published by Thomas Nelson, a firm for whom Hyatt had worked as an agent, and it reflected the themes that he and other theonomist writers were developing in anticipation of the so-called millennium bug. The plot was centered around an erstwhile musician who taught classes on history and literature to homeschooling families, who published a newsletter to advertise his pedagogical aspirations and achievements, and who established a school to which students migrated from across the United States for an education in classics, cultural leadership, and faith-based resistance in the expectation of an American crisis.[56] Of course, as the authors might have realized, a fellow traveler in northern Idaho was doing exactly that.

II

The reconstruction of Moscow was, of course, being driven by a distinctive media culture. Since the first issues of *Credenda Agenda*, the Moscow community had distinguished itself within the literary culture of evangelicalism by its distinctive theological style. It had distinguished itself within the literary cultures of Christian Reconstruction by developing new formats and new genres within which to articulate a theonomist vision that has gone much further than Rushdoony, North, and others in appropriating the values of high culture, in moving beyond didactic prose, and in gaining the attention of a wider reading public. In fact, one of the curious paradoxes of the literary culture that was promoted by the community was that it emphasized withdrawal from broader culture at the same time as it articulated some of the most high-brow values and achieved some of the most significant cultural impacts in the recent history of American evangelicalism.

The tone for this literary culture was set in the early issues of *Credenda Agenda*, which featured cultural commentary and biblical exposition alongside fora for theological debate and creative writing. The magazine's content was developed in the works that members of the Moscow community began to publish, which ranged from poetry and short stories to novels, works of history, and books about family life. What was so striking about the relation of the Moscow community to the evangelical publishing industry was its decision to step outside it. Hardly any of the Moscow authors have published books with major evangelical presses. With the exception of a handful of titles, such as Douglas Wilson's book on classical education, which was co-published by Crossway, writers from the Moscow community have published either with their own small publisher, Canon Press, or with one of the larger mainstream publishers, such as HarperCollins, Random House, or Oxford

University Press. Each author's choice of a publisher seems to be determined by the kind of material that they want to publish. Authors use Canon Press for material best suited to audiences that have already accepted their premises, while authors go to other publishers with less ostensibly theological material that might be of broader interest. The strategy was theological, Douglas Wilson explained. The

> problem here is not the use of jokes, figures of speech, parables, and so forth. The Scriptures point us in this direction. In the beginning was the Word, not the Pristine Formula. Banishing all fiction, poetry, metaphors, etc. as essential carriers of ultimate truth is how modernity went so grievously astray.[57]

Indeed, that is what is so striking about the literary culture of the Moscow community—the contrast between the emphatic didacticism of the materials that they circulate through Canon Press and the allusive, even elusive, quality of the materials they circulate through major publishing houses.

Canon Press operates as a gatekeeper and an intellectual clearinghouse within the Moscow community. Operated by community leaders, it achieves a doctrinal, cultural, and aesthetic consensus across a variety of voices and genres, articulating a consistent vision of individual, family, and congregational life, together with a sense of what an ideal national life ought to look like. Its toleration of doctrinal inconsistency is rare, strategic, and carefully calibrated. The title that Douglas Wilson coauthored with Christopher Hitchens, for example, *Is Christianity Good for the World?: A Debate* (2009), reprinted an exchange of emails that had initially appeared on the *Christianity Today* website. This book became the basis of a national lecture tour, which in turn became the subject of a documentary, *Collision* (dir. Darren Doane, 2009)—and the source of some good publicity that reinforced Wilson's reputation as a culture warrior of note. While the book, lecture tour, and documentary allowed the famous atheist to give full reign to his arguments against Christianity, and found the participants bonding over their shared enthusiasm for P. G. Wodehouse, it was a rare example of the ways in which the community's publisher could leverage its marginal situation to achieve some very big gains. Canon Press has published most of Douglas Wilson's writing, some of which was republished from articles that originally appeared in *Credenda Agenda*, including his teaching on family life, in such titles as *Reforming Marriage* (1995), *Standing on the Promises: A Handbook of Biblical*

Childrearing (1997), *Fidelity: What It Means to Be a One-Woman Man* (1999), and *Future Men* (2001), a book about raising boys. Canon Press published his biblical expositions, such as *Joy at the End of the Tether: The Inscrutable Wisdom of Ecclesiastes* (1999) and *Heaven Misplaced: Christ's Kingdom on Earth* (2008). Canon Press has also published Wilson's cultural commentary, including *Angels in the Architecture: A Protestant Vision for Middle Earth* (1998), which he coauthored with Douglas Jones, and *Black and Tan: Essays and Excursions on Slavery, Culture War, and Scripture in America* (2005), a revised version of *Southern Slavery as It Was* (1996), which had been cowritten with Steve Wilkins, and which appeared without the "atrocious errors . . . in the footnoting of that booklet" that had been the basis for earlier claims of plagiarism.[58] Canon Press has also published material by Douglas Wilson's wife, Nancy Wilson, including *The Fruit of Her Hands: Respect and the Christian Woman* (1997); by his father, Jim Wilson, including *Principles of War: A Handbook on Strategic Evangelism* (1964; rpt. 2009) and *Weapons & Tactics: A Handbook on Personal Evangelism* (2012); and by his son, Nathan D. Wilson, including his parodies of the Left Behind series, *Right Behind: A Parody of Last Days Goofiness* (2001) and *Supergeddon: A Really Big Geddon* (2003).[59]

However, the materials that these authors publish with major commercial presses tend to be entirely different in tone and content. The books that Nathan Wilson has placed with Canon Press and other Christian publishers are easily distinguished from his nine novels with Random House and his three novels with HarperCollins. His first novel with Random House was *Leepike Ridge* (2007). Writing as N. D. Wilson, he drew upon Homer, *Tom Sawyer*, and *The Swiss Family Robinson* to create a classic adventure tale of a boy who is sucked by a fast-flowing river under a mountain. The narrative plays with alternative historical ideas about pre-Columbian civilizations before toying with a plot that almost hinted at Christian allegory. Tom Robinson, the protagonist, experiences a metaphorical death and resurrection, and his escape from the mountain leads to miraculous reconciliations. The novel is a good example of the kind of cultural work that the Moscow community wants to promote—implicitly Christian, but, as might be expected of a novel published by Random House, never remotely proselytizing. An endnote did no more than gesture toward the kind of cultural commentary that Nathan Wilson had published in *Credenda Agenda*: "Civilizations rise and fall like tides . . . it can be difficult to tell whether they are at their height or have already fallen and are in decay."[60] But it was also difficult to tell how *Leepike Ridge* addressed that broader cultural problem. Nathan Wilson followed up on *Leepike Ridge* with a fantasy novel, *100 Cupboards* (2007), which draws upon plot structures from the Chronicles of Narnia and alludes to the Bible only insofar as including a character identified as the Witch of Endor. Any apologetic purpose was, at best, subtle.

Highly regarded by critics, and enormously popular with readers, it is not clear that the fiction of N. D. Wilson represents any kind of apologetic project. That may not be his intention. His fictional writing may be contributing to a more ambitious project of rebuilding culture, one children's novel at a time, developing as he does so the conceptual frameworks upon which the gospel might hang. N. D. Wilson's writing develops mythological structures that depend upon and reinforce the plot structure of the Christian faith. His thematic structures return to the question of fatherlessness even as they attempt to re-enchant the world. This approach approximates that of C. S. Lewis and J. R. R. Tolkien, whose work he admires, and represents a much higher view of the possibilities of mythological thinking than that allowed by, for example, Rushdoony.[61] But this approach also raises the question of the relationship between this kind of writing and that preferred within evangelical reading cultures. Jan Blodgett has observed that evangelical fiction tends to be "purposefully didactic."[62] Even when its plots are not structured around conversions, she explains, they intend to reinforce the social mores of the community and to mark out its "symbolic boundaries."[63] Yet, from his earliest satires of evangelical literary blockbusters, N. D. Wilson has rejected the sanitized and pragmatic qualities of much of this evangelical writing. This raises the question, of course, of whom he is writing for. While Christian readers may be primed to recognize his references to the complexities of the intermediate state in *Leepike Ridge* or to know how the Witch of Endor in *100 Cupboards* can pull individuals between worlds, these fictions contribute to a long-term strategy of reconstructing the imagination of readers, of creating the imaginative scaffolding that will make sense only when the gospel is presented as story—or as "true myth," as C. S. Lewis put it.[64] For all that the project of the Moscow community has been advanced by didactic accounts of theology, biblical commentary, and family life, and by their purpose in "defining, recruiting, and challenging" an ideal community, the interest in creative writing that has continued from the earliest issues of *Credenda Agenda* may provide it with its most impressive successes.[65] If, as Blodgett has suggested, evangelical fiction "continually straddles the line between secular and sacred," being "at once a part of the pattern of accommodation and a symbol of separation," then work by N. D. Wilson has shown just how cre-atively and commercially fruitful that tension can be.[66] After all, some of his Canon Press work has been able to break successfully into the mass culture mainstream: *Hello Ninja* (2013), published by Canon Press in a format for books for younger children, has become the basis for a new animated series on Netflix (2019). Fiction is always a social form: novels serve as "complex evidence of the interaction of publishers and authors within the larger com-munity of which they are also a part."[67] The commercial success of his work suggests that this new evangelical media is working to engineer a moment of radical engagement with mainstream culture that moves beyond older, more stately, models of dialogue between the political center and religious periphery—a work of reconstruction that may be all the more effective for being understated.

III

With its whimsical air, its gesturing toward G. K. Chesterton, P. G. Wodehouse, C. S. Lewis, and J. R. R. Tolkien, the literature of the Moscow community could not be further removed from the paramilitary focus of the novels that have done the most to promote the idea of the Redoubt, even though the Moscow community features within this literature. Some of the fiction that has been published to consolidate the idea of migration into the Pacific Northwest has made little explicit reference to the religious values that Rawles has attempted to promote. A. R. Shaw's *Surrender the Sun* (2016), for example, is an adventure story set around Coeur d'Alene during a sudden drop in global temperatures, and plays off local suspicions of the ends to which the town's development as a resort for the wealthy could be put.[68] But most of the writing to emerge from the Redoubt is self-consciously promoting the con-cept as a religious and political ideal. This writing draws from a long tradition in literature and historiography that assumes that the "center of American history . . . was actually to be found at its edges."[69] Redoubt writing intends to reopen that frontier, and to reinscribe the qualities of Turner's theory of the West.[70] Reviving the ideal of a muscular Christianity, these novels illustrate growing diversity within evangelical literary culture, while suggesting that the possibilities for developing that diversity are greatest outside the evangel-ical publishing industry, in self-published writing or in writing that appears under the auspices of a mainstream commercial press.[71]

These themes have become particularly prominent in the writing of one of the most successful and influential theorists of survival and resistance. James Wesley Rawles is one of the most widely read advocates of religious resistance to left-leaning modernity. His internet site, survivalblog.com, is considered to be the "guiding light of the prepper movement."[72] For all that he resists identification with the movement, his debt to the literature of Christian Reconstruction is clear.[73] Rawles's first novel, *Patriots* (2006), which he described as "a survival manual dressed as fiction," included Gary North in the acknowledgments.[74] Rawles followed his first effort with *Survivors* (2011), *Founders* (2013), *Expatriates* (2013), and *Liberators* (2014), which were published by Penguin and Simon & Schuster imprints, as well as with *How to Survive the End of the World as We Know It: Tactics, Techniques, and Technologies for Uncertain Times* (2010), which also listed Gary North in the acknowledgments, and *Tools for Survival: What You Need to Survive When You're on Your Own* (2014), both of which were published by Penguin.[75] While several of these books have become *New York Times* bestsellers, they have done nothing to conceal the conspiratorial worldview of which his broader media presence is both a cause and consequence.

Reinforcing the arguments of his website and survivalist manuals, Rawles's novels describe a near-future social collapse, in which those who would survive would need to draw upon their Christian faith as well as a vast store of materiel. His writing encodes the libertarian and anti-government impulse that is common throughout the survivalist cultures of the Pacific Northwest. His characters tend to be "dyed-in-the-wool conservatives," but their political theory looks a bit like bricolage.[76] While several of his characters speak appreciatively of the work of Ayn Rand, they do so without any real sense that her values might be incompatible with those of the evangelical faith they also recommend.[77] Some of his protagonists "felt that the Waco and Ruby Ridge incidents were nothing short of government massacres of law-abiding Christians who just wanted to be left alone."[78] Despite the events at Ruby Ridge, one of his characters "spoke in glowing terms about northern Idaho," praising the region's unassuming culture of self-sufficiency, hunting, home canning, home schooling, and home churching.[79] Despite their rejection of "that dispensational pre-tribulation rapture nonsense," his characters adopt highly separatist lifestyles that are driven by fears of the economic totalitarianism that also resonates in evangelical rapture fiction, as in the fear of "biochip" hand implants that can determine whether an individual may buy or sell.[80] Elsewhere his plots toy with the Rothschilds and Bilderberg conspiracy theories that recur in the literature of the far right.[81] But the most consistent set of values seem to be drawn from the print culture of Christian Reconstruction. One character sets out to work through the old theonomist books that are made available on Gary North's website, while other characters study *The True Meaning of Submission* (2011), an exposition of Romans 13 by Chuck Baldwin, a pastor and former Constitution Party presidential candidate who moved with his extended family to begin a new fellowship in Kalispell, Montana, and agree on the theory of armed resistance that he recommends.[82]

As this reference suggests, Rawles's novels advocate for their political and religious views with as much enthusiasm as they advocate for preparedness for crisis. For all that Rawles has disclaimed the Christian Reconstruction label, preferring to identify himself as a libertarian, his novels support theonomy and advertise the Ten Commandments as an ideal basis for social order.[83] Or, as he put it in one of his survivalist manuals: "The foundational morality of the civilized world is best summarized in the Ten Commandments."[84] But that kind of society is entirely aspirational in his fiction. The current social order is threatened by lawlessness: "we have seen what happens when man decides not to live according to God's law."[85] But it is also threatened by state power, for "governments tend to expand their power to the point that they do harm."[86] In this moment of crisis, as governments exceed their biblical responsibilities and citizens fail to live up to them, believers will become entitled to resist, becoming "pistol-packing Amish," as Rawles has described the migrants to the Redoubt, like the gun-toting Quakers he portrays in one of his books.[87] While providing tips for weapons acquisition and tactics for militia training, his works do not amount to a program for action. His characters recommend strategies of "leaderless resistance."[88] Neither does he argue that his conservative readers should throw themselves into political campaigns. Like the Reconstructionists, he rejects the top-down imposition of change, and encourages his readers to "re-form a limited, and in fact minimalist Constitutional government, from the grass roots up. The county governments are key to this."[89] Taking cues from Gary North, Rawles's goal is a God-fearing but libertarian America.

For all that they advance a radical religious and political program, Rawles's novels are populated with a diverse range of characters. His "radical Christian separatists" come from a variety of denominational backgrounds, including Anglican, Reformed, Presbyterian, Baptist, and home churches, as well as Douglas Wilson's Moscow congregation.[90] Unlike some earlier survivalist writing from the Pacific Northwest, he speaks positively of racial difference and insists that "racism ignores reason."[91] His characters can be religiously diverse. While the main protagonists in *Founders* are and remain Latin-mass Catholics, most of his Catholic characters embrace some form of evangelicalism. *Patriots* included a Roman Catholic "lay minister" who led daily Bible studies within his compound.[92] *Survivors* included a character who was "born and raised . . . Irish-Catholic" and still attended Mass, but admitted that, having "come to more of personal faith in Jesus Christ," he felt "no need of a mediator" and felt that he was "saved . . . by Jesus, by faith in him alone": as far as he was concerned, the Papacy and priesthood were only "fine for ceremony."[93] And the novels score doctrinal points too. *Founders* and *Liberators* included a critique of Catholic prayers for the dead and of the Catholic doctrine of purgatory.[94] *Founders* includes a "Reformed" Jew who becomes Messianic in one of the series' key moments of conversion:

> One day he got on his knees and cried out to Jesus to forgive him for his rebellion against God and for sins he had committee in his life. Ben recognized that he could never keep the Law perfectly, and that all men are sinners. He asked Jesus to come into his life and to save him. Jesus sent the Holy Spirit at that moment and Ben felt a glorious in-filling and cleansing. Immediately, Ben knew that he had become born-again.[95]

With this emphasis upon evangelical conversion, Rawles's novels become a vehicle for promoting discipleship among their readers. *Expatriates* begins with one character exhorting another to know Jesus Christ "as your personal savior" and to read the King James Bible.[96] The novel later reports this character's experience of reading through the New Testament and his conversion to evangelical faith.[97] Elsewhere, the novels recommend that Bible passages should be memorized, and that this work should be accompanied with prayer.[98] Bibles become symbolic objects in Rawles's novels, icons of the lost world as well as vehicles for born-again piety. One character includes an old family Geneva Bible in his list of survival essentials—hardly the most practical or accessible scriptural text.[99] Another wished that he had been able to pack a "pocket-sized Bible. A few memorized verses aren't enough. You need the Word to keep you going and to maintain your balance."[100] One character decides to sell his copies of Matthew Henry's commentary and the works of Jonathan Edwards, but retains his King James Bible and other essential religious texts.[101] As America descends into chaos, Bibles are valorized as of preeminent importance in the life of faith.

As these repeated references to the King James Version indicate, the religious style that the novels promote is intensely conservative. The novels dismiss modern worship songs as being "vain and repetitious," and as having a "shortage of good doctrine and a surplus of personal pronouns."[102] Throughout the series, "good doctrine" is defined in terms of Reformed theology.[103] But characters also listen for "God's quiet voice" in their hearts when making major life decisions.[104] The novels argue for the danger of popular culture: the Christian faith of one character is derailed by his watching too many episodes of *Seinfeld*, *Friends*, and *Desperate Housewives*.[105] In contrast to the morals of these popular television series, "well-educated Christians" do not believe in dating, the novels explain, but identify suitable marriage partners after making sure that differences in doctrine between prospective partners were "not fundamental . . . so they could be mutually overlooked."[106] And yet, during the social collapse, believers solemnize their marriages without reference to state certification, as the literature of Reconstruction has recommended.[107] Preferring to make private marriage covenants, they organize their families "in obedience to God's law . . . and under the Common Law."[108] *Survivors* ends with a section of exhortation: "I implore you: Get right with God, and get your Beans, Bullets, and Band-Aids together! Our only certain hope is in Christ Jesus."[109] Far more overtly Christian than most books published by Penguin and Simon & Schuster, and far more emphatically evangelical than the novels emanating from Moscow, Rawles's novels set out to describe the conditions of social collapse with the aim of converting their readers.

IV

The media products that emanate from Moscow and across the Redoubt curate an effective and persuasive vision for survival, resistance, and reconstruction. If the Moscow community has succeeded in creating a sustainable community around its educational endeavors, its use of media projects its soft power toward wider, more diverse audiences, like those who view Douglas Wilson's *Man Rampant* series (2019–) on Amazon Prime video. Addressing these different kinds of audiences with varying degrees of urgency, and with increasingly impressive publishers, the literary work of the migration varies in its sense of the seriousness and proximity of the threat it foresees; in its sense of the responsibility that threat presents to conservatives and Christians; and in its sense of the necessity of taking up defensive arms to restore or to renew the Constitution. Presented as fiction, and always with a knowing wink, these publications that promote narratives of "withdrawing in order to rebuild" are being consumed by a wider public. And there is little sense that their mainstream publishers are limiting what authors might want to say. The bottom line is the bottom line—and if there is a market for this kind of writing, mainstream publishers will want to find it.

The success of Rawles's novels, in particular, shows how the writers of the Redoubt can make explicit religious and political opinions that mainstream publishers might once have considered to be unthinkable. The commodification of evangelicalism in the 1970s pushed, with few exceptions, for the amelioration of distinctive theological claims, so that the faith-based products that entered into popular culture were largely evacuated of any kind of theological edge. But Rawles's work achieves commercial success while being emphatic in its religious message. In media, as in other areas, believers may be withdrawing from political culture at the same time as their presence in popular culture grows. But popular culture is changing, and changes in politics are likely to continue downstream. Cultural critics are sometimes concerned about the wider impact of the literary cultures of conservative evangelicals.[110] Perhaps it is time that they too considered strategies of survival, resistance, and reconstruction. There is always trouble ahead.

Conclusion

The moral capital of Christianity is rapidly disappearing; if it disap-
pears entirely, all culture and civilization will go with it, and the de-
cline and fall of the West will be more devastating than the decline and
fall of Rome.[1]

We must prepare . . . not for survival but for victory.[2]

One of the funniest charges leveled against us in Moscow was the charge
that everybody in our church was forced to make his own toothbrush.[3]

Electoral demographics change, culture evolves, liberalism fails, and democ-
racies die. What is to be done? The question is long-standing, but it seems increasingly urgent. "We are not in the dawn of a new civilization, but the twilight
of an old one," veteran activist Paul M. Weyrich admitted in February 1999,
in the immediate aftermath of the Senate's failure to impeach President Bill
Clinton, in a letter that circulated widely beyond his conservative Christians
supporters. The politics of national reform had failed and could not now succeed. The strategy of the Religious Right, which he had helped devise, had been
premised on the supposition that there did, in fact, exist a "moral majority,"
and it assumed that "if we could just elect enough conservatives . . . they would
fight to implement our agenda." The elected conservatives had failed to uphold their side of the deal. But the blame for this failure was not to be directed
merely at individuals. Conservative politics had failed because "politics itself
has failed . . . we are caught up in a cultural collapse of historic proportions,
a collapse so great that it simply overwhelms politics." The influence of cultural Marxism was now so pervasive that "I do not believe that a majority of
Americans actually share our values." His sense of devastation was obvious.
There were no grounds for further culture war. There was nothing left to win.
Instead, concerned Christians must "separate . . . from this hostile culture,"

Survival and Resistance in Evangelical America. Crawford Gribben, Oxford University Press (2021). © Oxford University Press. DOI: 10.1093/oso/9780199370221.003.0007

Weyrich exhorted, if they were to preserve any remnants of the "great Judeo-Christian civilization that we have known down through the ages." They did not need to "move to Idaho" in order to do so, he emphasized.[4] But many did. And many of those who made that move have been successful. For, in communities in the Pacific Northwest, after the strategic failures of the old Religious Right, evangelical cultural politics is being born again.

Of course, Weyrich's ideal of a Christian culture and his fear that it might never be realized have echoed in a great deal of conservative writing throughout the last century. As the world went to war, in 1939, T. S. Eliot set out to establish that the "only alternative to a progressive and insidious adaptation to totalitarian worldliness . . . is to aim at a Christian society."[5] The question resonated among theorists and commentators as the war continued, but after the armistice, solutions were developed in quite different ways on either side of the Atlantic, with the effect that British conservatism and American conservatism have become very different things.[6] As state powers expanded, and international treaty bodies emerged to work toward better global governance, the world sank into Cold War and geopolitics became a species of Manichean faith.[7] In the United States, a powerful coalition of grassroots reactionaries and libertarian elites drew from the wells of the emerging anti-communism to establish a new conservative movement. As Matthew Avery Sutton has noticed, born-again Protestants were never shy of making political interventions, even during the years of their supposed disengagement, after the fiasco of the Scopes trial.[8] But in the late 1940s and 1950s, as Southern evangelicals streamed into California, where their interests in conservative politics coalesced with those of wealthy think-tanks, born-again Protestants made some distinctive ideological claims. Cold War paranoia was reflected in new religious themes that emphasized the need to recapture the reins of power as often as they suggested that this pursuit of power might get in the way of short-term spiritual objectives as well as long-term cultural change. Mixing Christian faith with their trust in American institutions, these conservatives turned into a political force that moved from the fringe to the center of the Republican Party, and from coffee mornings and lunches in Orange County, California, to the centers of American power. This book reconstructs a chapter in this history of the American Right, a history of those ideas driven to the margins of conservative politics and of evangelical religion—where they have become more credible, and have begun to circulate more widely, than ever before.

I

Throughout the second half of the twentieth century, the arguments of Christian Reconstruction were advanced by their apologists with considerable rhetorical and philosophical force. They resonated with the declinist historiography and the rhetoric of the jeremiad that had become central to a great deal of the conservative discourse of the period. Responding to the loss of evangelical hegemony that he found so disorientating, Rushdoony turned to the Bible to find his predicament explained.[9] Drawing from Romans 1, he argued that "there is . . . in each degenerating culture, and in the totality of history as it matures, a progressive degeneration of the natural man, as a process of self-consciousness which makes the forms of conformity more and more irrelevant and absurd."[10] The "degeneration" of individuals enables and requires an expansion in the power of the state, he continued, but "a rise in the power of the state is the beginning of the breakdown of meaning and community and the social descent into hell." "Hell awaits culture after culture," he insisted, as, "torn by its inner tensions and schizophrenia, it collapses into frustration and evasion."[11] Nevertheless, while the "end of an age is always a time of turmoil, war, economic catastrophe, cynicism, lawlessness, and distress," it is also an "era of heightened challenge and creativity, and of intense vitality."[12] As the cultural collapse accelerates, "God alone can become the source of culture and meaning, and the Christian becomes the cultural force and agent."[13] That was not a message of easy reassurance for believers. For denominations that tolerated liberalism were sure to fail, until only true believers remained. The church would be purified as the wider culture crumbled around it. No longer "convinced of its own value," this culture would be "incapable of its own defense. Its energy is replaced by apathy, and its convictions by the torments of self-analysis."[14] And the outcome—at least in the first instance—would be terrible. "While the Christian, as a participant in the events, can share in the common dismay at the tragedies and mounting crises of history, he must nevertheless welcome these crises as the necessary and God-ordained shaking of history," Rushdoony declared.[15] As God shook history, the believer's responsibility was to survive, resist, and reconstruct. In the darkening "twilight of the American Enlightenment," Rushdoony had found his moment, turning Wordsworth's acclamation of the French Revolution on its head: "Never has an era faced a more demanding and exciting crisis. This then above all else is the great and glorious era to live in, a time of opportunity, one requiring fresh and vigorous thinking, indeed a glorious time to be alive."[16]

But for all his optimism, Rushdoony could not sustain the intellectual or organizational vigor with which the Christian Reconstruction movement began. For all that he emphasized in his scheme of renewal the centrality of the family unit, he was unable to keep together the movement that he had established. In the late 1970s, as he built his own ministry in Vallecito, California, his son-in-law, Gary North, began to gather in another community in Tyler, Texas, and, even in the close-knit circle of leaders, ideological differences began to emerge. The division between these camps of Christian Reconstruction was marked out by different views of church and family, but also by Rushdoony's promotion of some of the Old Testament dietary laws and even by his interest in geostationary theory.[17] There also developed some important differences in political style, if not actually in theological substance. North was concerned that Rushdoony's emphasis upon family over church "leads to familism, and then to clannism and even a kind of supposed Hebrew tribalism, all of which are features of one or another of the groups associated with the 'identity movement,' or 'Western destiny' movement, or 'British Israel' movement."[18] This was a serious charge, even if it did not rise above its hint of guilt by association. But the implication of guilt was unfounded: Michael Barkun found "no evidence of any connection between the small but influential Reconstructionist movement and the British-Israel or Identity groups" that he described in *Religion and the Racist Right* (1997).[19] While migrants influenced by Reconstructionist ideas continued to move into an area that has also been idealized by white separatists, they did so for very different reasons, and as Douglas Wilson and James Wesley Rawles, among other advocates of survival and resistance, reiterated their opposition to any form of racism. Nevertheless, when even its advocates were concerned by the similarities between Christian Reconstruction and the radical Right, the movement was facing an existential crisis. And so, by the mid-1990s, Molly Worthen has argued, Reconstructionism "trailed off."[20] Michael McVicar announced its death.[21] But the argument of this book is that Christian Reconstruction is not dead anymore. Paradoxically, the failure of the first generation of theonomists to cohere, either personally or ideologically, has worked in the movement's favor, creating an internal marketplace of ideas by means of which competing groupings within political and religious conservatism have been able to appropriate and adopt their central arguments.[22] "Christian Reconstructionist thought," Worthen observes, "has tempered itself for popular appeal," as the cultural work of the Moscow community and Redoubt advocates indicates, and its achievements have been subtler and more effective than many of its critics have seen.[23] The success of the Moscow theonomists has been so effective in reprofiling their ideology as to have it situated within the American mass market: Douglas Wilson's *Man Rampant* (2019–), is now a product that may be consumed on Amazon Prime video. Mass culture routinizes what was once regarded as radical, with effects that may not easily be predicted at the "end of white, Christian America."

For this tempered theonomy is being echoed in some very surprising locations. Readers of recent conservative writing will find unexpectedly prescient Rushdoony's views about the collapse of the liberal order, for conservative Catholic political theorists are now making some very similar claims. In one of the most important political theory books of the last few years, which made it onto Barack Obama's reading list in summer 2018, Patrick Deneen has argued that "liberalism has failed . . . because it was true to itself," and that the only solution to our most besetting political, cultural, social, technological, and environmental problems is our "liberation from liberalism itself."[24] The end that Deneen proposes is revolutionary, but the means to that end are not: "Political revolution . . . would produce only disorder and misery," he argues. "A better course will consist in smaller, local forms of resistance: practices more than theories, the building of resilient new cultures against the anti-culture of liberalism."[25] Calling for cohesive communities, and a renewal of religion and tradition from the grassroots up, Deneen's recipe for the American future shares important features of the Reconstructionist worldview. It may be true that the history of the evangelical movement has been bound up with a "struggle to shape America," as Frances Fitzgerald has claimed.[26] But perhaps evangelicals have made their greatest impact when they simply walked away from that goal, when the "meandering" influence of Rushdoony returned to center stage.[27] After all, what has Athens to do with Jerusalem, or Moscow, Idaho, with Washington, DC?

II

Deneen's reference to "political revolution" raises a sadly familiar question about other ways in which conservative evangelicals might respond to the "end of white Christian America"—whether this call to survival, resistance, and reconstruction is likely to lead to violence. There are obviously good reasons for fearing that it might. After all, a very small number of individuals associated with the movement of Christian Reconstruction have become involved in violence. Paul Jennings Hill studied with Greg Bahnsen at Reformed Theological Seminary, became a conservative Presbyterian minister, and for his assassination of an abortion doctor and his security guard ended up on death row. The Reconstructionist movement may have had no time for these "lone gunners for Jesus," as Gary North described this brand of terrorism, and examples of individuals turning toward a more radicalized politics are thankfully very rare.[28] But they may be becoming more commonplace. During the writing of this book, a bombing campaign in Austin, Texas, and the shooting at a synagogue in San Diego were attributed to young men who had grown up in highly religious and home-educating cultures that shared some elements of the program of withdrawal from wider society that this book's narrative describes.[29] In neither incident does the tragic violence appear to be connected to the experience of home education. Theonomist ideology does not appear to have a played a role in either of these tragedies, though its advocates may need to work out more clearly the difficult tension between their arguing for a smaller state and for their arguing that the state's role in capital punishment should greatly expand. Taking a broader view, the problem of religious violence may have much less to do with ideas and their implications than with the wider culture's obsession with retribution and identity politics and vulnerable individuals' easy access to guns. Sadly, given the ease with which dangerous weapons can be purchased, and given a sufficient disenchantment with prevailing norms, young men who combine high hopes for the future of America and who can identify those responsible for its short-term decline will likely continue to seek redress for their cognitive dissonance by assaulting scapegoats in acts of redemptive violence.

The prospect of violence should not surprise anyone, for the valorization of physical retribution has become intrinsic to American popular culture. After all, the "warrior dreams" that have emerged since the 1980s have promoted tropes in books and films that celebrate exactly this kind of behavior.[30] Aggression against the "other" and altruistic self-sacrifice on behalf of a community that may not realize its predicament is the narrative arc that connects cultural products as innocuous as *The Chronicles of Narnia* to several recent incidents of race-hate crime. Redemptive violence has become the stuff of cinematic revenge tragedy as well as a dominant theme in the manifestos of mass murderers. And whatever happens on the "dark web" is able to populate these popular cultural themes with sufficient quantities of paranoia and conspiracy to convince the epistemologically unwary that a single moment of social cleansing can "make America great again." For while religious behaviors inevitably shape elements of the wider culture, it may be that it is the broader cultural context, as much as any ideology circulating within it, that provides the trigger for violence. Themes of resistance and survival have circulated among American evangelicals at the same time as they have circulated in the popular cultural mainstream. And evangelicals, whose media artifacts mimic as much as they criticize that cultural mainstream, may be merely tuning in to a *Zeitgeist* in their practice of survival, resistance, and reconstruction.

It is not inevitable that conservative evangelicals should escalate resistance into violence. The intellectual tradition that this book has been describing also contains the tools by which this revolutionary impulse may be contained—and even eradicated. Rushdoony's program for action had as its goal the reconstruction of a Christian America. The vehicles by which he suggested that national revival would be accomplished were not the constitutional tools of politics, and were certainly not the extra-constitutional tools of revolutionary terror. His argument was, consistently, that the "weapons of our warfare are not carnal, but mighty through God to the pulling down of strong holds" (2 Corinthians 10:4). If the tradition he inspired emphasizes the centrality of preaching and the right use of the sacraments, those key themes within Reformed ecclesiology, then it contains within itself the ideas by which its adherents may continue to practice and share their faith without resorting to any unauthorized use of coercive power. In other words, one of the most effective ways of controlling what critics may describe as a propensity for violence within the cultures of Christian Reconstruction and the evangelical far-right may be to encourage the adherents of these idea-sets to pursue a closer reading of some of their key foundational texts. Rushdoony expected to see the reconstruction of America achieved by means of individual conversion, not by any attempt to wield political power, or to manipulate communities by compulsive means. He may not have approved of democracy, but neither did he approve of its violent subversion. Any turn toward redemptive violence is inconsistent with the theory of Christian Reconstruction, however much it echoes the preoccupations of the popular culture that this theological discourse critiques.

And what will happen in Moscow, Idaho? The largest, most enduring, and most successful community in the history of Christian Reconstruction may well continue to grow. As it does so, it may continue to moderate its theonomist ideals. That will happen as members of the community continue to more often take their theological and cultural cues from Canon Press than from the foundational theorists of Reconstruction. The Moscow community has survived, and has successfully resisted American modernity, and its greatest success may be found in its members' creative work. This attempt at cultural reconstruction has not yet made Moscow "a Christian town," as the goal is announced on the Christ Church order of service. But it has made sufficient impact on the locality to allow some of the earlier critiques to turn into comedy. "One of the funniest charges leveled against us in Moscow was the charge that everybody in our church was forced to make his own toothbrush," Douglas Wilson has joked.[31] But, as the New Saint Andrews students know only too well, a plot can only be identified as comedy when it provides a happy ending. Will there be a happy ending? Will the "wildly postmillennial" expectations of the New Saint Andrews students be realized? And would that be a happy ending for anybody else?

III

These are questions about whether the ideals and arguments that have sustained Christian Reconstruction within the cultures of American evangelicalism could be successful anywhere else. While the migration to the Redoubt has appealed to a small number of individuals and families from outside North America, the arguments of those who promote the ideals of resistance and survival make best sense within a domestic popular culture, where they are framed around polemical and often revisionist accounts of key moments in American history—the founding, the war of independence, and the Civil War. Turning away from national politics, toward strategies of survival and resistance, evangelicals are rejecting the American mainstream in terms that resonate within it.

Perhaps this is why the movement to the Pacific Northwest makes sense. These themes of resistance and survival were reiterated as the frontier was pushed from Plymouth Rock to the Pacific, and they resonate throughout the American canon. The language of resistance and survival is the language of the frontier, and it makes most sense where the threat of cultural assimilation into a liberal mainstream combines with a landscape and physical environment that reinforce the difficulty of this project. In Moscow, Idaho, and in the fictional worlds that have been elaborated around it, resistance and survival make sense of wide-open landscapes and the local predominance of the irreligious "nones."[32] But in their language, their most familiar tropes, and in their decision to move to this frontier, those born-again Protestants who aspire to withdraw from the American mainstream articulate their reasons for doing so in terms that it understands. After all, the foundational myth of the programs for action that this book describes is that human society can be improved, and that a "city on a hill" can be created. The vision is as old as America—and it is shared by the program's critics. For both the advocates of this program for action and its critics share the assumption that America should be leading the way to a better world. The "paranoid style" that is shared by the subjects of this book and their critics parallels their shared and almost utopian conviction that the experience of Americans will herald the future of humanity. This is a distinctively American vision, and it suggests why neither the program nor the critical response it has provoked will be easily transported elsewhere.

For it is not that the values of the Redoubt are internationally anomalous. In some parts of the world, the politics of evangelical conservatism have a long historical valence. In Northern Ireland, for example, there exist religious cultures that are very similar to those of this part of the Pacific Northwest— so much so that George Marsden has suggested that Protestant fundamentalism as a religious phenomenon was most obviously located in America and "Ulster."[33] Northern Ireland has never been home to a strong movement of theonomists, but its relatively conservative social fabric has often sustained the traditional values of the Old World in ways that Reconstructionists would understand. Many migrants to the Redoubt might be very happy to live in those parts of Northern Ireland in which home education is growing in popularity, in which conservative Presbyterian denominations have established their own networks of schools, in which evangelical culture is strong enough to sustain several university colleges, and in which several political parties represent to a greater or lesser degree a very militant species of this kind of worldview, with the result that the province was until late in 2019 the only region in the United Kingdom or Ireland where same-sex marriage was illegal and in which abortion was still very tightly controlled. Other of Northern Ireland's social factors might also appeal to migrants to the Redoubt. Gun ownership laws, despite or perhaps because of the tragic history of "the Troubles," are considerably more flexible than firearms legislation in the rest of the United Kingdom. The region is accessible, with plenty of available property, and the cost of that property is around half of that of the United Kingdom average. And, as some of my kinist interviewees noted, Northern Ireland has hardly been impacted by immigration, so that the province might represent the last, best hope for the white, evangelical, and conservative monoculture they want to protect. And yet, despite this claim made by one of my kinist interviewees that his next family move would be to Northern Ireland, the province is not the focus of any organized program of migration. In fact, the situation is quite the opposite—in Northern Ireland, the Protestant population is declining as its college-age young people leave for higher education in Great Britain, where they benefit from higher wages and a more atomistic culture, from which only a small proportion ever return. The counter-example of Northern Ireland suggests the extent to which the phenomena that this book describes may be understood as quintessentially American. The religious components of this program for action may be necessary, but they are not sufficient to encourage or warrant these radical strategies to survive, resist, and reconstruct. In other words, if these communities should be regarded as American fascists—which categorization my argument resists—it might only be because of their location. Only in America can there be *The Handmaid's Tale*.

Evangelicalism, after all, suffers from its own electoral discontents. Despite the concerns of many commentators, evangelicals do not share a common political vision. As a voluntarist and radically decentralized sequence of competing communities, evangelicalism lacks the infrastructure of compulsion or coercion by which such a political program could be rolled out. For, as Lydia Bean has put it, evangelicalism lacks a cockpit to storm.[34] So, in the absence of the disciplinary architecture of a religious denomination, as D. G. Hart has noted, born-again Protestants participate in a largely unregulated contest of ideas in which the gold standard of the historic creeds and confessions has given way to the laissez-faire opportunism that dominates in what Benjamin L. Huskinson has described as an "evangelical market."[35] Around the world, this market has many different economies, each of which are nationally peculiar, so that the radical convictions that drive culturally marginalized Protestants into the Pacific Northwest are fairly ordinary within the political mainstream in Northern Ireland. Neither is there any necessary link between these theological convictions and specific political goals. In the United States, politicians like Ben Sasse can share the Reformed theology that undergirds the politics of migration while operating firmly within the political mainstream. In the United Kingdom, a politician who shares these theological ideas—like Tim Farron—can become leader of the Liberal Party while refusing to develop legislation on the basis of his personal convictions. And the complexion of evangelical politics looks different again in Brazil, under President Jair Bolsonaro, and in Australia, under Prime Minister Scott Morrison. As D. G. Hart has argued, the idea of a unitary evangelical "movement" is an extraordinary confidence trick, in which both its participants and critics are victims. The trick has been played by pollsters and religious leaders, as they have sought to simplify, control, and project the influence of the complex and contradictory worlds that they seek to describe. But in simplifying and controlling, they have created a monster.

Now, of course, the "paranoid style" that Hofstadter observed among the postwar Right has become typical of a great deal of discourse and analysis across the political spectrum.[36] The radical Right is certainly on the rise, enjoying growing confidence if not yet in America enjoying political power, and descriptions of born-again Protestants as participants in a new American fascism are becoming very effective click-bait. This form of social messaging reinforces within mainstream media some very unhelpful stereotypes of the "repugnant cultural other," and works against the kinds of mutual understanding from which the collective temperature of the commentariat might eventually decline.[37] In describing one of the most important of modern evangelical cultures, and in allowing its participants to speak in their own words, this book has sought to establish what is at stake in the turn among born-again Protestants to resist and survive what they expect will be the structural crisis of American modernity.

IV

As their most prominent spokesmen recognize, the efforts of conservative evangelicals to find political solutions to what they might otherwise regard as spiritual problems have not succeeded, and genuine social change can only be achieved as a consequence of individual regeneration.[38] The experience of history suggests that all efforts tending toward the perfection of human society will eventually fail. As we noted in the Introduction, the long history of religious migration into the Pacific Northwest provides many examples that would support this conclusion. And, in fact, the first signs of this failure among some of the modern migrants may already be observed. This book has not engaged with the controversy about pastoral care within the largest community it has described, a controversy that had the effect, among other things, of having this community disappear from Rod Dreher's list of viable "Benedict options." Nor has this book offered any adjudication in the controversy about that community's proposals regarding the meaning and effect of baptism and its consequences for the Reformed doctrine of justification, although these debates have erupted in several conservative Presbyterian denominations and have been staging posts in at least one high-profile conversion to Roman Catholicism.[39] Readers will find substantial discussion of these issues in the lively online culture that has grown to promote and critique the experiment in Moscow. These websites include stories of individuals who have become victims in the very communities in which they were meant to find protection from a dangerous outside world. And while some of their claims have been disputed, these stories too are part of the narrative culture of the American Redoubt. It is not for nothing that the leaders of the principal congregation in Moscow have warned those who may be considering moving into the area not to have unreasonably high expectations of what they might discover. The effects of the Fall are as real in Moscow as anywhere else. But it is telling that the advocates of postmillennial social reconstruction feel the need to temper the expectations of their converts. Even in the town that some of its inhabitants regard as the "Reformed Mecca," the wheat and tares will grow together until harvest (Matthew 13:24–30). Those words from the Gospels are not likely to dampen the enthusiasm of those who seek to survive and resist the impending social and cultural crisis.

But, even if these projects do not succeed, they are certainly likely to continue—because the cultural conditions of American modernity are not likely to improve. Even in the 1970s, as American evangelicals were reclaiming their place in the public square, Alasdair MacIntyre predicted the social trend that is the subject of this book. MacIntyre argued that politics had become so fractured as to make the assumption of consensus entirely irrecoverable. Surveying the Left, alongside liberals and conservatives, he recognized the failure of Marxism but also the inadequacy of any other philosophical system to dismantle the "structures of late capitalism." Every "political tradition within our culture" had been "exhausted."[40] All that remained were competing discourses of virtue, utterly compelling to their devotees, and perfectly capable of making sense of their world. His conclusion was that "there seems to be no rational way of securing moral agreement in culture," because there exists

> no established way of deciding between these claims. . . . From our rival
> conclusions we can argue back to our rival premises; but when we do arrive
> at our premises argument ceases and the invocation of one premise against

another becomes a matter of pure assertion and counter-assertion. Hence perhaps the slightly shrill tone of so much moral debate.[41]

His fear, even in the 1970s, was that "we possess no unassailable criteria, no set of compelling reasons by means of which we may convince our opponents."[42] Government may assert a rhetoric of values or of virtues, but it cannot represent the "moral community of the citizens." Instead, it becomes "a set of institutional arrangements for imposing a bureaucratized unity on a society which lacks genuine moral consensus."[43] And when its government is a management tool, there can be little hope of generating feeling for or identification with the nation.

This is why the migration to the Redoubt is likely to continue. Migration into a monoculture provides one way of addressing the cognitive dissonance of American modernity. This valorization of monoculture might appear to be driven by some kind of racism—though this claim is almost always denied by those who promote the migration project. The individuals I encountered spoke forcefully about preserving traditional culture, and referred to racial differences only to claim their irrelevance to that task (an assumption that is, of course, loaded with political presuppositions of its own, though it might not be clear what happens to this claim when it is sustained by, for example, an African American). The "quest for community" that the migration represents uses the tools of modernity to break down the isolation that is being experienced by individuals, families, and even congregations that are moving together into the American Redoubt. The communities that they establish, discover, and promote offer the affirmation of normality to those who cannot find it anywhere else; these migrants buy into the ideals of the communities with which they affiliate long before they ever leave their home. These migrants understand that, for all that this book has used the labels, there is in reality no mainstream culture, and no "evangelical movement," just as there is no single kind of evangelical who is trying to escape from it. The Balkanization of modern politics finds its parallel in the collapse of a common culture, or even a common conversation between groups within that culture. And individuals, families, and small units of community will continue to gravitate to where they feel affirmed. Of course, participants in many subcultures have been doing this for a very long time. The hippie trail to San Francisco finds its parallel in the creation of distinctive religious enclaves in New York. In that context, the movement of conservative Protestants into regions in which their values are more widely shared should not come as any kind of surprise. Like continues to attract like. The regionalization of distinctive moral systems continues to be one of the most obvious consequences of modernity in the period that MacIntyre describes as being "after virtue." It is not the purpose of this book to inquire into the implications of the regionalization of morality for national government, for future trends in political participation, or for developing tensions between red states and blue. One of the most significant structural problems in American politics relates to the fact that these diverse and contradictory cultures wish to share a common infrastructure of law. As recent appointments to its bench have suggested, the Supreme Court may be not so much the "still point of turning world," as T. S. Eliot might have put it, but, as W. B. Yeats might have feared, the center that "cannot hold."

More than ever before, American evangelicals are thinking about the relationships between faith, politics, and the question for community. At this social, cultural, political, and demographic "turning point," at the "end of white, Christian America," what matters is the "construction of local forms of community within which civility and the intellectual and moral life can be sustained through the new dark ages which are already upon us."[44] The "continuation of civility and moral community" can no longer be identified with the "shoring up" of what might be considered to be the social, cultural, and political mainstream. MacIntyre concluded *After Virtue* with hope for a new St. Benedict. But other theorists, also developing their programs of renewal in the 1970s, were doing more to challenge dominant narratives and to inspire the creation of sustainable communities of survival, resistance, and reconstruction. Perhaps, in the person of Rushdoony, the evangelical St. Benedict had already arrived.

Glossary

Amillennialism

The belief that the period of one thousand years described in Revelation 20:1–10 does not refer to an end-time period and is instead a metaphor for all or a substantial part of the period between Christ's incarnation and second coming. This appears to be the reading of Revelation 20:1–10 assumed in the major reformation confessions of faith.[1]

Antichrist

The church's theological enemies are described as "antichrist" in several New Testament passages (1 John 2:18, 22; 1 John 4:3; 2 John 7). In popular discourse, however, "the Antichrist" is a single figure who tends to combine elements of the various eschatological enemies described in Daniel and Revelation. The older Protestant identification of the Antichrist as the Pope has given way to a range of other opinions under the influence of *futurist premillennialism* and *preterism*.

Apocalyptic

A biblical genre, with disputed characteristics, that has given its name to a wider approach to the understanding of world affairs. Apocalyptic literature emphasizes the sudden (and often imminent) end of all things. In contrast to the *millennium*, the apocalyptic mode can seem dualistic (evil is in constant struggle with goodness), pessimistic (world conditions are not likely to improve), deterministic (the future has been planned by God), ethically passive (if conditions are not likely to improve, there is little that can be done to make the world a better place), and final.

Christian Reconstruction

The belief, developed in the 1960s, that the *postmillennial* coming of Christ will be preceded by the establishment of "godly rule" on earth. This "godly rule" will be marked by an unprecedented revival of Christianity and the international adoption of the Mosaic judicial and penal codes.

Dispensationalism

A variety of *premillennialism* which emerged in the 1830s to argue for a radical disjunction between Israel and the church and which teaches that the "secret rapture" will precede the *tribulation*. Dispensationalists commonly mark seven distinct stages in the development of the history of redemption, which may or may not have different conditions of salvation. Dispensationalism has developed through three major stages: classical dispensationalism, which is best represented by the *Scofield Reference Bible* (1909; second edition 1917) and the writings of L. S. Chafer and J. Dwight Pentecost; revised dispensationalism, which is best represented by the *New Scofield Bible* (1967); and progressive dispensationalism, which is best represented by the writings of Craig Blaising and Darrell Bock.

Eschatology

Classically, the study of the "four last things"—death, judgment, heaven, and hell—but the term has been expanded in use to refer to other aspects of end of the world belief. Evangelical eschatology can be either pessimistic, in its expectation of *apocalyptic* events, or optimistic, in its expectation of the *millennium*.

Historicism

A system of hermeneutics that understands New Testament prophecies to detail all or part of the course of history in the period before the second coming. The identification of the Pope as the Antichrist is common in Protestant historicist interpretation; but the identification of the establishment of Israel in 1948 as a fulfillment of prophecy also represents a historicist interpretive approach. "Historicist" *premillennialism*, one variant of which is represented in the writings of Hal Lindsey, should be distinguished from "historic" (i.e., non-dispensational) *premillennialism*, as advanced by G. E. Ladd, which may or may not be historicist, and which Lindsey would certainly oppose.

Millenarian/Millennialist

Conventionally, scholars working in millennial studies have followed Ernest L. Tuveson in distinguishing "millennialists" (believers who adopt *postmillennial*, optimistic, and gradualist theologies) from "millenarians" (believers who adopt *premillennial*, pessimistic, and radical theologies). Ernest R. Sandeen has noted, however, that the terms are interchangeable in the literature of the emerging fundamentalist movement and a strict distinction should probably not therefore be imposed.[2]

Millennium

A utopian period whose general characteristics are based on the description of the binding of Satan in Revelation 20:1–10 and the prophecies of the renewal of the natural world in the Hebrew prophets. Its specific characteristics vary according to the interpreter, and the millennium can be used as a trope for a wide and sometimes contradictory range of political, cultural, and religious presuppositions. The three most common of evangelical millennial schemes—*amillennialism*, *premillennialism*, and *postmillennialism*—should not be anachronistically read into older material. Not every exegete would share the basic assumption of these schemes, the idea that Revelation 20:1–10 refers to only one thousand-year period. The *Oxford English Dictionary* dates the development of the *premillennial* and *postmillennial* terms to the mid-nineteenth century, though the interpretive paradigms they represent can be traced to the Reformation; it does not provide any information on the development of "amillennial," though it approximates to the eschatological position of the reformation creeds.

Postmillennialism

The belief that Christ will return after the *millennium* has substantially reformed life on earth. Postmillennialists can be either *apocalyptic* or gradualist, and vary in the extent to which they believe the *millennium* can be expedited by their own effort. Postmillennialism has been revived among some conservative Presbyterians, particularly those with interests in *Christian Reconstruction*, but, among evangelicals more generally, remains much less popular than *premillennialism*.

Premillennialism

The belief that the second coming of Christ will take place before the *millennium*. Historic premillennialism teaches that Christ will return after the *tribulation* (and is consequently designated "post-tribulational"); this was the view of, for example, C. H. Spurgeon and G. E. Ladd. *Dispensational* premillennialism, developed from the works of J. N. Darby, argues that Christ will return for the "secret rapture" before the *tribulation* (and is consequently designated "pre-tribulational"). This rapture will "catch up" believers in order to take them into heaven while the *Antichrist* rages on earth. The second coming proper will take place at the end of the tribulation, and Christ will then usher in the *millennium* and reign over the world for one thousand years. Premillennialists debate whether believers will live on earth during the *millennium* and debate the specific roles of Israel and a range of other powers in this end-times scenario.

Preterism

A system of hermeneutics that understands New Testament prophecies to be chiefly concerned with the Roman assault on Jerusalem and the end of Temple worship in AD 70. Preterism has influenced a number of recent evangelical *premillennial* and *postmillennial* Bible commentaries.

Tribulation

The belief (shared by many *premillennialists*) that the Bible predicts a final seven-year period of terrible suffering during which the *Antichrist* persecutes believers and God pours judgment on the world.

Notes

Preface

1. R. J. Rushdoony, *Intellectual schizophrenia: Culture, crisis and education* (Philadelphia, PA: Presbyterian & Reformed, 1961), p. 112.

2. For this concept, see Robert P. Jones, *The end of white Christian America* (New York: Simon & Schuster, 2016).

3. Julie J. Ingersoll, *Building God's kingdom: Inside the world of Christian Reconstruction* (New York: Oxford University Press, 2015), p. 5.

4. For early analysis, see Mark Juergensmeyer, *Terror in the mind of God: The global rise of religious violence* (Berkeley: University of California Press, 2000), pp. 27–30. For more detailed accounts, see Ingersoll, *Building God's kingdom*; Molly Worthen, *Apostles of reason: The crisis of authority in American evangelicalism* (New York: Oxford University Press, 2014); Michael J. McVicar, *Christian Reconstruction: R. J. Rushdoony and American religious conservatism* (Chapel Hill: University of North Carolina Press, 2015); Frances Fitzgerald, *The evangelicals: The struggle to shape America* (New York: Simon & Schuster, 2017); Gillis J. Harp, *Protestants and American conservatism* (New York: Oxford University Press, 2019); Benjamin L. Huskinson, *American creationism, creation science, and Intelligent Design in the evangelical market* (New York: Palgrave, 2020).

5. Ingersoll, by contrast, traces the continuity of Reconstructionist ideas into several evangelical ministries and political groups; Ingersoll, *Building God's kingdom, passim*.

6. The modification of Christian Reconstruction has been noted by Ingersoll, *Building God's kingdom*, pp. xiii, 167–88.

7. Queen's University Belfast, "Policy and principles of ethical research," available at https://www.qub.ac.uk/home/media/Media,600198,en.pdf, accessed June 26, 2019.

8. On gender within the cultures of theonomy, see McVicar, *Christian Reconstruction*, p. 234 n. 14.

9. On the use of composite characters, see the negative perspective of William F. Kelleher, *The Troubles in Ballybogoin: Memory and identity in Northern Ireland* (Ann Arbor: University of Michigan Press, 2003), pp. x, 2, 16, and the more positive perspective of Jason De Leon, *The land of open graves: Living and dying on the migrant trail* (Oakland: University of California Press, 2015). The use of composite characters has been developed by Nancy Scheper-Hughes, in *Saints, scholars and schizophrenics: Mental illness in rural Ireland* (Oakland: University of California Press, 1992), Lisa Malkki, *Purity and exile: Violence, memory, and national cosmology among Hutu refugees in Tanzania* (Chicago: University of Chicago Press, 1995),

and T. M. Luhrmann, *Of two minds: The growing disorder in American psychiatry* (New York: Alfred A. Knopf, 2000).

10. While James Wesley, Rawles prefers to include a comma in his name, I have followed the WorldCat citation of his name throughout this book, and have not included this comma.

11. For a striking example of this possibility, consider how Timothy McVeigh circulated copies of James Coates's *Armed and dangerous: The rise of the survivalist right* (New York: Farrar Straus & Giroux, 1988) in advance of the Oklahoma City bombing; Kathleen Belew, *Bring the war home: The White Power movement and paramilitary America* (Cambridge, MA: Harvard University Press, 2018), p. 223.

12. https://twitter.com/realDonaldTrump/status/1313823809150087168, accessed October 12, 2020.

13. Ingersoll, *Building God's kingdom*, p. 6.

14. McVicar, *Christian Reconstruction*, p. 230.

15. See, for good examples of these biographical, institutional and thematic approaches, McVicar, *Christian Reconstruction*; Ingersoll, *Building God's kingdom*; James K. Wellman, *Evangelical vs. liberal: The clash of Christian cultures in the Pacific Northwest* (New York: Oxford University Press, 2008); and Fitzgerald, *The evangelicals*.

16. Ingersoll, *Building God's kingdom*, pp. ix–xiii.

Introduction

1. Douglas Wilson, *Empires of dirt: Secularism, radical Islam, and the Mere Christendom alternative* (Moscow, ID: Canon Press, 2016), p. 2.

2. R. J. Rushdoony, *The institutes of Biblical law* (Nutley, NJ: Presbyterian & Reformed, 1973), p. 765.

3. See, for example, Rushdoony, *Institutes of Biblical law*, pp. 57, 186, 263, 283.

4. On the death of Christian Reconstruction, see Molly Worthen, "The Chalcedon problem: Rousas John Rushdoony and the origins of Christian Reconstruction," *Church History* 77:2 (2008), pp. 399–436.

5. Steven K. Green, *The third disestablishment: Church, state, and American culture, 1940–1975* (New York: Oxford University Press, 2019). For evangelicals' movement toward political pluralism, see Benjamin T. Lynerd, *Republican theology: The civil religion of American evangelicals* (New York: Oxford University Press, 2014), and Andrew R. Lewis, *The rights turn in conservative Christian politics: How abortion transformed the culture wars* (Cambridge: Cambridge University Press, 2017).

6. Crawford Gribben, *Writing the rapture: Prophecy fiction in evangelical America* (New York: Oxford University Press, 2009).

7. Todd M. Brenneman, *Homespun gospel: The triumph of sentimentality in contemporary American evangelicalism* (New York: Oxford University Press, 2014).

8. John Fea, *Believe me: The evangelical road to Donald Trump* (Grand Rapids, MI: Eerdmans, 2018).

NOTES   157

9. Patrick J. Deneen, *Why liberalism failed* (New Haven, CT: Yale University Press, 2018); Jones, *The end of white Christian America*.

10. For media coverage of the movement, see "The last big frontier," *The Economist*, August 6, 2016, available at http://www.economist.com/news/united-states/ 21703411-movement-staunch-conservatives-and-doomsday-watchers-inland- north-west?fsrc=scn/tw_ec/the_last_big_frontier, accessed June 26, 2019; Ryan Collingwood, "Welcome to the American Redoubt," *CDA Press*, August 14, 2016, available at http://cdapress.com/news/local_news/article_9caa9b9a-61d4-11e6- b131-871b50c47f7c.html#.V7F2yxmIhT0.twitter, accessed June 26, 2019; Kevin Sullivan, "A fortress against fear," *Washington Post*, August 27, 2016, available at https://www.washingtonpost.com/classic-apps/a-fortress-against-fear/2016/08/27/ 97a45992-5d60-11e6-8e45-477372e89d78_story.html?postshare=971147246246120 6&tid=ss_tw-bottom, accessed June 26, 2019.

11. Joe Carter, "Kinism, cultural Marxism, and the synagogue shooter," *The Gospel Coalition*, April 30, 2019, available at https://www.thegospelcoalition.org/article/ kinism-cultural-marxism-and-the-synagogue-shooter/, accessed June 26, 2019. On Reconstruction and violence, see Ingersoll, *Building God's kingdom*, pp. 213–35.

12. See, for example, Christopher (Chrissy) Stroop, "Is Christian homeschooling breeding a new kind of domestic terrorist?" *Playboy*, May 8, 2019, available at https:// www.playboy.com/read/is-christian-homeschooling-breeding-a-new-kind-of- domestic-terrorist, accessed June 26, 2019.

13. See, in this respect, D. G. Hart, *Deconstructing Evangelicalism: Conservative Protestantism in the age of Billy Graham* (Grand Rapids, MI: Baker, 2004); D. G. Hart, *From Billy Graham to Sarah Palin: Evangelicals and the betrayal of American conservatism* (Grand Rapids, MI: Eerdmans, 2011); Steven P. Miller, *The age of evangelicalism: America's born-again years* (New York: Oxford University Press, 2014); and Benjamin L. Huskinson, "The missing link between evangelicals and Trump," *The American Interest*, November 23, 2018, available at https://www.the-american- interest.com/2018/11/23/the-missing-link-between-evangelicals-and-trump/, accessed June 26, 2019.

14. Hart, *Deconstructing Evangelicalism*, passim.

15. See, for example, Miller, *The age of evangelicalism*, pp. 145–52; Brian Steensland and Philip Goff, "Introduction: The new evangelical social engagement," in Brian Steensland and Philip Goff (eds.), *The new evangelical social engagement* (New York: Oxford University Press, 2014), pp. 1–30. For an examination of political variety within individual evangelical congregations, as well as across the evangelical movement, the purported unity of which she questions, see Lydia Bean, *The politics of evangelical identity: Local churches and partisan divides in the United States and Canada* (Princeton, NJ: Princeton University Press, 2014).

16. For Wilson and Hitchens, see Ross Douthat, *Bad religion: How we became a nation of heretics* (New York: Free Press, 2012), p. 281.

17. See, for example, Kenneth Surin, "*Contemptus mundi* and the disenchanted world: Bonhoeffer's 'discipline of the secret' and Adorno's 'strategy of hibernation,'"

Journal of the American Academy of Religion 53:3 (1985), pp. 383–410, and *Captain Fantastic* (dir. Matt Ross, 2016).

18. Email from Gary North to the author, May 1, 2013. For North and Nisbet, see McVicar, *Christian Reconstruction*, p. 260 n. 27.

19. Steven Conn, *Americans against the city: Anti-urbanism in the twentieth century* (New York: Oxford University Press, 2014).

20. On recent histories of American conservatism, see Kim Phillips-Fein, "Conservatism: A state of the field," *Journal of American History* 98:3 (2011), pp. 723–43.

21. Joel A. Carpenter, *Revive us again: The reawakening of American fundamentalism* (New York: Oxford University Press, 1997); Matthew Avery Sutton, *American apocalypse: A history of modern evangelicalism* (Cambridge, MA: Belknap Press of Harvard University Press, 2014); and Markku Ruotsila, *Fighting fundamentalist: Carl McIntire and the politicization of American fundamentalism* (New York: Oxford University Press, 2016).

22. See Lisa McGirr, *Suburban warriors: The origins of the New American Right* (Princeton, NJ: Princeton University Press, 2001); Daniel K. Williams, *God's own party: The making of the Christian Right* (New York: Oxford University Press, 2010); and Darren Dochuk, *From Bible Belt to Sun Belt: Plain-folk religion, grassroots politics, and the rise of evangelical conservatism* (New York: W. W. Norton, 2011).

23. See Jones, *The end of white Christian America*; Green, *The third disestablishment*.

24. Gary North has claimed that the term "secular humanism" was coined by R. J. Rushdoony; Gary North, "The intellectual schizophrenia of the New Christian Right," in "The failure of the American Baptist culture," *Christianity and Civilisation 1* (1982), p. 14.

25. One of my interviewees at New Saint Andrews College, Moscow, ID, described the impact of the Obama administration as representing a "generational reversal"; interview, September 12, 2015.

26. For some discussion of the background to this election, see Fea, *Believe me*.

27. David Brooks, "The Benedict Option," *New York Times*, March 14, 2017, available at https://www.nytimes.com/2017/03/14/opinion/the-benedict-option.html?_r=0, accessed June 26, 2019.

28. Rod Dreher, "Scandal in Moscow," *American Conservative*, September 29, 2015, available at http://www.theamericanconservative.com/dreher/scandal-in-moscow/ , accessed June 26, 2019. Conservative theologians within the world of American Presbyterian and Reformed denominations debate whether Douglas Wilson and the religious movement he represents can be properly described as "Reformed." In using that descriptor without qualification, this book sidesteps the theological controversy to allow its subjects to identify themselves. For discussion of variety within the Reformed nomenclature, see Chris Caughey and Crawford Gribben, "History, identity politics, and the 'Recovery of the Reformed confession,'" in Matthew Bingham, Chris Caughey, R. Scott Clark, and Darryl G. Hart (eds.), *On being Reformed: Debates over a trans-Atlantic identity* (Basingstoke, UK: Palgrave, 2018), pp. 1–26.

29. Rod Dreher, *Crunchy cons: How Birkenstocked Burkeans, gun-loving organic gardeners, evangelical free-range farmers, hip homeschooling mamas, right-wing nature lovers, and their diverse tribe of countercultural conservatives plan to save America (or at least the Republican Party)* (New York: Crown Forum, 2006), *passim*; Alex R. Schäfer, *Countercultural conservatives: American evangelicalism from the postwar revival to the New Christian Right* (Madison: University of Wisconsin Press, 2011), *passim*.

30. McVicar, *Christian Reconstruction*, p. 4.

31. Ingersoll, *Building God's kingdom*, pp. 39, 238. Reconstructionists dispute who founded the movement, and whether Rushdoony and North were equal players in setting out its early agenda. North claims that he "co-founded" Christian Reconstructionism with Rushdoony; Gary North, "Geocentricity-Geostationism: The flat earth temptation," *Institute for Christian Economics Position Paper* (1992), p. 2.

32. John M. Frame, "The one, the many, and theonomy," in William S. Barker and W. Robert Godfrey (eds.), *Theonomy: A Reformed critique* (Grand Rapids, MI: Zondervan, 1990), p. 89.

33. Williams, *God's own party*, pp. 225–26; Miller, *The age of evangelicalism*, pp. 141–42; Max Blumenthal, *Republican Gomorrah: Inside the movement that shattered the party* (New York: Nation Books, 2009), pp. 17–27. For a discussion of the reception of Christian Reconstructionism in recent historical writing, see Brian J. Auten, "Narrating Christian transformationalism: Rousas J. Rushdoony and Christian Reconstruction in current histories of American religion and politics," in Peter Escalante and W. Bradford Littlejohn (eds.), *For the healing of the nations: Essays on creation, redemption, and neo-Calvinism* ([Moscow, ID]: The Davenant Trust, 2014), pp. 209–39.

34. Fitzgerald, *The evangelicals*, pp. 337–47.

35. Huskinson, *American creationism, creation science and Intelligent Design in the evangelical market*, pp. 50–55.

36. Ingersoll, *Building God's kingdom*, p. 242.

37. Randall Balmer, *Thy kingdom come: How the Religious Right distorts the faith and threatens America* (New York: Basic Books, 2006), pp. 64–66.

Chapter 1

1. R. J. Rushdoony, *Preparation for the future* (San Carlos, CA: The Pamphleteers, 1966), p. 23.

2. James Wesley Rawles, *Liberators: A novel of the coming global collapse* (New York: Dutton, 2014), p. 240.

3. Rawles refers to several real-life religious communities, apparently without having first secured their permission for his doing so: in conversation, on September 11, 2015, I discovered that the ministers of Christ Church, in Moscow, Idaho, were unaware that their congregation had been mentioned in his *Liberators* (2014).

4. James Wesley Rawles, "The American Redoubt: Move to the mountain states," March 28, 2011, available at https://survivalblog.com/redoubt/, accessed June 26, 2019.

5. Interview with James Wesley Rawles, May 14, 2013.

6. Rawles, "The American Redoubt: Move to the mountain states," available at https://survivalblog.com/redoubt/, accessed June 26, 2019.

7. As I noted earlier, it is not clear that each of these congregations has given permission for the display of their names in connection with the Redoubt movement—though one congregation has so identified with the concept of the Redoubt that they feature it in a self-composed hymn; see Lordship Church, Coeur d'Alene, "The Redoubt song," available at https://www.youtube.com/watch?v=HSB_EnQul90, accessed June 26, 2019.

8. James Wesley Rawles, *How to survive the end of the world as we know it: Tactics, techniques and technologies for uncertain times* (London: Penguin, 2009), pp. 13–14.

9. Interview with James Wesley Rawles, May 14, 2013.

10. Christ Church, Moscow, "Position Papers: Manners and life together: Moving to Moscow," available at https://www.christkirk.com/our-church/book-of-worship-faith-practice/, accessed June 26, 2019.

11. See, for example, Christopher Hitchens and Douglas Wilson, *Is Christianity good for the world?* (Moscow, ID: Canon Press, 2009), and the documentary film that recorded the debates that this book reflected, *Collision: Christopher Hitchens vs. Douglas Wilson* (dir. Darren Doane, 2009). For media coverage of the movement, see "The last big frontier," *The Economist*, August 6, 2016, available at http://www.economist.com/news/united-states/21703411-movement-staunch-conservatives-and-doomsday-watchers-inland-north-west?fsrc=scn/tw_ec/the_last_big_frontier, accessed June 26, 2019; Ryan Collingwood, "Welcome to the American Redoubt," *CDA Press*, August 14, 2016, available at http://cdapress.com/news/local_news/article_9caa9b9a-61d4-11e6-b131-871b50c47f7c.html#.V7F2yxmIhT0.twitter, accessed June 26, 2019; Kevin Sullivan, "A fortress against fear," *Washington Post*, August 27, 2016, available at https://www.washingtonpost.com/classic-apps/a-fortress-against-fear/2016/08/27/97a45992-5d60-11e6-8e45-477372e89d78_story.html?postshare=9711472462461206&tid=ss_tw-bottom, accessed June 26, 2019.

12. Surin, "*Contemptus mundi* and the disenchanted world," pp. 383–410; Sam Haselby, *The origins of American religious nationalism* (Oxford: Oxford University Press, 2015); Jones, *The end of white Christian America*.

13. Michael J. McVicar, "Apostles of deceit: Ecumenism, fundamentalism, surveillance, and the contested loyalties of Protestant clergy during the Cold War," in Sylvester A. Johnson and Steven Weitzman (eds.), *The FBI and religion: Faith and national security before and after 9/11* (Oakland: University of California Press, 2017), pp. 85–107.

14. See Bean, *The politics of evangelical identity*; James K. Wellman, Jr, *Evangelical vs. liberal: The clash of Christian cultures in the Pacific Northwest* (New York: Oxford University Press, 2008); Daniel K. Williams, "Prolifers of the left: Progressive evangelicals' campaign against abortion," in Brian Steensland and Philip Goff (eds.), *The new evangelical social engagement* (New York: Oxford University Press, 2014), pp. 200–20; Lynerd, *Republican theology*, pp. 193–95.

15. Interview with two anonymous kinists, Coeur d'Alene, September 10, 2015.

16. Email to the author, September 15, 2015.

17. See "The last big frontier," *The Economist*, August 6, 2016, available at http://www.economist.com/news/united-states/21703411-movement-staunch-conservatives-and-doomsday-watchers-inland-north-west?fsrc=scn/tw_ec/the_last_big_frontier, accessed June 26, 2019; Ryan Collingwood, "Welcome to the American Redoubt," *CDA Press*, August 14, 2016, available at http://cdapress.com/news/local_news/article_9caa9b9a-61d4-11e6-b131-871b50c47f7c.html#.V7F2yxmIhT0.twitter, accessed June 26, 2019; Kevin Sullivan, "A fortress against fear," *Washington Post*, August 27, 2016, available at https://www.washingtonpost.com/classic-apps/a-fortress-against-fear/2016/08/27/97a45992-5d60-11e6-8e45-477372e89d78_story.html?postshare=9711472462461206&tid=ss_tw-bottom, accessed June 26, 2019.

18. Ingersoll, *Building God's kingdom*, pp. xii, 6. Gary North has estimated that between 25,000 and 40,000 individuals were involved in the movement of Christian Reconstruction; McVicar, *Christian Reconstruction*, p. 201.

19. See, for example, Daniel T. Rogers, "In search of progressivism," *Reviews in American history 10*:4 (1982), pp. 113–32.

20. David Sabean, *Power in the blood: Popular culture and village discourse in early modern Germany* (Cambridge: Cambridge University Press, 1988), p. 29. I owe this point to Chris Schlect.

21. James Wesley Rawles, "Addenda: Reformed churches in the American Redoubt states," available at https://survivalblog.com/redoubt/, accessed June 26, 2019.

22. Jill K. Gill, "The power and the glory: Idaho's religious history," in Adam M. Sowards (ed.), *Idaho's place: A new history of the Gem State* (Seattle: University of Washington Press, 2014), p. 110.

23. Gill, "The power and the glory: Idaho's religious history," p. 108; Adam M. Sowards, "Reckoning with history," in Sowards (ed.), *Idaho's place*, p. 4.

24. See, for example, James A. Aho, *The politics of righteousness: Idaho Christian patriotism* (Seattle: University of Washington Press, 1990); Jonathan Raban, *Bad Land: An American romance* (London: Picador, 1996); Martin Fletcher, *Almost heaven: Travels through the backwoods of America* (London: Little, Brown, 1998); Philip Melling, *Fundamentalism in America: Millennialism, identity and militant religion* (Edinburgh: Edinburgh University Press, 1999), pp. 135–67; Richard G. Mitchell, *Dancing at Armageddon: Survivalism and chaos in modern times* (Chicago: University of Chicago Press, 2002); Belew, *Bring the war home*.

25. See especially the essays contained in Philip Lockley (ed.), *Protestant communalism in the trans-Atlantic world, 1650–1850* (London: Palgrave Macmillan, 2016).

26. Philip Lockley, "Introduction," in Lockley (ed.), *Protestant communalism in the trans-Atlantic world, 1650–1850*, p. 2; The Church of Jesus Christ of Latter-Day Saints, "Facts and statistics," available at http://www.mormonnewsroom.org/facts-and-statistics/country/united-states/state/idaho, accessed May 29, 2019.

27. Robert J. Hendricks, *Bethel and Aurora: An experiment in communalism as practical Christianity* (New York: Pioneer Press, 1933); David Nelson Duke, "The evolution of religion in Wilhelm Keil's community: A new reading of old testimony," *Communal Societies 13* (1993), pp. 84–98; James Kopp, *Eden within Eden: Oregon's utopian*

heritage (Corvallis: Oregon State University Press, 2009), pp. 39–50; Philip Lockley, "Mapping Protestant communalism, 1650–1850," in Lockley (ed.), *Protestant communalism in the trans-Atlantic world, 1650–1850*, pp. 25–26.

28. Gill, "The power and the glory," pp. 117–18. The Psychiana papers are in Special Collections of the University of Idaho, available at http://www.lib.uidaho.edu/special-collections/Manuscripts/mg101.htm, accessed June 26, 2019.

29. Gill, "The power and the glory," p. 127; Michael W. Cuneo, *The smoke of Satan: Conservative and traditionalist dissent in contemporary American Catholicism* (Baltimore, MD: Johns Hopkins University Press, 1999), p. 100.

30. Garrison Keillor, *Lake Wobegon Days* (1985; London: Faber, 1997), p. vii.

31. Alex Hannaford, "Wayne Bent: The cult of the man they call messiah," *Sunday Times Magazine*, June 14, 2009, pp. 42–47; "Accusations against sect in New Mexico," *New York Times*, May 4, 2004, available at http://www.nytimes.com/2008/05/04/us/04church.html, accessed June 26, 2019; see also *The cult at the end of the world* (dir. Ben Anthony, 2007).

32. Mitchell, *Dancing at Armageddon*, pp. 33–34, https://news.google.com/newspapers?nid=950&dat=19811219&id=XsNaAAAAIBAJ&sjid=nlkDAAAAIBAJ&pg=6844,1178471

33. Kopp, *Eden within Eden*, pp. 169–79.

34. Belew, *Bring the war home*, p. 53.

35. Alan W. Bock, *Ambush at Ruby Ridge: How government agents set Randy Weaver up and took his family down* (Irvine, CA: Dickens Press, 1995), p. 56; Belew, *Bring the war home*, pp. 51–53, 105, 115–16, 125, 127.

36. R. E. Miles and R. Butler, *From the Mountain Newsletter* (Spring 1985).

37. Belew, *Bring the war home*, pp. 161–62. See E. Toy, "'Promised land' or Armageddon? History, survivalists, and the Aryan Nations in the Pacific Northwest," *Montana: The Magazine of Western History* 36:3 (Summer 1986), pp. 80–82; R. Velarde, "Preparing for the Apocalypse: A look at the rise of doomsday preppers," *Christian Research Journal* 36:4 (2013), available at http://www.equip.org/PDF/JAF5364.pdf, accessed June 26, 2019.

38. Mark S. Hamm, *Apocalypse in Oklahoma: Waco and Ruby Ridge avenged* (Boston, MA: Northeastern University Press, 1997), p. 14.

39. Raphael S. Ezekiel, *The racist mind: Portraits of American neo-Nazis and Klansmen* (London: Penguin, 1995), pp. 37–57, 122–42; Mitchell, *Dancing at Armageddon*, p. 176.

40. Bock, *Ambush at Ruby Ridge*, p. 56; Gill, "The power and the glory," p. 130.

41. Bock, *Ambush at Ruby Ridge*.

42. Melling, *Fundamentalism in America*, p. 156.

43. Melling, *Fundamentalism in America*, p. 157.

44. Melling, *Fundamentalism in America*, p. 155. Some accounts claim that Gritz decried race-mixing even as he lived with "two half-Chinese children and an African-American godchild"; Melling, *Fundamentalism in America*, p. 155.

45. George Marsden, *The twilight of the American Enlightenment: The 1950s and the crisis of liberal belief* (New York: Basic Books, 2014).

46. Michael Barkun, *Chasing phantoms: Reality, imagination, and Homeland Security since 9/11* (Chapel Hill: University of North Carolina Press, 2014), pp. 29–30.

47. Sutton, *American apocalypse*, p. 327.

48. Melling, *Fundamentalism in America*, p. 77.

49. Barkun, *Chasing phantoms*, p. 30.

50. See, in particular, Wellman, *Evangelical vs. liberal.*

51. Gill, "The power and the glory," p. 108.

52. Gill, "The power and the glory," pp. 123–24. See also John Kevin Olson and Ann C. Beck, "Religion and political realignment in the Rocky Mountain States," *Journal for the Scientific Study of Religion 29* (1990), pp. 198–204; Stephanie Witt and Gary Moncrief, "Religion and roll call voting in Idaho: The 1990 abortion controversy," *American Politics Quarterly 21* (1993), pp. 140–49; Sowards, "Reckoning with history," p. 9.

53. Kathryn Joyce, *Quiverfull: Inside the Christian Patriarchy movement* (Boston, MA: Beacon Press, 2009), p. 176; "Of holidays and domestic violence," *The Spokesman-Review*, November 21, 2007, available at http://www.spokesman.com/blogs/boise/2007/nov/21/of-holidays-and-domestic-violence/, accessed June 26, 2019.

54. "Republican Matt Shea 'participated in act of domestic terrorism,' says report," in https://www.theguardian.com/us-news/2019/dec/20/matt-shea-domestic-terrorism-washington-state-report, accessed February 17, 2020.

55. Christ Church, Moscow, "Position Papers: Manners and life together: Moving to Moscow," available at https://www.christkirk.com/our-church/book-of-worship-faith-practice/, accessed June 26, 2019.

56. For Rushdoony's biography, see McVicar, *Christian Reconstruction.*

57. R. J. Rushdoony, "Christian missions and Indian culture," *Westminster Theological Journal 12*:1 (1949), pp. 1–12.

58. McVicar, *Christian Reconstruction*, pp. 4, 7, 112–15.

59. R. J. Rushdoony, *The mythology of science* (Nutley, NJ: Craig Press, 1967), p. 14.

60. McVicar, *Christian Reconstruction*, p. 3.

61. Mike Lorenz, "Wolves in sheep's clothing: Gary North, Y2K, and hidden agendas," available at http://www.sweetliberty.org/garynorth.htm, accessed June 26, 2019.

62. Rushdoony, *Preparation for the future*, p. 1.

63. Rushdoony, *Preparation for the future*, pp. 9–10, 15–17, 19.

64. Rushdoony, *Preparation for the future*, p. 19.

65. Rushdoony, *Preparation for the future*, p. 22.

66. Rushdoony, *Preparation for the future*, pp. 7–8.

67. Rushdoony, *Preparation for the future*, p. 23.

68. McVicar, *Christian Reconstruction*, p. 104.

69. Rushdoony, *Preparation for the future*, p. 23.

70. Gary North and David Chilton, "Apologetics and strategy," in *Tactics of Christian Resistance, Christianity & Civilization 3* (1983), pp. 125–26; Barry Hankins, *Francis Schaeffer and the shaping of evangelical America* (Grand Rapids, MI: Eerdmans, 2008), p. 193; Auten, "Narrating Christian transformationalism," pp. 227–28; McVicar, *Christian Reconstruction*, pp. 210–13; Fea, *Believe me*, p. 58. See also Joel McDurmon,

"Fitzgerald's *Evangelicals* and the repeat-failure of the Christian Right," available at https://americanvision.org/16700/fitzgeralds-evangelicals-and-the-repeat-failure-of-the-christian-right/, accessed June 26, 2019.

71. McVicar, *Christian Reconstruction*, p. 7.
72. Rushdoony merits only a passing reference in D. G. Hart, *Between the times: The Orthodox Presbyterian Church in transition, 1945–1990* (Willow Grove, PA: The Committee for the Historian of the Orthodox Presbyterian Church, 2011), pp. 191–92.
73. Ingersoll, *Building God's kingdom*, p. 34; McVicar, *Christian Reconstruction*, pp. 218–19. See also Lorenz, "Wolves in sheep's clothing: Gary North, Y2K, and hidden agendas."
74. Gary North, "The sabbath millennium," *Biblical Economics Today* 8:2 (1985), pp. 1–3; Gary North, *The Sinai strategy: Economics and the Ten Commandments* (Tyler, TX: Institute for Christian Economics, 1986), pp. 86–93.
75. McVicar, *Christian Reconstruction*, pp. 150–51, 187–91; Ingersoll, *Building God's kingdom*, p. 34; Martin G. Selbrede, "You can't split rotten wood," *The Journal of Christian Reconstruction 9* (1982–83), p. 207.
76. See, for example, an article in the journal that North edited: Michael R. Gilstrap, "The Biblical basis for survival preparation," *The Journal of Christian Reconstruction 8* (1981), pp. 155–65.
77. Gary North recommended the Moscow-Pullman area as "the best Y2K survival location in North America, if you have a water well less than 300 feet deep"; http://www.sullivan-county.com/nf0/fundienazis/y2k_gary.htm, accessed June 26, 2019.
78. Joyce, *Quiverfull*, p. 163.
79. For a critical review of this endeavor, see "Behind the walls," *SPLC Intelligence Report* (Summer 2013), available at https://www.splcenter.org/fighting-hate/intelligence-report/2013/behind-walls, accessed June 26, 2019.
80. Melling, *Fundamentalism in America*, p. 145; Arthur Bestor, *Backwoods utopias: The sectarian and Owenite phases of communitarian socialism in America, 1663–1829* (Philadelphia: University of Philadelphia Press, 1950).
81. Hitchins, as cited in Melling, *Fundamentalism in America*, p. 136.
82. Ezekiel makes a similar point about racist groups in *The racist mind*, p. xxi.
83. Richard Hofstadter, *The paranoid style in American politics and other essays* (New York: Knopf, 1965).
84. Melling, *Fundamentalism in America*, p. xiii.
85. Melling, *Fundamentalism in America*, p. x.
86. See, for example, Conn, *Americans against the city*.
87. Kopp, *Eden within Eden*, p. 141.
88. Melling argues that this is typical of fundamentalisms; *Fundamentalism in America*, p. 1.
89. Rawles, *Liberators*, p. 240.
90. Susan Harding, "Representing fundamentalism: The problem of the repugnant cultural other," *Social Research* 58:2 (1991), pp. 373–93.

91. Kopp, *Eden within Eden*, p. 4; Marilynne Robinson, *Housekeeping* (1980; rpt. London: Faber, 2005), p. 164.
92. Barkun deploys the expression "coercive re-enchantment" in a different context in *Chasing phantoms*, p. 18.

Chapter 2

1. Gary North, "Editor's introduction," *The Journal of Christian Reconstruction* 3:2 (1976–77), p. 1.
2. Interview with kinists, September 10, 2015.
3. Rushdoony, *Institutes of Biblical law*, p. 375. In this discussion of kinists, none of whom in my fieldwork wished to go on record, I refer the reader to the statement in the preface about my occasional use of the composite character device.
4. On Rushdoony and Holocaust denial, see Gary North, "Notes on the history of Christian Reconstruction: Clarifying the so-called 'Hitler connection,'" *Institute for Christian Economics Position Papers* (1992), pp. 1–2, and Carl Trueman, *Histories and fallacies: Problems faced in the writing of history* (Wheaton, IL: Crossway, 2009), p. 30. Ingersoll, in *Building God's kingdom*, p. 218, states that Rushdoony "does not deny the Holocaust occurred and, in fact, he calls it evil. He does draw on the work of anti-Semite Vicomte Leon de Poncins, but he labels him anti-Semitic and uses him as an example of those who are desensitized to evil." The most informed discussion of Rushdoony's interest in and withdrawal from Holocaust denial may be found in McVicar, *Christian Reconstruction*, p. 256 n. 113. For a broader discussion of Holocaust denial in the theonomist movement, see Joyce, *Quiverfull*, pp. 146–52.
5. For details of the Rushdoony family, see McVicar, *Christian Reconstruction, passim*.
6. The kinist narrative does not take account of Mark Rushdoony's observation that his father, when at seminary in the early 1940s, defied the racist prejudices of his peers and shared a room with an African-American student, who became a close friend; see Mark R. Rushdoony, "Rousas John Rushdoony: A brief history, part II: 'You are going to be a writer,'" available at https://chalcedon.edu/magazine/rousas-john-rushdoony-a-brief-history-part-ii-you-are-going-to-be-a-writer, accessed June 26, 2019. Similarly, Rushdoony spoke highly of "Rev. E.V. Hill and the Mount Zion Missionary Baptist Church," *The Journal of Christian Reconstruction* 9:1–2 (1982–83), p. 86; Rushdoony also served with Hill on the Council for National Policy, McVicar, *Christian Reconstruction*, pp. 146. Rushdoony spoke positively of certain aspects of Native American cultures in contrast to those of the "white man . . . a cold and inhospitable monster"; Rushdoony, *Intellectual schizophrenia*, p. 95. Ingersoll describes Rushdoony as an opponent of mixed-race marriage, in Ingersoll, *Building God's kingdom*, pp. 226–27, but McVicar claims that Rushdoony did officiate in at least one mixed-race wedding, in McVicar, *Christian Reconstruction*, pp. 274–75 n. 48. For examples of R. J. Rushdoony's multiple perspectives on race, see Rushdoony, *Institutes of Biblical law*, pp. 121, 157, 537; Rushdoony, *The mythology of science*, p. 53. These discussions of race need to be balanced against more nuanced references to racial

difference and race-based slavery in, for example, R. J. Rushdoony, *The politics of guilt and pity* (Nutley, NJ: Craig Press, 1970), pp. 25, 46. This theme is explored in John Frame, review of Rushdoony, *Institutes of Biblical law*, in *Westminster Theological Journal* 38:2 (1976), pp. 195–217, available at https://frame-poythress.org/the-institutes-of-biblical-law-a-review-article/, accessed June 26, 2019.

7. On kinism, see Mark Potok, "The year in hate, 2004," available at https://www.splcenter.org/fighting-hate/intelligence-report/2005/year-hate-2004, accessed June 26, 2019; Joyce, *Quiverfull*, pp. 122–23; for scholarly discussion, see Ingersoll, *Building God's kingdom*, pp. 226–27.

8. Philip Jenkins, *Mystics and messiahs: Cults and new religions in American history* (New York: Oxford University Press, 2000), p. 5.

9. For the emergence of postmillennialism, and a discussion of Edwards's role within it, see Crawford Gribben, *Evangelical millennialism in the trans-Atlantic world, 1500–2000* (Basingstoke, UK: Palgrave, 2011), pp. 71–91.

10. Gary North, "Editor's introduction," *The Journal of Christian Reconstruction* 3:2 (1976–77), p. 34.

11. See Haselby, *The origins of American religious nationalism, passim.*

12. James Moorhead, *World without end: Mainstream American Protestant visions of the last things, 1880–1925* (Bloomington: Indiana University Press, 1999), *passim.*

13. Gribben, *Evangelical millennialism in the trans-Atlantic world*, pp. 91–109.

14. For this concept, see Eric Hobsbawm (ed.), *The invention of tradition* (Cambridge: Cambridge University Press, 1993).

15. Gribben, *Evangelical millennialism in the trans-Atlantic world*, pp. 91–109; Darren Dochuk, *Anointed with oil: How Christianity and crude made modern America* (New York: Basic Books, 2019), *passim*; Daniel Vaca, *Evangelicals incorporated: Books and the business of religion in America* (Cambridge, MA: Harvard University Press, 2019), p. 100.

16. Gribben, *Evangelical millennialism in the trans-Atlantic world*, pp. 91–109.

17. The argument of Carpenter, *Revive us again*, is nuanced by Dochuk, *From Bible belt to sun belt.*

18. Maurice Isserman and Michael Kazin, *America divided: The civil war of the 1960s* (Oxford: Oxford University Press, 1999), pp. 254–55; John W. Whitehead, *Slaying dragons: The truth behind the man who defended Paula Jones* (Nashville, TN: Thomas Nelson, 2006), pp. 135–36; Larry Eskridge, *God's forever people: The Jesus People movement in America* (New York: Oxford University Press, 2013), p. 76; McVicar, *Christian Reconstruction*, pp. 139–41.

19. Gribben, *Evangelical millennialism in the trans-Atlantic world, 1500–2000*, pp. 110–24.

20. Whitehead, *Slaying dragons*, p. 136.

21. Hal Lindsey, *The late great planet earth* (Grand Rapids, MI: Zondervan, 1970), p. 5.

22. Lindsey, *The late great planet earth*, pp. 7–8.

23. Lindsey, *The late great planet earth*, p. 54.

24. Lindsey, *The late great planet earth*, p. 176.

25. Gary North has confirmed the significance of the 1970s as providing for the reformulation of postmillennialism; *Millennialism and social theory* (Tyler, TX: Institute for

Christian Economics, 1991), p. 21. Lindsey later attacked postmillennial theory in *The road to Holocaust* (New York: Bantam, 1990).

26. Peter J. Leithart, "Old Geneva & the New World: The Reverend Rousas J. Rushdoony, 1916–2001," *The Weekly Standard*, March 26, 2001, pp. 36–37.

27. Whitehead, *Slaying dragons*, pp. 136–37; Hankins, *Francis Schaeffer and the shaping of evangelical America*, pp. 192–227.

28. Harp, *Protestants and American Conservatism*, p. 201.

29. R. J. Rushdoony, *By what standard? An analysis of the philosophy of Cornelius Van Til* (Philadelphia, PA: Presbyterian & Reformed, 1959). For a more recent exposition of Van Til's ideas, from another Reconstructionist, see Greg Bahnsen, *Van Til's apologetic: Readings and analysis* (Philipsburg, NJ: Presbyterian & Reformed, 1998).

30. R. J. Rushdoony, "Introduction," in J. Marcellus Kik, *An eschatology of victory* (Philadelphia, PA: Presbyterian & Reformed, 1971). The volume republished material that had earlier appeared as J. Marcellus Kik, *Matthew XXIV: An exposition* (Philadelphia, PA: Presbyterian & Reformed, 1948) and *Revelation twenty: An exposition* (Philadelphia, PA: Presbyterian & Reformed, 1955).

31. Rushdoony, "Introduction," in Kik, *An eschatology of victory*, p. viii.

32. Lindsey, *The late great planet earth*, p. 176.

33. Rushdoony, *Thy kingdom come*, p. 39.

34. Rushdoony, *Thy kingdom come*, p. 214.

35. Rushdoony, *Thy kingdom come*, p. 84.

36. Rushdoony, *Thy kingdom come*, p. 210.

37. Rushdoony, *Thy kingdom come*, p. 89.

38. Rushdoony, *Thy kingdom come*, p. 89.

39. Rushdoony, *Thy kingdom come*, pp. 84, 238.

40. Rushdoony, *Thy kingdom come*, p. 83.

41. Rushdoony, *Institutes of Biblical law*, n.p. [Preface].

42. Worthen, "The Chalcedon problem," p. 409.

43. Daniel K. Williams, *Defenders of the unborn: The pro-life movement before Roe v. Wade* (New York: Oxford University Press, 2016), pp. 39–57.

44. Lewis, *The rights turn in conservative Christian politics*, pp. 16–19.

45. Milton Gaither, *Homeschool: An American history* (New York: Palgrave Macmillan, 2008), p. 106.

46. John Frame, "Abortion and the Christian," *The Presbyterian Guardian* (November 1970), pp. 78, 80; John Frame, "The law, theology and abortion," *The Christian Lawyer* 4:3 (1972), pp. 24–27.

47. Rushdoony, *Institutes of Biblical law*, pp. 186, 263.

48. Balmer, *Thy kingdom come*, pp. 5–17.

49. Chalcedon Archive, Letter from Iain H. Murray to Gary North, May 3, 1972.

50. Worthen, "The Chalcedon problem: Rousas John Rushdoony and the origins of Christian Reconstruction," p. 424. See Rushdoony, *Institutes of Biblical law*, p. 264.

51. Rushdoony, *Institutes of Biblical law*, p. 263, citing Bruce K. Waltke, "The Old Testament and birth control," *Christianity Today* 13:3 (November 8, 1968), p. 3. See

also Allan C. Carlson, *Godly seed: American evangelicals confront birth control, 1873–1973* (London: Transaction, 2012), p. 135.

52. Email from Mark R. Rushdoony to the author, October 19, 2016. My inquiry addressed to Hal Lindsey and the Hal Lindsey Report did not provide any further information; email from the Hal Lindsey Report to the author, October 19, 2016.

53. Rushdoony may have spoken at the Jesus Christ Light and Power house on several occasions, according to Whitehead, *Slaying dragons*, pp. 143–45.

54. This text was published in *Chalcedon Report* 124 (December 1975) and *Chalcedon Report* 125 (January 1976), and reprinted in R. J. Rushdoony, *The roots of Reconstruction* (Vallecito, CA: Ross House Books, 1991), pp. 919–22. I am grateful to Mark Rushdoony for identifying the speaking engagement in his father's diary, and for providing scans of the material he used in his address.

55. Rushdoony, *The roots of Reconstruction*, p. 920.

56. Rushdoony, *The roots of Reconstruction*, p. 920.

57. Rushdoony, *The roots of Reconstruction*, p. 922.

58. Rushdoony, *The roots of Reconstruction*, p. 922.

59. Eskridge, *God's forever family*, p. 305.

60. North, *Millennialism and social theory*, pp. 196–98.

61. Gary North, "Editor's introduction," *The Journal of Christian Reconstruction* 3:2 (1976–77), p. 4; Gary North, *75 Bible questions your instructors pray you won't ask* (Tyler, TX: Spurgeon Press, 1984), pp. 10–11. See also Joel McDurmon, "Understanding Gary North," available at https://www.youtube.com/watch?v=TyBUEadyiws, accessed June 26, 2019; John Murray, *The epistle to the Romans*, The New International Commentary on the New Testament (Grand Rapids, MI: Eerdmans, 1959, 1965), 2:75–103; John Murray, *Principles of conduct* (London: Tyndale Press, 1957), p. 13.

62. The first issue of the journal was devoted to the issue of Creationism; *The Journal of Christian Reconstruction* 1:1 (1974).

63. Gary North, "Editor's introduction," *The Journal of Christian Reconstruction* 3:2 (1976–77), p. 3.

64. Gary North, "Towards the recovery of hope," *Banner of Truth 88* (1971), pp. 12–16; Tommy W. Rogers, review of Iain H. Murray, *The puritan hope: A study in revival and the interpretation of* prophecy, *Journal of Christian Reconstruction* 3:2 (1976–77), pp. 178–81.

65. Chalcedon Archive, Letter from Iain H. Murray to Gary North, May 3, 1972.

66. Gary North, "Editor's introduction," *The Journal of Christian Reconstruction* 5:2 (1978–79), pp. 1–3.

67. Gary North, "Editor's introduction," *The Journal of Christian Reconstruction* 5:2 (1978–79), p. 4.

68. Gary North, "Editor's introduction," *The Journal of Christian Reconstruction* 3:2 (1976–77), p. 2.

69. Gary North, "Editor's introduction," *The Journal of Christian Reconstruction* 3:2 (1976–77), p. 3.

70. On trends in evangelical millennialism in the 1980s and 1990s, see Gribben, *Evangelical millennialism in the trans-Atlantic world*, pp. 110–24.

71. Ingersoll, *Building God's kingdom*, p. xii.

72. Worthen, "The Chalcedon problem: Rousas John Rushdoony and the origins of Christian Reconstruction," p. 429.

73. Worthen, "The Chalcedon problem: Rousas John Rushdoony and the origins of Christian Reconstruction," pp. 433, 435.

74. Steensland and Goff, "Introduction: The new evangelical social engagement," pp. 12–13.

75. James Aho, *Far-right fantasy: A sociology of American religion and politics* (London: Routledge, 2016), pp. 87–88.

76. Joel McDurmon, *Restoring America one county at a time* (Athens, GA: American Vision Press, 2012). On McDurmon and the work of American Vision, see Ingersoll, *Building God's kingdom*, pp. 167–88.

77. Whitehead, *Slaying dragons*, pp. 266–85.

78. Lindsey, *The late great planet earth*, p. 7.

79. North, *Millennialism and social theory*, p. 313.

80. For North's recommendation of Moscow, ID, see "Y2K doomsday scenario," available at http://www.sullivan-county.com/nf0/fundienazis/y2k_gary.htm, accessed on June 26, 2019.

81. Anonymous archived discussion board, available at http://www.verycomputer.com/7_d72bc918d334a1be_1.htm, accessed June 26, 2019.

82. Douglas Wilson, book review, *Credenda Agenda* [hereafter *CA*] 8:1 (1996), p. 31; Douglas Jones and Marc Dupont, "Disputatio: Prophecy old and new," *CA* 7:6 (1995), pp. 28–29.

83. Jim Wilson, *Principles of war: A handbook on strategic evangelism* (1964; rpt. Moscow, ID: Canon Press, 2009), p. 20; Jim Wilson, *Weapons and tactics: A handbook on personal evangelism* (Moscow, ID: Canon Press, 2012), p. 88.

84. Douglas Wilson, *Black and tan: Essays and excursions on slavery, culture war, and Scripture in America* (Moscow, ID: Canon Press, 2005), p. 1.

85. Support letter included in *CA* 11:5 (1999), stapled insert; "Mother of all From Us's," *CA* 12:3 (2000), p. 8.

86. See, for example, David Chilton, *Paradise restored: A biblical theology of dominion* (Ft Worth, TX: Dominion Press, 1984), and David Chilton, *Days of vengeance: An exposition of the Book of Revelation* (Ft Worth, TX: Dominion Press, 1990).

87. Douglas Wilson, book review, *CA* 9:1 (1997), p. 34. See further commentary on North in Chris Schlect, "Schlect's top ten," *CA* 9:2 (1997), p. 30; Letters page, *CA* 10:1 (1998), p. 9; Douglas Wilson, "Okay, okay, Y2K," *CA* 10:1 (1998), p. 10.

88. Chris Schlect, book review, *CA* 10:1 (1998), p. 31.

89. Douglas Wilson, "THE interview," available at https://dougwils.com/s7-engaging-the-culture/the-interview.html, accessed June 26, 2019.

90. "From us," *CA* 11:5 (1999), p. 6.

91. Douglas Jones and Douglas Wilson, *Angels in the architecture: A Protestant vision for Middle Earth* (Moscow, ID: Canon Press, 1998), p. 17.

92. Jones and Wilson, *Angels in the architecture*, p. 18.

93. Douglas Wilson, "Gender warriors," *CA* 10:3 (1998), p. 14.

94. Douglas Wilson, "And this, just in," *CA* 9:2 (1997), p. 10.
95. Greg Dickison, "Knowing enough to start a country," *CA* 7:6 (1995), p. 12.
96. "Cave of Adullam," *CA* 7:5 (1995), p. 39; Jim Nance, "The courage of the cross," *CA* 7:5 (1995), p. 20; Douglas Wilson, review of Ambrose Evans-Pritchard, *The Secret Life of Bill Clinton*, *CA* 10:3 (1998), p. 32.
97. Douglas Wilson, "Bad moon rising," *CA* 8:1 (1996), pp. 4–5.
98. Wilson, "Gender warriors," p. 14.
99. Douglas Wilson, "That Y2K thing," *CA* 10:2 (1998), p. 37.
100. Wilson, "That Y2K thing," pp. 38–39.
101. Wilson, "That Y2K thing," p. 39.
102. Wilson, "That Y2K thing," p. 39.
103. "From us," *CA* 11:2 (1999), p. 6.
104. Wilson, "That Y2K thing," p. 39.
105. Jack Van Deventer, "Feminize the clergy," *CA* 11:2 (1999), p. 24.
106. Douglas Wilson, letters page, *CA* 11:1 (1999), p. 7.
107. Douglas Wilson, "Rattle and hum," *CA* 11:3 (1999), p. 20.
108. "Mutterings on the regnant follies," *CA* 11:5 (1999), p. 22; Douglas Wilson, "Tinkerty Tonk," *CA* 12:3 (2000), p. 22.
109. Support letter included in *CA* 11:5 (1999), stapled insert; "Mother of all From Us's," *CA* 12:3 (2000), p. 8.
110. Peter Leithart, "Worship first and last," *CA* 12:2 (2000), p. 16; "A little help for our friends," *CA* 12:1 (2000), p. 23; advertisement, *CA* 12:2 (2000), p. 21; Leithart, "Old Geneva & the New World."
111. A sample church brochure is held in the author's archive.
112. Interviews, September 12, 2015.
113. Interviews, September 12, 2015.
114. Douglas Wilson, "The nose under Joe Camel's tent," *CA* 7:6 (1995), p. 10.
115. Wilson, *Heaven misplaced*, p. 84.
116. Interviews, September 12, 2015.
117. Wilson, *Heaven misplaced*, p. 76.
118. Interview with New Saint Andrews College faculty member, September 30, 2016.
119. Interview with Douglas Wilson, September 12, 2015.
120. Douglas Wilson, *Heaven misplaced: Christ's kingdom on earth* (Moscow, ID: Canon Press, 2008), p. 42.
121. Gribben, *Writing the rapture*, pp. 129–44; Gribben, *Evangelical millennialism in the trans-Atlantic world*, pp. 92–109.
122. Wilson, *Heaven misplaced*, pp. 9–10.
123. Sutton, *American apocalypse, passim*.
124. See Craig A. Blaising and Darrell L. Bock, *Progressive dispensationalism* (Wheaton, IL: BridgePoint, 1993), *passim*.
125. Wilson, *Heaven misplaced*, p. 86.
126. North, *Millennialism and social theory*, p. 124.
127. Gary North, *Unconditional surrender: God's program for victory* (Tyler, TX: Institute for Christian Economics, 1983), p. 100.

128. North, *The Sinai strategy*, p. 48; North, *Millennialism and social theory*, p. 321; North, *Unconditional surrender*, p. 117.
129. North, *Unconditional surrender*, p. 141.
130. Rawles, *How to survive the end of the world as we know it, passim.*

Chapter 3

1. Greg Dickison, "Nursing fathers pt. 2," *CA 13*:2 (2001), p. 13.
2. Jones and Wilson, *Angels in the architecture*, p. 112.
3. "God or man conference 2015," available at https://www.youtube.com/watch?v=-feBAZGB7kQ, accessed June 26, 2019; Ehud Would, "The pro-life movement and political correctness," *Faith & Heritage*, available at http://faithandheritage.com/2015/10/the-pro-life-movement-and-political-correctness/, accessed June 26, 2019.
4. "God or man conference 2015," accessed at https://www.youtube.com/watch?v=-feBAZGB7kQ, at 21:30 and 36:31.
5. "Chet Gallagher arrest arrested as Las Vegas on duty police officer" [*sic*], available at https://www.youtube.com/watch?v=T3ij0e_mfWs, accessed June 26, 2019; "Police officer is arrested in anti-abortion protest," *Deseret News*, January 29, 1989, available at http://www.deseretnews.com/article/32365/POLICE-OFFICER-IS-ARRESTED-IN-ANTI-ABORTION-PROTEST.html, accessed June 26, 2019.
6. Ehud Would, "The pro-life movement and political correctness."
7. "Classic dystopian novels' popularity surges in Trump's America," *Entertainment Weekly*, January 31, 2017, available at http://ew.com/books/2017/01/31/classic-dystopian-novels-trump/, accessed June 26, 2019; Rebecca Nicholson, "The Handmaid's Tale review—timely adaptation scares with dystopian dread," *The Guardian*, April 26, 2017, available at https://www.theguardian.com/tv-and-radio/2017/apr/26/the-handmaids-tale-tv-show-hulu-review, accessed June 26, 2019.
8. These fears were perhaps justified by the sackcloth processions of the Children of God, a radical "Jesus People" community, in the early part of the previous decade; Eskridge, *God's forever people*, p. 190.
9. Chris Hedges, *American fascists: The Christian Right and the war on America* (New York: Free Press, 2006), p. 10.
10. Hedges, *American fascists*, pp. 12, 28–29.
11. Hedges, *American fascists*, pp. 19, 21.
12. Hedges, *American fascists*, p. 36.
13. Hedges, *American fascists*, pp. 10–11, 13.
14. Hedges, *American fascists*, pp. 11, 36; Chip Berlet, "How we coined the term 'dominionism,'" *Talk to Action*, August 31, 2011, available at http://www.talk2action.org/story/2011/8/31/17047/5683/, accessed June 26, 2019.
15. Balmer, *Thy kingdom come*, pp. 65–68, 71–108.
16. For a discussion of the history, philosophy, and strategy of this institution, see Hanna Rosin, *God's Harvard: A Christian college on a mission to save America* (New York: Houghton Mifflin Harcourt, 2008).

17. Rawles, *How to survive the end of the world as we know it*, pp. 13–14.

18. Kathryn Stewart, *The Good News Club: The Christian Right's stealth assault on America's children* (New York: PublicAffairs, 2012), p. 79.

19. For a broader history of the relationship between American Protestants and conservative culture, see Harp, *Protestants and American conservatism*; Green, *The third disestablishment*.

20. On the revitalization of evangelicalism see Carpenter, *Revive us again, passim*; Williams, *God's own party, passim*.

21. Sutton, *American apocalypse, passim*.

22. Dochuk, *From the Bible Belt to the Sun Belt*, p. xvi.

23. See George Marsden, *Reforming fundamentalism: Fuller Seminary and the new evangelicalism* (Grand Rapids, MI: Eerdmans, 1995), and Grant Wacker, *America's pastor: Billy Graham and the shaping of a nation* (Cambridge, MA: Harvard University Press, 2014).

24. K. Healan Gaston, "The Cold War romance of religious authenticity: Will Herberg, William F. Buckley Jr., and the rise of the new right," *Journal of American History* 99:4 (2013), pp. 1133–58; Lynerd, *Republican theology*, pp. 159–90.

25. Nancy MacLean, *Democracy in chains: The deep history of the radical right's stealth plan for America* (London: Scribe, 2017), pp. 116, 127. MacLean's book has been widely criticized by reviewers; see Ilya Somin, "Who wants to put democracy in chains?" *Washington Post*, July 10, 2017, available at https://www.washingtonpost.com/news/volokh-conspiracy/wp/2017/07/10/who-wants-to-put-democracy-in-chains/?utm_term=.9e775df7064b, accessed June 26, 2019.

26. MacLean, *Democracy in chains*, pp. 142, 152.

27. Lynerd, *Republican theology*, pp. 190–92; MacLean, *Democracy in chains*, pp. 159, 169.

28. McVicar, *Christian Reconstruction*, pp. 57–58; Chalcedon Archive, "Activities of Chalcedon, January, 1965–May, 1966," typescript; Chalcedon Archive, undated letters from Charles H. Craig, director of the Presbyterian & Reformed Publishing Company, to R. J. Rushdoony, concerning editorial decisions and the establishing of Craig Press.

29. Rushdoony, *The mythology of science*, p. 50.

30. For the broader relationship between American evangelicals and abortion activism, see Williams, *Defenders of the unborn, passim*; Lewis, *The rights turn in conservative Christian politics, passim*.

31. Balmer, *Thy kingdom come*, pp. 9–15.

32. "The right: A house divided," *Newsweek*, February 2, 1981.

33. MacLean, *Democracy in chains*, pp. 176–77, 192.

34. Whitehead, *Slaying dragons*, pp. 197–98, 228.

35. David Usborne, "Nobel honour stuns Obama and the world," *The Independent*, October 10, 2009, available at https://www.independent.co.uk/news/world/americas/nobel-honour-stuns-obama-ndash-and-the-world-1800567.html, accessed June 26, 2019.

36. Joyce, *Quiverfull*, p. 6.

37. My reading of Rushdoony is that his opposition to democracy was less nuanced that Ingersoll has suggested; Ingersoll, *Building God's kingdom*, p. 67.

38. R. J. Rushdoony, "Foreword," in Raymond O. Zorn, *Church and kingdom* (Philadelphia, PA: Presbyterian & Reformed, 1962), p. xx. A revised edition of this book was published, without Rushdoony's foreword, as Raymond O. Zorn, *Christ triumphant: Biblical perspectives on his church and kingdom* (Edinburgh: Banner of Truth, 1997).

39. Rushdoony, *The messianic character of American education*, p. 31.

40. On Singer, see McVicar, *Christian Reconstruction*, pp. 116, 118, 120. For a list of Singer's papers, see Presbyterian Church in America Historical Center, "Charles Gregg Singer, Manuscript collection #021 Box #319," http://www.pcahistory.org/findingaids/singer.html, accessed June 26, 2019.

41. C. Gregg Singer, *A theological interpretation of American history* (Nutley, NJ: Craig Press, 1975), p. 41.

42. Singer, *A theological interpretation of American history*, pp. 38, 41.

43. Singer, *A theological interpretation of American history*, pp. 36–37.

44. Singer, *A theological interpretation of American history*, pp. 67, 78.

45. Singer, *A theological interpretation of American history*, pp. 19–21.

46. Singer, *A theological interpretation of American history*, pp. 73–76, 87–88.

47. Singer, *A theological interpretation of American history*, p. 123.

48. Singer, *A theological interpretation of American history*, pp. 124–25, 282.

49. Singer, *A theological interpretation of American history*, pp. 297–98.

50. Singer, *A theological interpretation of American history*, pp. 240–41.

51. Singer, *A theological interpretation of American history*, p. 294.

52. Singer's book was recommended in *Credenda Agenda*; *CA* 9:4 (1997), p. 33, and *CA* 10:3 (1998), p. 34.

53. On Singer's relationship with Rushdoony, see McVicar, *Christian Reconstruction*, pp. 116, 118, 120.

54. Chalcedon Archive, undated letters, Charles H. Craig to R. J. Rushdoony.

55. Rushdoony, *The politics of guilt and pity*, p. 320.

56. Rushdoony, *The politics of guilt and pity*, p. 315.

57. Rushdoony, *The politics of guilt and pity*, p. 321.

58. Gary North, "Editor's introduction," in Gary North (ed.), *Theonomy: An informed response* (Tyler, TX: Institute for Christian Economics, 1991), p. 18.

59. Balmer, *Thy kingdom come*, p. 9; Ingersoll *Building God's kingdom*, p. 40.

60. John Frame, review of Rushdoony, *Institutes of Biblical law*, in *Westminster Theological Journal* 38:2 (1976), pp. 195–217.

61. Gary North, "Publisher's preface," in Greg Bahnsen, *No other standard: Theonomy and its critics* (Tyler, TX: Institute for Christian Economics, 1991), p. ix.

62. Gary North, *Unholy spirits: Occultism and New Age humanism* (Fort Worth, TX: Dominion Press, 1986), pp. 392–93; Lindsey, *The road to holocaust*, p. 36.

63. Gary North, "Prologue," in Greg L. Bahnsen, *By this standard: The authority of God's law today* (Tyler, TX: Institute for Christian Economics, 1985), p. xxvi.

64. Gary North, "Reconstructionist renewal and charismatic renewal," *Christian Reconstruction* 61:4 (May–June 1988), pp. 1–2.

65. Bahnsen, *No other standard*, pp. 37, 40.

66. Bahnsen, *No other standard*, p. 1.

67. Ingersoll, *Building God's kingdom*, p. 40.

68. Rodney Clapp, "Democracy as heresy," *Christianity Today 20* (February 1987), pp. 17–20; Lindsey, *The road to holocaust*, p. 246.

69. Lindsey, *The road to holocaust*, pp. 3, 157, 159, 161, 164, 278.

70. Chalcedon Archive, R. J. Rushdoony work journal, November 12, 1987; the year is erroneously represented as 1991 on Mark Rushdoony, "Rousas John Rushdoony: A brief history: Part vii: He is on the Lord's side," available at https://chalcedon.edu/magazine/rousas-john-rushdoony-a-brief-history-part-vii-hes-on-the-lords-side, accessed June 26, 2019. I am grateful to Mark Rushdoony for his advice about the chronology of this part of his father's life.

71. Email from Douglas Wilson to the author, July 4, 2019.

72. "Free Kirk in uproar over heresy; Church report calling for crackdown on a controversial doctrine likely to reopen old wounds," *The Herald*, May 12, 1997, available at http://www.heraldscotland.com/news/12325919.Free_Kirk_in_uproar_over__apos_heresy_apos__Church_report_calling_for_crackdown_on_a_controversial_doctrine_likely_to_reopen_old_wounds/, accessed June 26, 2019; Martin A. Foulner, "The Free Kirk of Scotland against theonomy," *Chalcedon Report* (August 1998), available at https://chalcedon.edu/magazine/the-free-kirk-of-scotland-against-theonomy, accessed June 26, 2019.

73. William S. Barker and W. Robert Godfrey, "Preface," in William S. Barker and W. Robert Godfrey (eds.), *Theonomy: A Reformed critique* (Grand Rapids, MI: Zondervan, 1990), p. 9.

74. Gary North, "Editor's preface," in North (ed.), *Theonomy: An informed response*, p. xv; idem, "Editor's introduction," in Gary North (ed.), *Theonomy: An informed response*, p. 3.

75. Vern S. Poythress, "A Biblical view of mathematics," in Gary North (ed.), *Foundations of Christian scholarship* (Vallecito, CA: Ross House, 1976), pp. 156–88; Vern S. Poythress, *The shadow of Christ in the law of Moses* (Phillipsburg, NJ: P&R Publishing, 1991), pp. xii, 314.

76. Bahnsen, *No other standard*, p. 1.

77. McVicar, *Christian Reconstruction*, pp. 194–97.

78. Gary North, *Baptized patriarchy: The cult of the family* (Tyler, TX: Institute for Christian Economics, 1995), pp. 13–17; Selbrede, "You can't split rotten wood," pp. 207–8.

79. Gary DeMar, *Something greater is here: Christian Reconstruction in Biblical perspective* (Fort Worth, TX: Dominion Press, 1988), p. 28.

80. Douglas Wilson, "A mouth full of teeth," *CA 17*:5 (2005), p. 33; Douglas Wilson, "Son of Fort Sumpter," *CA 14*:3 (2002), p. 10.

81. Chris Schlect, book review, *CA 7*:5 (1995), p. 32.

82. Wilson, *Black and tan*, p. 116.

83. Douglas Wilson, *Joy at the end of the tether: The inscrutable wisdom of Ecclesiastes* (Moscow, ID: Canon Press, 1999), p. 99.
84. Wilson, *Joy at the end of the tether*, p. 25.
85. Wilson, *Joy at the end of the tether*, p. 51.
86. Andrew Sullivan, "Does Bill Kristol like the Taliban?" *The Dish*, March 12, 2001, available at http://dish.andrewsullivan.com/2001/03/23/does-bill-kristol-like-the-taliban/, accessed June 26, 2019. This point was noted in "Mutterings on the regnant follies," *CA 13*:3 (2001), p. 39. Readers of *CA* described the Moscow community in similar terms; letters page, *CA 11*:4 (1999), p. 6; letters page, *CA 13*:3 (2001), p. 8.
87. Wilson, *Black and tan*, p. 82.
88. Jones and Wilson, *Angels in the architecture*, p. 157.
89. Bahnsen, *By this standard*, pp. 36, 257.
90. Bahnsen, *By this standard*, p. 322.
91. Wilson, *Black and tan*, p. 103.
92. Wilson, *Black and tan*, pp. 92–93.
93. Douglas Wilson, "Life and death of *Homo pervertens*," *CA 16*:2 (2004), p. 5.
94. Douglas Jones, "Christian Coalition takes the easy path," *CA 7*:4 (1995), p. 10.
95. Douglas Wilson, "The trampled church," *CA 8*:1 (1996), p. 13.
96. Wilson, *Black and tan*, p. 82.
97. Douglas Wilson, "Militias on a toot," *CA 8*:1 (1996), p. 10.
98. Greg Dickison, "The sin of lawlessness," *CA 8*:1 (1996), p. 12.
99. Wilson, *Black and tan*, p. 21.
100. Douglas Wilson, "Life, liberty, property," *CA 21*:1 (2011), p. 19.
101. Greg Dickison, "Nursing fathers," *CA 12*:3 (2000), p. 9.
102. Gregory C. Dickison, "Courtroom culture," *CA 14*:6 (2002), p. 19.
103. Douglas Wilson, "Clan jamfry," *CA 14*:3 (2002), p. 27.
104. Douglas Jones, "Just say 'no' to politics," *CA 10*:2 (1998), p. 11.
105. Gregory C. Dickison, "Courtroom culture," *CA 14*:6 (2002), p. 19.
106. Nathan Wilson, "Picking one's poison," *CA 12*:2 (2000), p. 10.
107. Nathan Wilson, "Picking one's poison," p. 10.
108. Douglas Wilson, "God struck America," *CA 13*:4 (2001), p. 5.
109. Wilson, "God struck America," p. 13.
110. Wilson, "God struck America," p. 7.
111. Wilson, "God struck America," p. 16.
112. Douglas Wilson, "Chonklit cake," *CA 14*:2 (2002), p. 31.
113. Douglas Jones, "Pre-Adamite yearnings," *CA 9*:1 (1997), p. 18; Douglas Jones, "An interracial cross," *CA 9*:1 (1997), p. 20; Douglas Jones, "Debunking racial rights," *CA 9*:1 (1997), p. 22; Douglas Wilson and Charles Weisman, "Disputatio: Christianity and race," *CA 9*:1 (1997), pp. 30–31; "A new skinist movement," *CA 17*:3 (2005), p. 28.
114. Wilson, *Black and tan*, p. 120.
115. Douglas Wilson, "Clowns to the left of me, jokers to the right . . . ," *CA 8*:2 (1996), p. 10.
116. For background to this relationship, see Wilson, *Black and tan*, pp. 62–63.
117. Wilson, *Black and tan*, pp. 47, 63.

118. Greg Dickison, "Civil disobedience," *CA 7*:2 (1995), p. 8.

119. Douglas Wilson, "In the system, not of it," *CA 13*:5 (2001), p. 6.

120. Nathan Wilson, "Patience," *CA 11*:1 (1999), p. 10.

121. Interview with recent graduates of New Saint Andrews College, September 12, 2015.

122. Interview with recent graduates of New Saint Andrews College, September 12, 2015.

123. Interview with recent graduates of New Saint Andrews College, September 12, 2015.

124. Interview with current students of New Saint Andrews College, September 12, 2015.

125. Interview with recent graduates of New Saint Andrews College, September 12, 2015.

126. Interview with current students of New Saint Andrews College, September 12, 2015.

127. Greg Dickison, "Nursing fathers," *CA 12*:3 (2000), p. 9.

128. Dickison, "Nursing fathers," p. 9.

129. "A joint Federal Vision profession," *CA 19*:3 (2007), p. 7; Douglas Wilson, "Cruciform politics," *CA 19*:1 (2007), p. 5.

130. Wilson, *Empires of dirt*, p. 9.

131. Wilson, *Empires of dirt*, pp. 31, 58.

132. Wilson, *Empires of dirt*, p. 62.

133. Wilson, *Empires of dirt*, pp. 143, 176, where Wilson states that an "explicitly Christian settlement would do a better job of protecting the true rights of Muslims and secularists than secularists do in protecting the rights of Christians."

134. See Wilson, *Empires of dirt*, *passim*.

135. See, for example, http://dnews.com/opinion/letter-doug-wilson-and-slavery/article_58b00388-d37b-5c8d-9066-51748948068c.html, http://dnews.com/opinion/letter-wilson-not-representative-of-christians/article_82ce8582-fb0e-5e12-b8bc-6b2915513a3c.html,

136. Duck Schuler, "You will have songs," *CA 16*:2 (2004), p. 16; Peter J. Leithart, "Being scary," *CA 13*:2 (2001), p. 11.

137. McDurmon, *Restoring America one county at a time*, p. 2.

138. McDurmon, *Restoring America one county at a time*, p. ix.

139. McDurmon, *Restoring America one county at a time*, p. 202.

140. McDurmon, *Restoring America one county at a time*, p. 143.

141. McDurmon, *Restoring America one county at a time*, p. 289.

142. McDurmon, *Restoring America one county at a time*, p. 148.

143. McDurmon, *Restoring America one county at a time*, p. 151.

144. McDurmon, *Restoring America one county at a time*, p. 337.

145. McDurmon, *Restoring America one county at a time*, p. 342.

146. McDurmon, *Restoring America one county at a time*, p. 339.

147. Matthew J. Trewhella, *The doctrine of the lesser magistrates* (n.p., 2013), p. 63.

148. Trewhella, *The doctrine of the lesser magistrates*, p. xiv.

149. Trewhella, *The doctrine of the lesser magistrates*, p. xiv.

150. Trewhella, *The doctrine of the lesser magistrates*, p. 15.

151. Trewhella, *The doctrine of the lesser magistrates*, p. 23.

152. Trewhella, *The doctrine of the lesser magistrates*, pp. 66–67.

153. Trewhella, *The doctrine of the lesser magistrates*, p. 100.

154. Trewhella, *The doctrine of the lesser magistrates*, p. xiii.

155. Gordan Runyan, *Resistance to tyrants: Romans 13 and the Christian duty to oppose wicked rulers* (n.p., 2012), p. 27.
156. Runyan, *Resistance to tyrants*, p. 63.
157. Runyan, *Resistance to tyrants*, p. 31.
158. Runyan, *Resistance to tyrants*, p. 28.
159. Runyan, *Resistance to tyrants*, p. 28.
160. Runyan, *Resistance to tyrants*, pp. 3, 5, 52, 74.
161. Runyan, *Resistance to tyrants*, p. 33.
162. Runyan, *Resistance to tyrants*, p. 34.
163. Runyan, *Resistance to tyrants*, pp. 3, 5, 74.
164. Runyan, *Resistance to tyrants*, pp. 45, 65, 68, 70.
165. Runyan, *Resistance to tyrants*, p. 54.
166. Interview with James Wesley Rawles, May 14, 2013.
167. Interview with James Wesley Rawles, May 14, 2013.
168. Interview with James Wesley Rawles, May 14, 2013.
169. Federal News Service, "Transcript of the Republican presidential debate," *New York Times*, February 14, 2016, available at https://www.nytimes.com/2016/02/14/us/politics/transcript-of-the-republican-presidential-debate.html, accessed June 26, 2019.
170. John Fea, "Ted Cruz's campaign is fueled by a dominionist vision for America," *Washington Post*, February 4, 2016.
171. "Donald Trump, abortion foe, eyes 'punishment' for women, then recants," *New York Times*, March 30, 2016.
172. "Mutterings on the regnant follies," *CA 11*:5 (1999), p. 22.

Chapter 4

1. Rushdoony, *The messianic character of American education*, pp. 294–95.
2. Douglas Wilson, *Recovering the lost tools of learning: An approach to distinctively Christian education* (Wheaton, IL: Crossway, 1991), p. 112.
3. Rawles, *Liberators*, pp. 25, 51. On Reconstructionist thinking about education, see Ingersoll, *Building God's kingdom*, pp. 79–118.
4. Stewart, *The Good News Club*, pp. 2, 147.
5. Katherine Stewart, "Betsy DeVos and God's plan for schools," *New York Times*, December 13, 2016, available at https://www.nytimes.com/2016/12/13/opinion/betsy-devos-and-gods-plan-for-schools.html, accessed June 26, 2019.
6. Jennifer Lois, *Home is where the school is: The logic of homeschooling and the emotional labor of mothering* (New York: New York University Press, 2013), p. 1. On the history of the legalization of home education, see Gaither, *Homeschool*, pp. 175–200.
7. Jeremy Redford, Danielle Battle, Stacey Bielick, and Sarah Grady, *Homeschooling in the United States: 2012* (NCES 2016-096) (Washington, DC: United States Department of Education, 2016); Robert Kunzman, *Write these laws on your children: Inside the world of conservative Christian homeschooling* (Boston, MA: Beacon Press, 2009), p. 1.

178   NOTES

8. See, for example, the variety of teaching and learning described in Kunzman, *Write these laws on your children.*
9. Gaither, *Homeschool*, p. 202.
10. Kunzman, *Write these laws on your children*, pp. 163–64.
11. Edward C. Facey, "Accelerated Christian Education: An alternative to state schools," *The Journal of Christian Reconstruction* 4:1 (1977), pp. 61, 63–64.
12. Gaither, *Homeschool*, p. 153.
13. Worthen, "The Chalcedon problem: Rousas John Rushdoony and the origins of Christian Reconstruction," p. 413.
14. Lee Grady, "God's emerging army," *The Journal of Christian Reconstruction* 9:1–2 (1982-83), p. 157.
15. Joseph Murphy, *Homeschooling in America: Capturing and assessing the movement* (Thousand Oaks, CA: Corwin, 2012).
16. Kunzman, *Write these laws on your children*, p. 17,
17. Susan Wise Bauer and Jessie Wise, *The well-trained mind: A guide to classical education in the home* (New York: Norton, 1999, 2004); Leigh A. Bortins, *The core: Teaching your child the foundations of classical education* (New York: Palgrave Macmillan, 2010). On Bauer's criticisms of homeschool patriarchy, see Joyce, *Quiverfull*, pp. 31–34.
18. Redford, Battle, Bielick, and Grady, *Homeschooling in the United States: 2012.*
19. Robert Kunzman, "Homeschooling and religious fundamentalism," *International Journal of Elementary Education* 3:1 (2010), pp. 17–28; Rachana Bhatt, "Home is where the school is: The impact of homeschool legislation on school choice," *Journal of School Choice* 8:2 (2014), pp. 192–212.
20. Andrea Vieux, "The politics of homeschools: Religious conservatives and regulation requirements," *The Social Science Journal* 51:4 (2014), pp. 556–63.
21. Kunzman, *Write these laws on your children*, p. 2.
22. Lois, *Home is where the school is*, p. 2.
23. See, for example, Gregory and Martine Millman, *Home schooling: A family's journey* (London: Penguin, 2008), pp. 7–13.
24. Stewart, *The Good News Club*, pp. 7, 32–33, 58, 247.
25. Balmer, *Thy kingdom come*, p. 93.
26. Stroop, "Is Christian homeschooling breeding a new kind of domestic terrorist?"
27. Adam Laats, "Forging a fundamentalist 'One Best System': Struggles over curriculum and educational philosophy for Christian day schools, 1970–1989," *History of Education Quarterly* 50:1 (2010), pp. 55–83; Albert Cheng, "Does homeschooling or private schooling promote political intolerance? Evidence from a Christian university," *Journal of School Choice* 8:1 (2014), pp. 49–68; Kunzman, *Write these laws on your children*, p. 107, citing Christian Smith and David Sikkink, "Is private school privatizing?" *First Things* 92 (April 1999), pp. 16–20.
28. Kunzman, *Write these laws on your children*, pp. 97–99, 126.
29. Lewis, *The rights turn in conservative Christian politics, passim.*
30. Gaither, *Homeschool*, p. 44.
31. Gaither, *Homeschool*, p. 70.
32. Marsden, *The twilight of the American Enlightenment, passim.*

33. Kunzman, *Write these laws on your children*, p. 3; Gaither, *Homeschool*, pp. 122–27.

34. Gaither, *Homeschool*, pp. 2, 85, 95.

35. Gaither, *Homeschool*, p. 112–13.

36. Balmer, *Thy kingdom come*, pp. 13–17, 88; Ingersoll, *Building God's kingdom*, pp. 83–88. See also Kunzman, *Write these laws on your children*, p. 160.

37. Rushdoony, *The messianic character of American education*, p. 108 n. 36.

38. Tommy W. Rogers, review of Lino A. Graglia, *Disaster by decree: The Supreme Court decisions on race and the schools* (Ithaca, NY: Cornell University Press, 1976), in *The Journal of Christian Reconstruction* 4:1 (1977), pp. 205–10. See also Samuel L. Blumenfeld, "Is public education necessary?" *The Journal of Christian Reconstruction* 4:1 (1977), p. 109.

39. Thoburn, *The children trap*, p. 65; Ingersoll, *Building God's kingdom*, pp. 54–78.

40. Thoburn, *The children trap*, pp. 65, 109.

41. Gaither, *Homeschool*, p. 112.

42. Rushdoony, *The messianic character of American education*, pp. 294–95; Worthen, "The Chalcedon problem: Rousas John Rushdoony and the origins of Christian Reconstruction," p. 411; McVicar, *Christian Reconstruction*, pp. 2, 69.

43. McVicar, *Christian Reconstruction*, pp. 2, 169. A transcript of Rushdoony's testimony at the Leeper trial is available at http://rushdoony.sitewave.net/rushdoony-leeper-transcript-texas-homeschool-trial/, accessed June 26, 2019.

44. Milton Gaither, review of McVicar, *Christian Reconstruction*, available at https://gaither.wordpress.com/2018/03/19/christian-reconstruction-a-new-biography-of-rousas-rushdoony/#more-2735, accessed June 26, 2019. Gaither makes the same point in Gaither, *Homeschool*, pp. 134–40; Ingersoll makes the same point in *Building God's kingdom*, pp. 79–118.

45. Rushdoony, *Intellectual schizophrenia*, pp. 75, 82, 113.

46. Rushdoony, *Intellectual schizophrenia*, pp. 2, 5.

47. Rushdoony, *Intellectual schizophrenia*, p. 10.

48. Rushdoony, *Intellectual schizophrenia*, p. xi.

49. Rushdoony, *Intellectual schizophrenia*, p. 57.

50. Rushdoony, *Intellectual schizophrenia*, p. 28.

51. Rushdoony, *Intellectual schizophrenia*, p. 76.

52. Rushdoony, *Intellectual schizophrenia*, p. 100.

53. Rushdoony, *Intellectual schizophrenia*, p. 112.

54. Rushdoony, *Intellectual schizophrenia*, p. 37.

55. Rushdoony, *The messianic character of American education*, p. 108.

56. Rushdoony, *The messianic character of American education*, p. 108 n. 36.

57. Rushdoony, *By what standard?*

58. Rushdoony, *The messianic character of American education*, p. 16.

59. Rushdoony, *The messianic character of American education*, p. 3.

60. Rushdoony, *The messianic character of American education*, p. 4.

61. Rushdoony, *The messianic character of American education*, p. 45.

62. Rushdoony, *The messianic character of American education*, p. 288.

63. Rushdoony, *The messianic character of American education*, p. 329.

64. Rushdoony, *The messianic character of American education*, p. 1.
65. Rushdoony, *The mythology of science*, p. 31.
66. Rushdoony, *The messianic character of American education*, p. 314.
67. Rushdoony, *Intellectual schizophrenia*, p. 112; Gary North, "Editor's introduction," *The Journal of Christian Reconstruction* 4:1 (1977), p. 1.
68. North, "Editor's introduction," p. 2.
69. North, "Editor's introduction," p. 2.
70. North, "Editor's introduction," p. 9.
71. North, "Editor's introduction," p. 3.
72. William N. Blake, "A Christian philosophy of method in education," *The Journal of Christian Reconstruction* 4:1 (1977), p. 42.
73. North, "The intellectual schizophrenia of the New Christian Right," p. 20.
74. North, "The intellectual schizophrenia of the New Christian Right," p. 24.
75. North, "The intellectual schizophrenia of the New Christian Right," p. 25.
76. Stewart, *The Good News Club*, pp. 7, 32–33, 58, 247.
77. Grady, "God's emerging army," p. 157.
78. Gaither, *Homeschool*, p. 142.
79. Kunzman, *Write these laws on your children*, p. 4.
80. Kunzman, *Write these laws on your children*, p. 3; Whitehead, *Slaying dragons*, pp. 197–98.
81. On the change in editors of *The Journal of Christian Reconstruction*, see Gary North, "Chilton, Sutton, and dominion theology," *Institute for Christian Economics Position Paper* (1987), p. 2.
82. Douglas F. Kelly, "Editor's introduction," *The Journal of Christian Reconstruction* 9:1–2 (1982–83), p. 16.
83. Douglas F. Kelly, "The present struggle for Christian Reconstruction in the United States," *The Journal of Christian Reconstruction* 9:1–2 (1982–83), p. 32.
84. Kelly, "Editor's introduction," p. 17.
85. Kelly, "Editor's introduction," p. 17.
86. Kelly, "Editor's introduction," p. 18.
87. Gary North (ed.), *The tactics of Christian resistance, Christianity & Civilization* 3 (1983) (Tyler, TX: Geneva Divinity School Press, 1983).
88. Gary North, "Editor's introduction," in Gary North (ed.), *The tactics of Christian resistance, Christianity & Civilization* 3 (1983) (Tyler, Texas: Geneva Divinity School Press, 1983), p. ix.
89. North, "Editor's introduction," in North (ed.), *The tactics of Christian resistance, Christianity & Civilization* 3, p. xii.
90. North, "Editor's introduction," in North (ed.), *The tactics of Christian resistance, Christianity & Civilization* 3, p. xxxv.
91. Robert L. Thoburn, *The children trap: Biblical principles for education* (Ft Worth, TX: Dominion Press / Nashville, TN: Thomas Nelson, 1986), p. 40.
92. Thoburn, *The children trap*, p. 5.
93. Thoburn, *The children trap*, p. 37.
94. North, "Editor's introduction," in Thoburn, *The children trap*, p. xv.

95. Thoburn, *The children trap*, p. 65.
96. Thoburn, *The children trap*, pp. 96, 143.
97. North, "Editor's introduction," in Thoburn, *The children trap*, p. ix.
98. North, "Editor's introduction," in Thoburn, *The children trap*, p. xvii.
99. North, "Editor's introduction," in Thoburn, *The children trap*, p. xi.
100. Kunzman, *Write these laws on your children*, p. 4.
101. Balmer, *Thy kingdom come*, pp. 102–4; Rosin, *God's Harvard, passim*.
102. Wilson, *Recovering the lost tools of learning*, p. 49; Wilson, *Black and tan*, pp. 23–25.
103. Wilson, *Recovering the lost tools of learning*, p. 13.
104. Wilson provides two different numbers for the first enrolment; see *Recovering the lost tools of learning*, pp. 14, 104.
105. Wilson, *Recovering the lost tools of learning*, p. 14.
106. Wilson, *Recovering the lost tools of learning*, p. 124.
107. Wilson, *Recovering the lost tools of learning*, p. 104.
108. Wilson, *Recovering the lost tools of learning*, pp. 113, 125.
109. Wilson, *Recovering the lost tools of learning*, p. 51.
110. Dorothy L. Sayers, "The lost tools of learning (1947)," *The Journal of Christian Reconstruction* 4:1 (1977), pp. 10–25; Dorothy L. Sayers, *The lost tools of learning* (Moscow, ID: Canon Press, 1990); Wilson, *Recovering the lost tools of learning*, pp. 92, 145–64. For the background to Wilson's engagement with Sayers's work, see John J. Miller, "Back to basics," *National Review*, October 19, 2015, available at https://www.nationalreview.com/magazine/2015/10/19/back-basics-2/, accessed June 26, 2019.
111. Email from Douglas Wilson to the author, July 4, 2019.
112. Wilson, *Recovering the lost tools of learning*, pp. 83, 97.
113. Wilson, *Recovering the lost tools of learning*, pp. 74, 85.
114. Wilson, *Recovering the lost tools of learning*, p. 77.
115. Wilson, *Recovering the lost tools of learning*, pp. 190 n. 49, 193–94 n. 2, 199 n. 25, 201 n. 7, 206 n. 1, 207 n. 13.
116. Wilson, *Recovering the lost tools of learning*, p. 59.
117. Wilson, *Recovering the lost tools of learning*, p. 97.
118. Wilson, *Recovering the lost tools of learning*, pp. 134–35.
119. Wilson, *Recovering the lost tools of learning*, p. 30.
120. Wilson, *Recovering the lost tools of learning*, p. 41.
121. Wilson, *Recovering the lost tools of learning*, p. 57.
122. Wilson, *Recovering the lost tools of learning*, p. 42.
123. Wilson, *Recovering the lost tools of learning*, pp. 141–43.
124. Advert, *CA* 17:1 (2005), p. 33.
125. Wesley Callihan, Douglas Jones, and Douglas Wilson, *Classical education and the homeschool* (Moscow, ID: Canon Press, 2001), pp. 61, 64.
126. Email from Douglas Wilson to the author, July 4, 2019.
127. Douglas Wilson, "Gary North and classical education," *CA* 7:4 (1995), p. 11.
128. Joyce, *Quiverfull*, p. 27.
129. McVicar, *Christian Reconstruction*, pp. 80, 82, 98, 143.

130. "Christ College" advert, *Chalcedon Report* 419 (June 2000), p. 20.

131. Robert J. Bailey, "Christ College begins fall semester in Greenville, SC," *The Counsel of Chalcedon* (October 1993), pp. 18–19.

132. R. J. Rushdoony, "Random notes, 84," *Chalcedon Report 419* (June 2000), p. 15.

133. "New St. Andrews College," *CA* 7:1 (1995), p. 30.

134. Jack Van Deventer, "The Christians mean business," *CA 15*:4 (2003), p. 32.

135. Molly Worthen, "Onward Christian soldiers," *New York Times Magazine* (September 30, 2007), available at http://www.nytimes.com/2007/09/30/magazine/30Christian-t.html?_r=1&scp=1&sq=molly%20worthen%20moscow&st=cse, accessed June 26, 2019.

136. Douglas Wilson, "Marriage and community," *CA 17*:2 (2005), p. 15.

137. Jones and Wilson, *Angels in the architecture*, p. 200.

138. Benjamin R. Merkle, *Defending the Trinity in the Reformed Palatinate: The Elohistae* (New York: Oxford University Press, 2015).

139. Dreher, *The Benedict Option*, p. 146.

140. See the discussion of the Ron Paul Curriculum in McVicar, *Christian Reconstruction*, pp. 226–27, Ingersoll, *Building God's kingdom*, p. 56, and the discussion of the Sonlight curriculum in Kunzman, *Write these laws on your children*, pp. 132–35, 146–47.

141. Worthen, "The Chalcedon problem: Rousas John Rushdoony and the origins of Christian Reconstruction," p. 413.

Chapter 5

1. Jared Miller, "Reading for keeps," *CA 14*:3 (2002), p. 17.

2. Christ Church, Moscow, "Position Papers: Manners and life together: Moving to Moscow," available at https://www.christkirk.com/our-church/book-of-worship-faith-practice/, accessed June 26, 2019.

3. Interview with Douglas Wilson, September 12, 2015.

4. Support letter included in *CA* 11:5 (1999), stapled insert; "Mother of all From Us's," *CA 12*:3 (2000), p. 8.

5. Advertisement for Logos School, *CA 17*:1 (2005), p. 33.

6. For this concept, see Benedict Anderson, *Imagined communities: Reflections on the origin and spread of nationalism* (London: Verso, 1983), *passim*.

7. For this concept, see Nathan Hatch, *The democratization of American Christianity* (New Haven, CT: Yale University Press, 1989), *passim*.

8. Douglas Wilson, "Clan jamfry," *CA 14*:3 (2002), p. 27.

9. Jared Miller, "Reading for keeps," *CA 14*:3 (2002), p. 17.

10. Christ Church, Moscow, "Position Papers: Manners and life together."

11. Ingersoll, *Building God's kingdom*, p. xii.

12. Vaca, *Evangelicals incorporated*, p. 171.

13. For a general history, see Vaca, *Evangelicals incorporated*, *passim*.

14. For this argument, see Gribben, *Writing the rapture*.

15. Vaca, *Evangelicals incorporated*, p. 12.
16. Grady, "God's emerging army," p. 157.
17. See Isabel Hofmeyr, *The Portable Bunyan: A trans-national history of The Pilgrim's Progress* (Princeton, NJ: Princeton University Press, 2003).
18. Jan Blodgett, *Protestant evangelical literary culture and contemporary society* (Westport, CT: Greenwood, 1997), p. 20; Gaither, *Homeschool*, p. 37.
19. Crawford Gribben, "Rethinking the rise of prophecy fiction: H.R.K.'s *Life in the Future* (?1879)," *Brethren Historical Review 7* (2011), pp. 68–80.
20. John P. Ferré, *A social gospel for millions: The religious bestsellers of Charles Sheldon, Charles Gordon, Howard Bell Wright* (Bowling Green, OH: Bowling Green University Popular Press, 1988), pp. 43–63; Uwe Zagratzki, "Ralph Connor, Hugh MacLennan and Alice Munro: Three Scottish-Canadian authors," *Scottish Tradition 23* (1998), pp. 3–47; Blodgett, *Protestant evangelical literary culture and contemporary society*, p. 13.
21. Erin A. Smith, *What would Jesus read? Popular religious books and everyday life in twentieth-century America* (Chapel Hill, NC: University of North Carolina Press, 2015).
22. On O'Connor, see Vaca, *Evangelicals incorporated*, pp. 53–54.
23. Ferré, *A social gospel for millions*, pp. 43–63.
24. J. Lee Thompson and John H. Thompson, "Ralph Connor and the Canadian identity," *Queen's Quarterly 79*:2 (1972), pp. 159–70.
25. Frederick Jackson Turner, *The significance of the frontier in American history* (1894; rpt. Mansfield Centre, CT: Martino, 2014), p. 4.
26. Turner, *The significance of the frontier in American history*, p. 12.
27. D. G. Hart, *Damning words: The life and religious times of H. L. Mencken* (Grand Rapids, MI: Eerdmans, 2016), pp. 131–43.
28. Marsden, *The twilight of the American Enlightenment*.
29. Marsha Orgeron and Skip Elsheimer, "'Something different in science films': The Moody Institute of Science and the canned missionary movement," *The Moving Image 7*:1 (2007), pp. 1–26.
30. Orgeron and Elsheimer, "Something different in science films," p. 2.
31. Orgeron and Elsheimer, "Something different in science films," p. 20; Fred Nadis, *Wonder Shows: Performing science, magic, and religion in America* (New Brunswick, NJ: Rutgers University Press, 2005), *passim*; James Gilbert, *Redeeming the culture: American religion in an age of science* (Chicago: University of Chicago Press, 1997), pp. 121–45.
32. For different stages of the commodification of evangelical culture, see Heather Hendershot, *Shaking the world for Jesus: Media and conservative evangelical culture* (Chicago: University of Chicago Press, 2004), and Gribben, *Writing the rapture*.
33. Gribben, *Writing the rapture*, p. 28.
34. Hendershot, *Shaking the world for Jesus*, pp. 2, 11, 21; Eskridge, *God's forever family*, pp. 145–78.
35. See, for example, Larry Norman, in Hendershot, *Shaking the world for Jesus*, p. 22.
36. Smith, *What would Jesus read?*, pp. 201–48.
37. Smith, *What would Jesus read?*, p. 202.

38. Smith, *What would Jesus read?*, p. 221.
39. Blodgett, *Protestant evangelical literary culture and contemporary society*, p. 42.
40. Blodgett, *Protestant evangelical literary culture and contemporary society*, p. 47.
41. Blodgett, *Protestant evangelical literary culture and contemporary society*, p. 1.
42. Blodgett, *Protestant evangelical literary culture and contemporary society*, pp. 94, 98.
43. Jones and Wilson, *Angels in the architecture*, p. 102.
44. Hendershot, *Shaking the world for Jesus*, pp. 17–51.
45. For the concept of "moralistic, therapeutic deism," see Christian Smith and Melinda Lundquist Denton, *Soul searching: The religious and spiritual lives of American teenagers* (Oxford: Oxford University Press, 2005), *passim*.
46. For this argument, see Gribben, *Writing the rapture*.
47. "Thank God, it's doomsday," *The Simpsons* episode 19, series 16 (2005).
48. This idea of divergent reading is explored in Amy Johnson Frykholm, *Rapture culture: Left Behind in evangelical America* (New York: Oxford University Press, 2004).
49. "Diamond award: 10 million in sales (2009)," Christian Book Expo, available at http://christianbookexpo.com/salesawards/, accessed June 26, 2019.
50. Christy Ellen Mesaros-Winckles, "Christian patriarchy life: TLC's *19 kids and counting*," in Alena Amato Ruggerio (ed.), *Media depictions of brides, wives, and mothers* (Lanham, MD: Lexington Books, 2012), pp. 63–75. See Stewart, *Quiverfull*, passim.
51. Ross McDonagh, "The Duggar children 'liked being recognized and hate that *19 kids and counting* has been cancelled' due to molestation scandal," *The Daily Mail*, July 22, 2015, available at https://www.dailymail.co.uk/tvshowbiz/article-3171022/Duggar-children-gutted-s-cancellation-amid-molestation-scandal.html, accessed June 26, 2019.
52. Blodgett, *Protestant evangelical literary culture and contemporary society*, pp. 144, 154.
53. Blodgett, *Protestant evangelical literary culture and contemporary society*, p. ix; Jane Tompkins, *Sensational designs: The cultural work of American fiction, 1790–1860* (New York: Oxford University Press, 1985), p. xi.
54. David Chilton, *Productive Christians in an age of guilt-manipulation: A biblical response to Ronald J. Sider* (Tyler, TX: Institute for Christian Economics, 1981).
55. George Grant, *In the shadow of plenty: Biblical principles for welfare and poverty* (Forth Worth, TX: Dominion Press, and Nashville, TN: Thomas Nelson, 1986); George Grant, *The changing of the guard: Biblical principles for political action* (Forth Worth, TX: Dominion Press, 1987).
56. Michael S. Hyatt and George Grant, *Y2K: The day the world shut down* (Nashville, TN: Word, 1998), p. 89; Gribben, *Writing the rapture*, pp. 146–47, 151–53. On Hyatt, see Ingersoll, *Building God's kingdom*, p. 23.
57. Douglas Wilson writing in Douglas Wilson and Randy Booth, *A justice primer*, second edition (Moscow, ID: Blog and Mablog Press, Nacogdoches, TX: Covenant Media Press, 2018), p. 152.
58. Wilson, *Black and tan*, p. 41 n. 1.
59. For a discussion of Nathan D. Wilson's rapture fiction satires, see Gribben, *Writing the rapture*, p. 134.

60. N. D. Wilson, *Leepike Ridge* (New York: Yearling, 2007), p. 225. Douglas Wilson outlined his pre-Columbian theories in *5 cities that ruled the world: How Jerusalem, Athens, Rome, London & New York Shaped Global History* (Nashville: Thomas Nelson, 2009), pp. 8–9.

61. See Rushdoony's rejection of mythological thinking in *The myth of science, passim.*

62. Blodgett, *Protestant evangelical literary culture and contemporary society*, p. 2.

63. Blodgett, *Protestant evangelical literary culture and contemporary society*, p. 6.

64. For this idea, see James W. Menzies, *True myth: C. S. Lewis and Joseph Campbell on the veracity of Christianity* (London: Lutterworth Press, 2014).

65. Blodgett, *Protestant evangelical literary culture and contemporary society*, p. 2.

66. Blodgett, *Protestant evangelical literary culture and contemporary society*, p. 13.

67. Blodgett, *Protestant evangelical literary culture and contemporary society*, p. 14.

68. A. R. Shaw, *Surrender the sun* (n.p., 2016).

69. Patricia Nelson Limerick, *The legacy of conquest: The unbroken past of the American West* (New York: Norton, 1987), p. 20.

70. See Rawles, *Tools for survival*; Limerick, *The legacy of conquest*, p. 24.

71. For discussion of this diversity, see Blodgett, *Protestant evangelical literary culture and contemporary society*, p. 65.

72. Jim Forsyth, "Subculture of Americans prepares for civilization's collapse," *Reuters*, January 21, 2012, available at https://www.reuters.com/article/us-usa-civilization-collapse/subculture-of-americans-prepares-for-civilizations-collapse-idUSTRE80K0LA20120121, accessed June 26, 2019.

73. Interview with James Wesley Rawles, May 14, 2013.

74. Interview with James Wesley Rawles, May 14, 2013; Rawles, *Patriots*, p. 8.

75. Rawles, *How to survive the end of the world as we know it*; James Wesley Rawles, *Tools for survival: What you need to survive when you're on your own* (London: Penguin, 2014).

76. Rawles, *Patriots*, p. 72.

77. Rawles, *Patriots*, pp. 90, 167; Rawles, *Survivors*, p. 165; Rawles, *Liberators*, p. 228; Lynerd, *Republican theology*, pp. 190–92. Contrast Wilson's rejection of Rand in *Empires of dirt*, p. 19.

78. Rawles, *Patriots*, p. 72.

79. Rawles, *Patriots*, p. 39.

80. Rawles, *Patriots*, p. 351; Rawles, *Founders*, p. 225. See also Rawles, *Liberators*, p. 310.

81. Rawles, *Patriots*, p. 288.

82. Rawles, *Expatriates*, pp. 49, 53, 178; Rawles, *Liberators*, p. 108.

83. Rawles, *Liberators*, p. 34. Interview with James Wesley Rawles, May 14, 2013.

84. Rawles, *How to survive the end of the world as we know it*, p. 13.

85. Rawles, *Liberators*, p. 88.

86. Rawles, *How to survive the end of the world as we know it*, p. 14.

87. G. Jeffrey Macdonald, "Secession theology runs deep in American religious, political thought," *Washington Post*, November 29, 2012; Rawles, *Founders*, p. 131.

88. Rawles, *Founders*, p. 178.

89. Rawles, *Founders*, p. 338.

90. Rawles, *Founders*, pp. 90, 358; Rawles, *Patriots*, p. 269; Rawles, *Expatriates*, pp. 172–73, 189; Rawles, *Liberators*, p. 239.
91. Rawles, *Patriots*, p. 369; Rawles, *How to survive the end of the world as we know it*, p. 13.
92. Rawles, *Founders*, p. 18; Rawles, *Patriots*, p. 58.
93. Rawles, *Survivors*, p. 219.
94. Rawles, *Founders*, p. 145; Rawles, *Liberators*, p. 166.
95. Rawles, *Founders*, pp. 26–28.
96. Rawles, *Expatriates*, p. 13.
97. Rawles, *Expatriates*, p. 36.
98. Rawles, *Patriots*, p. 225; Rawles, *Expatriates*, p. 230.
99. Rawles, *Patriots*, p. 24.
100. Rawles, *Patriots*, p. 135.
101. Rawles, *Survivors*, p. 102.
102. Rawles, *Expatriates*, p. 160.
103. Rawles, *Founders*, p. 116.
104. Rawles, *Founders*, pp. 35–36.
105. Rawles, *Liberators*, p. 48.
106. Rawles, *Founders*, p. 111; Rawles, *Liberators*, p. 146.
107. Ingersoll, *Building God's kingdom*, p. 70.
108. Rawles, *Patriots*, p. 107.
109. Rawles, *Survivors*, p. 372.
110. Jason C. Bivins, *Religion of fear: The politics of horror in conservative evangelicalism* (New York: Oxford University Press, 2008), pp. 213–36.

Conclusion

1. Rushdoony, *The mythology of science*, p. 57.
2. Rushdoony, *Preparation for the future*, p. 23.
3. Douglas Wilson writing in Wilson and Booth, *A justice primer*, 2nd edition, p. 23.
4. Paul M. Weyrich, "Letter to conservatives," available at https://nationalcenter.org/ncppr/1999/02/16/letter-to-conservatives-by-paul-m-weyrich/, accessed June 26, 2019.
5. T. S. Eliot, *The idea of a Christian society* (London: Faber and Faber, 1939), pp. 20–21.
6. Alan Jacobs, *The Year of Our Lord 1943: Christian humanism in an age of crisis* (Oxford: Oxford University Press, 2018), pp. 5–36.
7. Odd Arne Westad, *The Cold War: A world history* (London: Allen Lane, 2017), pp. 617–30.
8. Sutton, *American apocalypse*, passim.
9. Balmer, *Blessed assurance*, p. 104.
10. Rushdoony, *Intellectual schizophrenia*, p. 94.
11. Rushdoony, *Intellectual schizophrenia*, pp. 62–63, 99.
12. Rushdoony, *Intellectual schizophrenia*, p. 114.

13. Rushdoony, *Intellectual schizophrenia*, pp. 62–63, 99.

14. Rushdoony, *Intellectual schizophrenia*, p. 101.

15. Rushdoony, *Intellectual schizophrenia*, p. 93.

16. Marsden, *The twilight of the American enlightenment*; Rushdoony, *Intellectual schizo-phrenia*, p. 114. For Wordsworth's view of the French Revolution—"Bliss it was in that dawn to be alive/But to be young was very heaven"—see "The Prelude" x. 692–93, in *William Wordsworth: The major works*, ed. Stephen Gill (Oxford: Oxford University Press, 2008), p. 550.

17. North, "Geocentricity-Geostationism: The flat earth temptation," p. 8; Gary North, "The annulment of the dietary laws," *Institute for Christian Economics Position Paper* (1994), pp. 1–2.

18. North, "Chilton, Sutton, and dominion theology," p. 2.

19. Michael Barkun, *Religion and the racist right: The origins of the Christian Identity movement*, 2nd edition (Chapel Hill: University of North Carolina Press, 1997), p. 209.

20. Worthen, "The Chalcedon problem: Rousas John Rushdoony and the origins of Christian Reconstruction," p. 430.

21. McVicar, *Christian Reconstruction*, pp. 175, 217–31.

22. McVicar, *Christian Reconstruction*, p. 12.

23. Worthen, "The Chalcedon problem: Rousas John Rushdoony and the origins of Christian Reconstruction," p. 433.

24. Deneen, *Why liberalism failed*, pp. 3, 18; Clare Foran, "Here's what's on Barack Obama's reading list," *CNN Politics*, June 16, 2018, available at https://edition.cnn.com/2018/06/16/politics/barack-obama-reading-list-mitch-landrieu/index.html, accessed June 26, 2019.

25. Deneen, *Why liberalism failed*, pp. 19–20.

26. Fitzgerald, *The evangelicals: The struggle to shape America*.

27. Ingersoll, *Building God's kingdom*, p. 211.

28. Gary North, *Lone gunners for Jesus: Letters to Paul J. Hill* (Tyler, TX: Institute for Christian Economics, 1994), *passim*.

29. Stroop, "Is Christian homeschooling breeding a new kind of domestic terrorist?"

30. James William Gibson, *Warrior dreams: Paramilitary culture in post-Vietnam America* (New York: Hill and Wang, 1994), pp. 121–94.

31. Douglas Wilson writing in Wilson and Booth, *A justice primer*, 2nd edition, p. 23.

32. For irreligion in the Pacific Northwest, see Wellman, *Evangelical vs. liberal*.

33. George M. Marsden, "Fundamentalism as an American phenomenon," *Church History* 46:2 (1977), pp. 215–32, reprinted in D. G. Hart (ed.), *Reckoning with the Past: Historical essays on American evangelicalism from the Institute for the Study of American Evangelicals* (Grand Rapids, MI: Baker, 1995), p. 304 n. 3.

34. Bean, *The politics of evangelical identity*, p. 2.

35. D. G. Hart, *The lost soul of American Protestantism* (Lanham, MD: Rowman & Littlefield, 2002), pp. 1–28; Huskinson, "The missing link between evangelicals and Trump."

36. Hofstader, *The paranoid style in American politics*.

37. Harding, "Representing fundamentalism: The problem of the repugnant cultural other," pp. 373–93.
38. Lynerd, *Republican theology*, pp. 196–207.
39. This debate about the Reformed doctrine of justification has been continued among Christian Reconstructionists over many years; see David L. Bahnsen, "Greg Bahnsen and Norm Shepherd—the final word," *Viewpoint: Politics, economics, and culture through the eyes of David L. Bahnsen*, April 28, 2008, available at https://www.davidbahnsen.com/index.php/2008/04/28/greg-bahnsen-and-norm-shepherd-the-final-word/, accessed June 26, 2019. A number of Christian Reconstructionists contributed chapters to P. Andrew Sandlin and John Barach (eds.), *Obedient faith: A festschrift for Norman Shepherd* (Mount Hermon, CA: Kerygma Press, 2012).
40. Alasdair MacIntyre, *After virtue: A study in moral theory* (1981; rpt. London: Bloomsbury, 2011), p. 304.
41. MacIntyre, *After virtue*, pp. 7, 9.
42. MacIntyre, *After virtue*, p. 10.
43. MacIntyre, *After virtue*, p. 294.
44. MacIntyre, *After virtue*, p. 305.

Glossary

1. This glossary is revised and expanded from an earlier version which I first published in Gribben, *Writing the rapture*, pp. 171–74, and Gribben, *Evangelical millennialism in the trans-Atlantic world, 1500–2000*, pp. xi–xv.
2. Ernest L. Tuveson, *Redeemer nation: The idea of America's millennial role* (Chicago: University of Chicago Press, 1968), 33–34; Ernest R. Sandeen, *The roots of fundamentalism: British and American millenarianism, 1800–1930* (Chicago: University of Chicago Press, 1970), 5 n. 3.

Bibliography

Archives

Chalcedon Archive, Vallecito, CA.
Undated letters from Charles H. Craig to R. J. Rushdoony.
"Activities of Chalcedon, January, 1965–May, 1966."
Letter from Iain H. Murray to Gary North, May 3, 1972.
R. J. Rushdoony work journal, November 12, 1987.
Presbyterian Church in America Historical Center, St Louis, MO.
Charles Gregg Singer, Manuscript collection #021, Box #319.

Primary Sources

Advertisement for "Christ College," *Chalcedon Report 419* (June 2000), p. 20.
Advertisement for Logos School, *CA 17*:1 (2005), p. 33.
Anonymous archived discussion board, available at http://www.verycomputer.com/7_d72bc918d334a1be_1.htm, accessed June 26, 2019.
Bailey, Robert J., "Christ College begins fall semester in Greenville, SC," *The Counsel of Chalcedon 8* (October 1993), pp. 18–19.
Blake, William N., "A Christian philosophy of method in education," *The Journal of Christian Reconstruction 4*:1 (1977), pp. 26–43.
Blumenfeld, Samuel L., "Is public education necessary?" *The Journal of Christian Reconstruction 4*:1 (1977), p. 108–20.
Callihan, Wesley, Douglas Jones, and Douglas Wilson, *Classical education and the home-school* (Moscow, ID: Canon Press, 2001).
"Cave of Adullam," *CA 7*:5 (1995), p. 39.
"Chet Gallagher arrest arrested as Las Vegas on duty police officer" [*sic*], available at https://www.youtube.com/watch?v=T3ij0e_mfWs, accessed June 26, 2019.
Chilton, David, *Productive Christians in an age of guilt-manipulation: A Biblical response to Ronald J. Sider* (Tyler, TX: Institute for Christian Economics, 1981).
Chilton, David, *Paradise restored: A biblical theology of dominion* (Fort Worth, TX: Dominion Press, 1984).
Chilton, David, *Days of vengeance: An exposition of the Book of Revelation* (Fort Worth, TX: Dominion Press, 1990).
Christ Church, Moscow, "Position Papers: Manners and life together: Moving to Moscow," available at https://www.christkirk.com/our-church/book-of-worship-faith-practice/, accessed June 26, 2019.

Church of Jesus Christ of Latter-day Saints, "Facts and statistics," available at http://www.mormonnewsroom.org/facts-and-statistics/country/united-states/state/idaho, accessed May 29, 2019.

Clapp, Rodney, "Democracy as heresy," *Christianity Today 20* (February 1987), pp. 17–20.

Collision: Christopher Hitchens vs. Douglas Wilson (dir. Darren Doane, 2009).

DeMar, Gary, *Something greater is here: Christian Reconstruction in Biblical perspective* (Fort Worth, TX: Dominion Press, 1988).

Dickison, Greg, "Civil disobedience," *CA 7*:2 (1995), p. 8.

Dickison, Greg, "Knowing enough to start a country," *CA 7*:6 (1995), p. 12.

Dickison, Greg, "The sin of lawlessness," *CA 8*:1 (1996), p. 12.

Dickison, Greg, "Nursing fathers pt. 2," *CA 13*:2 (2001), p. 13.

Dickison, Greg, "Courtroom culture," *CA 14*:6 (2002), p. 19.

Eliot, T. S., *The idea of a Christian society* (London: Faber and Faber, 1939).

Facey, Edward C., "Accelerated Christian Education: An alternative to state schools," *The Journal of Christian Reconstruction 4*:1 (1977), pp. 61, 63–64.

"From us," *CA 11*:5 (1999), p. 6.

Gilstrap, Michael R., "The Biblical basis for survival preparation," *The Journal of Christian Reconstruction 8* (1981), pp. 155–65.

"God or man conference 2015," available at https://www.youtube.com/watch?v=-feBAZGB7kQ, accessed June 26, 2019.

Grady, Lee, "God's emerging army," *The Journal of Christian Reconstruction 9*:1–2 (1982–83), pp. 157–63.

Grant, George, *In the shadow of plenty: Biblical principles for welfare and poverty* (Forth Worth, TX: Dominion Press; Nashville, TN: Thomas Nelson, 1986).

Grant, George, *The changing of the guard: Biblical principles for political action* (Forth Worth, TX: Dominion Press, 1987).

Hitchens, Christopher, and Douglas Wilson, *Is Christianity good for the world?* (Moscow, ID: Canon Press, 2009).

Hyatt, Michael S., and George Grant, *Y2K: The day the world shut down* (Nashville, TN: Word, 1998).

"A joint Federal Vision profession," *CA 19*:3 (2007), pp. 7–13.

Jones, Douglas, "Christian Coalition takes the easy path," *CA 7*:4 (1995), p. 10.

Jones, Douglas, "Debunking racial rights," *CA 9*:1 (1997), p. 22.

Jones, Douglas, "An interracial cross," *CA 9*:1 (1997), p. 20.

Jones, Douglas, "Pre-Adamite yearnings," *CA 9*:1 (1997), p. 18.

Jones, Douglas, "Just say 'no' to politics," *CA 10*:2 (1998), p. 11.

Jones, Douglas, and Marc Dupont, "Disputatio: Prophecy old and new," *CA 7*:6 (1995), pp. 28–29.

Jones, Douglas, and Douglas Wilson, *Angels in the architecture: A Protestant vision for Middle Earth* (Moscow, ID: Canon Press, 1998).

Kelly, Douglas F., "Editor's introduction," *The Journal of Christian Reconstruction 9*:1–2 (1982–83), p. 16.

Kelly, Douglas F., "The present struggle for Christian Reconstruction in the United States," *The Journal of Christian Reconstruction 9*:1–2 (1982–83), pp. 30–42.

Leithart, Peter J., "Worship first and last," *CA 12*:2 (2000), p. 16.

Leithart, Peter J., "Being scary," *CA 13*:2 (2001), p. 11.

Leithart, Peter J. , "Old Geneva & the New World: The Reverend Rousas J. Rushdoony, 1916–2001," *The Weekly Standard*, March 26, 2001, pp. 36–37.

"A little help for our friends," *CA 12*:1 (2000), p. 23.

Lordship Church, Coeur d'Alene, "The Redoubt song," available at https://www.youtube.com/watch?v=HSB_EnQul90, accessed June 26, 2019.

Merkle, Benjamin R., *Defending the Trinity in the Reformed Palatinate: The Elohistae* (New York: Oxford University Press, 2015).

Miller, Jared, "Reading for keeps," *CA 14*:3 (2002), p. 17.

"Mutterings on the regnant follies," *CA 11*:5 (1999), p. 22.

Nance, Jim, "The courage of the cross," *CA 7*:5 (1995), p. 20.

"A new skinist movement," *CA 17*:3 (2005), p. 28.

"New St. Andrews College," *CA 7*:1 (1995), p. 30.

North, Gary, "Towards the recovery of hope," *Banner of Truth 88* (1971), pp. 12–16.

North, Gary, "Editor's introduction," *The Journal of Christian Reconstruction 3*:2 (1976–77), pp. 1–5.

North, Gary, "Editor's introduction," *The Journal of Christian Reconstruction 4*:1 (1977), pp. 1–13.

North, Gary, "Editor's introduction," *The Journal of Christian Reconstruction 5*:2 (1978–79), pp. 1–7.

North, Gary, "The intellectual schizophrenia of the New Christian Right," *The failure of the American Baptist culture, Christianity and civilisation* 1 (1982), pp. 1–40.

North, Gary, *Unconditional surrender: God's program for victory* (Tyler, TX: Institute for Christian Economics, 1983).

North, Gary, *75 Bible questions your instructors pray you won't ask* (Tyler, TX: Spurgeon Press, 1984).

North, Gary, "Prologue," in Greg L. Bahnsen, *By this standard: The authority of God's law today* (Tyler, TX: Institute for Christian Economics, 1985), pp. i–xxvi.

North, Gary, "The sabbath millennium," *Biblical Economics Today 8*:2 (1985), pp. 1–3.

North, Gary, *The Sinai strategy: Economics and the Ten Commandments* (Tyler, TX: Institute for Christian Economics, 1986).

North, Gary, *Unholy spirits: Occultism and New Age humanism* (Fort Worth, TX: Dominion Press, 1986).

North, Gary, "Chilton, Sutton, and dominion theology," *Institute for Christian Economics Position Paper* (1987).

North, Gary, "Reconstructionist renewal and charismatic renewal," *Christian Reconstruction 61*:4 (May–June 1988), pp. 1–2.

North, Gary, "Editor's introduction," in Gary North (ed.), *Theonomy: An informed response* (Tyler, TX: Institute for Christian Economics, 1991), pp. 1–18.

North, Gary, *Millennialism and social theory* (Tyler, TX: Institute for Christian Ecomomics, 1991).

North, Gary, "Publisher's preface," in Greg Bahnsen, *No other standard: Theonomy and its critics* (Tyler, TX: Institute for Christian Economics, 1991), p. ix–xv.

North, Gary, "Geocentricity-Geostationism: The flat earth temptation," *Institute for Christian Economics Position Paper* (1992).

North, Gary, "Notes on the history of Christian Reconstruction: Clarifying the so-called 'Hitler connection,'" *Institute for Christian Economics Position Papers* (1992).

North, Gary, "The annulment of the dietary laws," *Institute for Christian Economics Position Paper* (1994).

North, Gary, *Lone gunners for Jesus: Letters to Paul J. Hill* (Tyler, TX: Institute for Christian Economics, 1994).

North, Gary, *Baptized patriarchy: The cult of the family* (Tyler, TX: Institute for Christian Economics, 1995).

North, Gary (ed.), *The tactics of Christian resistance, Christianity & Civilization* 3 (1983) (Tyler, Texas: Geneva Divinity School Press, 1983).

North, Gary, and David Chilton, "Apologetics and strategy," in Gary North (ed.), *Tactics of Christian resistance, Christianity & Civilization* 3 (1983), pp. 100–40.

McDurmon, Joel, *Restoring America one county at a time* (Athens, GA: American Vision Press, 2012).

McDurmon, Joel, "Fitzgerald's *Evangelicals* and the repeat-failure of the Christian Right," available at https://americanvision.org/16700/fitzgeralds-evangelicals-and-the-repeat-failure-of-the-christian-right/, accessed June 26, 2019.

McDurmon, Joel, "Understanding Gary North," available at https://www.youtube.com/watch?v=TyBUEadyiws, accessed June 26, 2019.

"Mother of all From Us's," *CA 12*:3 (2000), p. 8.

"Police officer is arrested in anti-abortion protest," *Deseret News*, January 29, 1989, available at http://www.deseretnews.com/article/32365/POLICE-OFFICER-IS-ARRESTED-IN-ANTI-ABORTION-PROTEST.html, accessed June 26, 2019.

Poythress, Vern S., "A Biblical view of mathematics," in Gary North (ed.), *Foundations of Christian scholarship* (Vallecito, CA: Ross House, 1976), pp. 156–88.

Poythress, Vern S., *The shadow of Christ in the law of Moses* (Phillipsburg, NJ: P&R, 1991).

Rawles, James Wesley, *How to survive the end of the world as we know it: Tactics, techniques and technologies for uncertain times* (London: Penguin, 2009).

Rawles, James Wesley, *Liberators: A novel of the coming global collapse* (New York: Dutton, 2014).

Rawles, James Wesley, *Tools for survival: What you need to survive when you're on your own* (London: Penguin, 2014).

Rawles, James Wesley, *Land of promise: Volume one of the Counter-Caliphate Chronicles* (Moyie Springs, ID: Liberty Paradigm Press, 2015).

Rawles, James Wesley, "Addenda: Reformed churches in the American Redoubt states," available at https://survivalblog.com/redoubt/, accessed June 26, 2019.

Rawles, James Wesley, "The American Redoubt: Move to the mountain states," March 28, 2011, available at https://survivalblog.com/redoubt/, accessed June 26, 2019.

Rogers, Tommy W., "Review of Iain H. Murray, *The puritan hope: A study in revival and the interpretation of* prophecy," *Journal of Christian Reconstruction* 3:2 (1976–77), pp. 178–81.

Rogers, Tommy W., "Review of Lino A. Graglia, *Disaster by decree: The Supreme Court decisions on race and the schools* (Ithaca, NY: Cornell University Press, 1976)," in *The Journal of Christian Reconstruction* 4:1 (1977), pp. 205–210.

Runyan, Gordan, *Resistance to tyrants: Romans 13 and the Christian duty to oppose wicked rulers* (n.p., 2012).

Rushdoony, Mark R., "Rousas John Rushdoony: A brief history, Part II: 'You are going to be a writer,'" available at https://chalcedon.edu/magazine/rousas-john-rushdoony-a-brief-history-part-ii-you-are-going-to-be-a-writer, accessed June 26, 2019.

Rushdoony, Mark R., "Rousas John Rushdoony: A brief history: Part VII: He is on the Lord's side," available at https://chalcedon.edu/magazine/rousas-john-rushdoony-a-brief-history-part-vii-hes-on-the-lords-side, accessed June 26, 2019.

Rushdoony, R. J., "Christian missions and Indian culture," *Westminster Theological Journal* 12:1 (1949), pp. 1–12.

Rushdoony, R. J., *By what standard? An analysis of the philosophy of Cornelius Van Til* (Philadelphia, PA: Presbyterian & Reformed, 1959).

Rushdoony, R. J., *Intellectual schizophrenia: Culture, crisis and education* (Philadelphia, PA: Presbyterian & Reformed, 1961),

Rushdoony, R. J., "Foreword," in Raymond O. Zorn, *Church and kingdom* (Philadelphia, PA: Presbyterian & Reformed, 1962), p. xix–xxii.

Rushdoony, R. J., *The messianic character of American education* (Nutley, NJ: Presbyterian & Reformed, 1963).

Rushdoony, R. J., *Preparation for the future* (San Carlos, CA: The Pamphleteers, 1966).

Rushdoony, R. J., *The mythology of science* (Nutley, NJ: Craig Press, 1967).

Rushdoony, R. J., *The politics of guilt and pity* (Nutley, NJ: Craig Press, 1970).

Rushdoony, R. J., "Introduction," in J. Marcellus Kik, *An eschatology of victory* (Philadelphia, PA: Presbyterian & Reformed, 1971).

Rushdoony, R. J., *The institutes of Biblical law* (Nutley, NJ: Presbyterian & Reformed, 1973).

Rushdoony, R. J., "Rev. E.V. Hill and the Mount Zion Missionary Baptist Church," *The Journal of Christian Reconstruction* 9:1–2 (1982–83), pp. 86–87.

Rushdoony, R. J., *The roots of Reconstruction* (Vallecito, CA: Ross House Books, 1991).

Rushdoony, R. J., unpublished testimony at the Leeper trial, available at http://rushdoony. sitewave.net/rushdoony-leeper-transcript-texas-homeschool-trial/, accessed June 26, 2019.

Rushdoony, R. J., "Random notes, 84," *Chalcedon Report* 419 (June 2000), p. 15.

Sandlin, P. Andrew, and John Barach (eds.), *Obedient faith: A festschrift for Norman Shepherd* (Mount Hermon, CA: Kerygma Press, 2012).

Sayers, Dorothy L., "The lost tools of learning (1947)," *The Journal of Christian Reconstruction* 4:1 (1977), pp. 10–25.

Sayers, Dorothy L., *The lost tools of learning* (Moscow, ID: Canon Press, 1990).

Schlect, Chris, "Book review," *CA* 7:5 (1995), p. 32.

Schlect, Chris, "Schlect's top ten," *CA* 9:2 (1997), p. 30.

Schuler, Duck, "You will have songs," *CA* 16:2 (2004), p. 16.

Selbrede, Martin G., "You can't split rotten wood," *The Journal of Christian Reconstruction* (1982–83), pp. 207–15.

Shaw, A. R., *Surrender the sun* (n.p., 2016).

Thoburn, Robert L., *The children trap: Biblical principles for education* (Fort Worth, TX: Dominion Press; Nashville, TN: Thomas Nelson, 1986).

Trewhella, Matthew J., *The doctrine of the lesser magistrates* (n.p., 2013).

Van Deventer, Jack, "Feminize the clergy," *CA* 11:2 (1999), p. 24.

Van Deventer, Jack, "The Christians mean business," *CA* 15:4 (2003), p. 32.

Weyrich, Paul M., "Letter to conservatives," available at https://nationalcenter.org/ncppr/ 1999/02/16/letter-to-conservatives-by-paul-m-weyrich/, accessed June 26, 2019.

Wilson, Douglas, *Recovering the lost tools of learning: An approach to distinctively Christian education* (Wheaton, IL: Crossway, 1991).

Wilson, Douglas, "Gary North and classical education," *CA* 7:4 (1995), p. 11.

Wilson, Douglas, "Bad moon rising," *CA* 8:1 (1996), pp. 4–5.

Wilson, Douglas, "Clowns to the left of me, jokers to the right . . . ," *CA* 8:2 (1996), p. 10.

Wilson, Douglas, "Militias on a toot," *CA* 8:1 (1996), p. 10.

Wilson, Douglas, "The trampled church," *CA* 8:1 (1996), p. 13.

Wilson, Douglas, "And this, just in," *CA* 9:2 (1997), p. 10.

Wilson, Douglas, "Gender warriors," *CA* 10:3 (1998), p. 14.

Wilson, Douglas, "Okay, okay, Y2K," *CA* 10:1 (1998), p. 10.

Wilson, Douglas, "Review of Ambrose Evans-Pritchard," *The Secret Life of Bill Clinton, CA* 10:3 (1998), p. 32.

Wilson, Douglas, "That Y2K thing," *CA 10*:2 (1998), pp. 36–39.

Wilson, Douglas, *Joy at the end of the tether: The inscrutable wisdom of Ecclesiastes* (Moscow, ID: Canon Press, 1999).

Wilson, Douglas, "Rattle and hum," *CA 11*:3 (1999), p. 20.

Wilson, Douglas, "Tinkerty Tonk," *CA 12*:3 (2000), p. 22.

Wilson, Douglas, "God struck America," *CA 13*:4 (2001), pp. 5–13.

Wilson, Douglas, "In the system, not of it," *CA 13*:5 (2001), p. 6.

Wilson, Douglas, "Chonklit cake," *CA 14*:2 (2002), p. 31.

Wilson, Douglas, "Clan jamfry," *CA 14*:3 (2002), p. 27.

Wilson, Douglas, "Son of Fort Sumpter," *CA 14*:3 (2002), p. 10.

Wilson, Douglas, "Life and death of *Homo pervertens*," *CA 16*:2 (2004), pp. 4–5.

Wilson, Douglas, *Black and tan: Essays and excursions on slavery, culture war, and Scripture in America* (Moscow, ID: Canon Press, 2005).

Wilson, Douglas, "Marriage and community," *CA 17*:2 (2005), p. 14.

Wilson, Douglas, "A mouth full of teeth," *CA 17*:5 (2005), p. 33.

Wilson, Douglas, "Cruciform politics," *CA 19*:1 (2007), pp. 4–7.

Wilson, Douglas, *Heaven misplaced: Christ's kingdom on earth* (Moscow, ID: Canon Press, 2008).

Wilson, Douglas, *5 cities that ruled the world: How Jerusalem, Athens, Rome, London & New York Shaped Global History* (Nashville, TN: Thomas Nelson, 2009).

Wilson, Douglas, "Life, liberty, property," *CA 21*:1 (2011), p. 19.

Wilson, Douglas, *Empires of dirt: Secularism, radical Islam, and the Mere Christendom alternative* (Moscow, ID: Canon Press, 2016).

Wilson, Douglas, "THE interview," available at https://dougwils.com/s7-engaging-the-culture/the-interview.html, accessed June 26, 2019.

Wilson, Douglas, and Randy Booth, *A justice primer*, 2nd edition (Moscow, ID: Blog and Mablog Press; Nacogdoches, TX: Covenant Media Press, 2018).

Wilson, Douglas, and Charles Weisman, "Disputatio: Christianity and race," *CA 9*:1 (1997), pp. 30–31.

Wilson, Jim, *Principles of war: A handbook on strategic evangelism* (1964; rpt. Moscow, ID: Canon Press, 2009).

Wilson, Jim, *Weapons and tactics: A handbook on personal evangelism* (Moscow, ID: Canon Press, 2012).

Wilson, N. D., *Leepike Ridge* (New York: Yearling, 2007).

Wilson, Nathan, "Patience," *CA 11*:1 (1999), p. 10.

Wilson, Nathan, "Picking one's poison," *CA 12*:2 (2000), p. 10.

Would, Ehud, "The pro-life movement and political correctness," *Faith & Heritage*, available at http://faithandheritage.com/2015/10/the-pro-life-movement-and-political-correctness/, accessed June 26, 2019.

Secondary Sources

"Accusations against sect in New Mexico," *New York Times*, May 4, 2004, available at http://www.nytimes.com/2008/05/04/us/04church.html, accessed June 26, 2019.

Aho, James A., *The politics of righteousness: Idaho Christian patriotism* (Seattle: University of Washington Press, 1990).

Aho, James A., *Far-right fantasy: A sociology of American religion and politics* (London: Routledge, 2016).

Anderson, Benedict, *Imagined communities: Reflections on the origin and spread of nationalism* (London: Verso, 1983).

Auten, Brian J., "Narrating Christian transformationalism: Rousas J. Rushdoony and Christian Reconstruction in current histories of American religion and politics," in Peter Escalante and W. Bradford Littlejohn (eds.), *For the healing of the nations: Essays on creation, redemption, and neo-Calvinism* ([Moscow, ID]: The Davenant Trust, 2014), pp. 209–39.

Bahnsen, David L., "Greg Bahnsen and Norm Shepherd—the final word," *Viewpoint: Politics, economics, and culture through the eyes of David L. Bahnsen*, April 28, 2008, available at https://www.davidbahnsen.com/index.php/2008/04/28/greg-bahnsen-and-norm-shepherd-the-final-word/, accessed June 26, 2019.

Bahnsen, Greg, *Van Til's apologetic: Readings and analysis* (Philipsburg, NJ: Presbyterian & Reformed, 1998).

Balmer, Randall, *Thy kingdom come: How the Religious Right distorts the faith and threatens America* (New York: Basic Books, 2006).

Barker, William S., and W. Robert Godfrey, "Preface," in William S. Barker and W. Robert Godfrey (eds.), *Theonomy: A Reformed critique* (Grand Rapids, MI: Zondervan, 1990), pp. 9–16.

Barkun, Michael, *Religion and the racist right: The origins of the Christian Identity movement*, 2nd edition (Chapel Hill: University of North Carolina Press, 1997).

Barkun, Michael, *Chasing phantoms: Reality, imagination, and Homeland Security since 9/11* (Chapel Hill: University of North Carolina Press, 2014).

Bauer, Susan Wise, and Jessie Wise, *The well-trained mind: A guide to classical education in the home* (New York: W. W. Norton, 1999, 2004).

Bean, Lydia, *The politics of evangelical identity: Local churches and partisan divides in the United States and Canada* (Princeton, NJ: Princeton University Press, 2014).

"Behind the walls," *SPLC Intelligence Report* (Summer 2013), available at https://www.splcenter.org/fighting-hate/intelligence-report/2013/behind-walls, accessed June 26, 2019.

Belew, Kathleen, *Bring the war home: The White Power movement and paramilitary America* (Cambridge, MA: Harvard University Press, 2018).

Berlet, Chip, "How we coined the term 'dominionism,'" *Talk to Action*, August 31, 2011, available at http://www.talk2action.org/story/2011/8/31/17047/5683/, accessed June 26, 2019.

Bestor, Arthur, *Backwoods utopias: The sectarian and Owenite phases of communitarian socialism in America, 1663–1829* (Philadelphia: University of Philadelphia Press, 1950).

Bhatt, Rachana, "Home is where the school is: The impact of homeschool legislation on school choice," *Journal of School Choice* 8:2 (2014), pp. 192–212.

Bivins, Jason C., *Religion of fear: The politics of horror in conservative evangelicalism* (New York: Oxford University Press, 2008).

Blaising, Craig A., and Darrell L. Bock, *Progressive dispensationalism* (Wheaton, IL: BridgePoint, 1993).

Blodgett, Jan, *Protestant evangelical literary culture and contemporary society* (Westport, CT: Greenwood, 1997).

Blumenthal, Max, *Republican Gomorrah: Inside the movement that shattered the party* (New York: Nation Books, 2009).

Bock, Alan W., *Ambush at Ruby Ridge: How government agents set Randy Weaver up and took his family down* (Irvine, CA: Dickens Press, 1995).

Bortins, Leigh A., *The core: Teaching your child the foundations of classical education* (New York: Palgrave Macmillan, 2010).

Brenneman, Todd M., *Homespun gospel: The triumph of sentimentality in contemporary American evangelicalism* (New York: Oxford University Press, 2014).

Brooks, David, "The Benedict Option," *New York Times*, March 14, 2017, available at https://www.nytimes.com/2017/03/14/opinion/the-benedict-option.html?_r=0, accessed June 26, 2019.

Captain Fantastic (dir. Matt Ross, 2016).

Carlson, Allan C., *Godly seed: American evangelicals confront birth control, 1873–1973* (London: Transaction, 2012).

Carpenter, Joel A., *Revive us again: The reawakening of American fundamentalism* (New York: Oxford University Press, 1997).

Carter, Joe, "Kinism, cultural Marxism, and the synagogue shooter," *The Gospel Coalition*, April 30, 2019, available at https://www.thegospelcoalition.org/article/kinism-cultural-marxism-and-the-synagogue-shooter/, accessed June 26, 2019.

Caughey, Chris, and Crawford Gribben, "History, identity politics, and the 'Recovery of the Reformed confession,'" in Matthew Bingham, Chris Caughey, R. Scott Clark, and Darryl G. Hart (eds.), *On being Reformed: Debates over a trans-Atlantic identity* (Basingstoke, UK: Palgrave, 2018), pp. 1–26.

Cheng, Albert, "Does homeschooling or private schooling promote political intolerance? Evidence from a Christian university," *Journal of School Choice* 8:1 (2014), pp. 49–68.

"Classic dystopian novels' popularity surges in Trump's America," *Entertainment Weekly*, January 31, 2017, available at http://ew.com/books/2017/01/31/classic-dystopian-novels-trump/, accessed June 26, 2019.

Coates, James, *Armed and dangerous: The rise of the survivalist right* (New York: Farrar Straus & Giroux, 1988).

Collingwood, Ryan, "Welcome to the American Redoubt," *CDA Press*, August 14, 2016, available at http://cdapress.com/news/local_news/article_9caa9b9a-61d4-11e6-b131-871b50c47f7c.html#.V7F2yxmIhT0.twitter, accessed June 26, 2019.

Conn, Steven, *Americans against the city: Anti-urbanism in the twentieth century* (New York: Oxford University Press, 2014).

The cult at the end of the world (dir. Ben Anthony, 2007).

Cuneo, Michael W., *The smoke of Satan: Conservative and traditionalist dissent in contemporary American Catholicism* (Baltimore, MD: Johns Hopkins University Press, 1999).

De Leon, Jason, *The land of open graves: Living and dying on the migrant trail* (Oakland: University of California Press, 2015).

Deneen, Patrick J., *Why liberalism failed* (New Haven, CT: Yale University Press, 2018).

"Diamond award: 10 million in sales (2009)," Christian Book Expo, available at http://christianbookexpo.com/salesawards/, accessed June 26, 2019.

Dochuk, Darren, *From Bible Belt to Sun Belt: Plain-folk religion, grassroots politics, and the rise of evangelical conservatism* (New York: W. W. Norton, 2011).

Dochuk, Darren, *Anointed with oil: How Christianity and crude made modern America* (New York: Basic Books, 2019).

"Donald Trump, abortion foe, eyes 'punishment' for women, then recants," *New York Times*, March 30, 2016, available at https://www.nytimes.com/2016/03/31/us/politics/donald-trump-abortion.html, accessed June 26, 2019.

Douthat, Ross, *Bad religion: How we became a nation of heretics* (New York: Free Press, 2012).

Dreher, Rod, *Crunchy cons: How Birkenstocked Burkeans, gun-loving organic gardeners, evangelical free-range farmers, hip homeschooling mamas, right-wing nature lovers, and their diverse tribe of countercultural conservatives plan to save America (or at least the Republican Party)* (New York: Crown Forum, 2006).

Dreher, Rod, *The Benedict option: A strategy for Christians in a post-Christian nation* (New York: Sentinel, 2017).

Dreher, Rod, "Scandal in Moscow," *The American Conservative*, September 29, 2015, available at http://www.theamericanconservative.com/dreher/scandal-in-moscow/, accessed June 26, 2019.

Duke, David Nelson, "The evolution of religion in Wilhelm Keil's community: A new reading of old testimony," *Communal Societies 13* (1993), pp. 84–98.

Eskridge, Larry, *God's forever people: The Jesus People movement in America* (New York: Oxford University Press, 2013).

Ezekiel, Raphael S., *The racist mind: Portraits of American neo-Nazis and Klansmen* (London: Penguin, 1995).

Fea, John, "Ted Cruz's campaign is fueled by a dominionist vision for America," *Washington Post*, February 4, 2016.

Fea, John, *Believe me: The evangelical road to Donald Trump* (Grand Rapids, MI: Eerdmans, 2018).

Federal News Service, "Transcript of the Republican presidential debate," *New York Times*, February 14, 2016, available at https://www.nytimes.com/2016/02/14/us/politics/transcript-of-the-republican-presidential-debate.html, accessed June 26, 2019.

Ferré, John P., *A social gospel for millions: The religious bestsellers of Charles Sheldon, Charles Gordon, Howard Bell Wright* (Bowling Green, OH: Bowling Green University Popular Press, 1988).

Fitzgerald, Frances, *The evangelicals: The struggle to shape America* (New York: Simon & Schuster, 2017).

Fletcher, Martin, *Almost heaven: Travels through the backwoods of America* (London: Little, Brown, 1998).

Foran, Clare, "Here's what's on Barack Obama's reading list," *CNN Politics*, June 16, 2018, available at https://edition.cnn.com/2018/06/16/politics/barack-obama-reading-list-mitch-landrieu/index.html, accessed June 26, 2019.

Forsyth, Jim, "Subculture of Americans prepares for civilization's collapse," *Reuters*, January 21, 2012, available at https://www.reuters.com/article/us-usa-civilization-collapse/subculture-of-americans-prepares-for-civilizations-collapse-idUSTRE80K0LA20120121, accessed June 26, 2019.

Foulner, Martin A., "The Free Kirk of Scotland against theonomy," *Chalcedon Report* (August 1998), available at https://chalcedon.edu/magazine/the-free-kirk-of-scotland-against-theonomy, accessed June 26, 2019.

Frame, John M., "Abortion and the Christian," *The Presbyterian Guardian* (November 1970), pp. 78, 80.

Frame, John M., "The law, theology and abortion," *The Christian Lawyer* 4:3 (1972), pp. 24–27.

Frame, John M., "Review of Rushdoony, *Institutes of Biblical law*," *Westminster Theological Journal* 38:2 (1976), pp. 195–217, available at https://frame-poythress.org/the-institutes-of-biblical-law-a-review-article/, accessed June 26, 2019.

Frame, John M., "The one, the many, and theonomy," in William S. Barker and W. Robert Godfrey (eds.), *Theonomy: A Reformed critique* (Grand Rapids, MI: Zondervan, 1990).

"Free Kirk in uproar over heresy; Church report calling for crackdown on a controversial doctrine likely to reopen old wounds," *The Herald*, May 12, 1997, available at http://www.heraldscotland.com/news/12325919.Free_Kirk_in_uproar_over__apos_heresy_apos__Church_report_calling_for_crackdown_on_a_controversial_doctrine_likely_to_reopen_old_wounds/, accessed June 26, 2019.

Frykholm, Amy Johnson, *Rapture culture: Left Behind in evangelical America* (New York: Oxford University Press, 2004).

Gaither, Milton, *Homeschool: An American history* (New York: Palgrave Macmillan, 2008).

Gaston, K. Healan, "The Cold War romance of religious authenticity: Will Herberg, William F. Buckley Jr., and the rise of the new right," *Journal of American History* 99:4 (2013), pp. 1133–58.

Gibson, James William, *Warrior dreams: Paramilitary culture in post-Vietnam America* (New York: Hill and Wang, 1994).

Gilbert, James, *Redeeming the culture: American religion in an age of science* (Chicago: University of Chicago Press, 1997).

Gill, Jill K., "The power and the glory: Idaho's religious history," in Adam M. Sowards (ed.), *Idaho's place: A new history of the Gem State* (Seattle: University of Washington Press, 2014), pp. 108–35.

Green, Steven K., *The third disestablishment: Church, state, and American culture, 1940–1975* (New York: Oxford University Press, 2019).

Gribben, Crawford, *Writing the rapture: Prophecy fiction in evangelical America* (New York: Oxford University Press, 2009).

Gribben, Crawford, *Evangelical millennialism in the trans-Atlantic world, 1500–2000* (Basingstoke, UK: Palgrave, 2011).

Gribben, Crawford, "Rethinking the rise of prophecy fiction: H.R.K.'s *Life in the Future* (?1879)," *Brethren Historical Review* 7 (2011), pp. 68–80.

Hamm, Mark S., *Apocalypse in Oklahoma: Waco and Ruby Ridge avenged* (Boston, MA: Northeastern University Press, 1997).

Hankins, Barry, *Francis Schaeffer and the shaping of evangelical America* (Grand Rapids, MI: Eerdmans, 2008).

Hannaford, Alex, "Wayne Bent: The cult of the man they call messiah," *Sunday Times Magazine*, June 14, 2009, pp. 42–47.

Harding, Susan, "Representing fundamentalism: The problem of the repugnant cultural other," *Social Research* 58:2 (1991), pp. 373–93.

Harp, Gillis J., *Protestants and American conservatism* (New York: Oxford University Press, 2019).

Hart, D. G., *The lost soul of American Protestantism* (Lanham, MD: Rowman & Littlefield, 2002).

Hart, D. G., *Deconstructing Evangelicalism: Conservative Protestantism in the age of Billy Graham* (Grand Rapids, MI: Baker, 2004).

Hart, D. G., *Between the times: The Orthodox Presbyterian Church in transition, 1945–1990* (Willow Grove, PA: The Committee for the Historian of the Orthodox Presbyterian Church, 2011).

Hart, D. G., *From Billy Graham to Sarah Palin: Evangelicals and the betrayal of American conservatism* (Grand Rapids, MI: Eerdmans, 2011).

Hart, D. G., *Damning words: The life and religious times of H. L. Mencken* (Grand Rapids, MI: Eerdmans, 2016).

Haselby, Sam, *The origins of American religious nationalism* (Oxford: Oxford University Press, 2015).

Hatch, Nathan, *The democratization of American Christianity* (New Haven, CT: Yale University Press, 1989).

Hedges, Chris, *American fascists: The Christian Right and the war on America* (New York: Free Press, 2006).

Hendershot, Heather, *Shaking the world for Jesus: Media and conservative evangelical culture* (Chicago: University of Chicago Press, 2004).

Hendricks, Robert J., *Bethel and Aurora: An experiment in communalism as practical Christianity* (New York: Pioneer Press, 1933).

Hobsbawm, Eric (ed.), *The invention of tradition* (Cambridge: Cambridge University Press, 1993).

Hofmeyr, Isabel, *The Portable Bunyan: A trans-national history of The Pilgrim's Progress* (Princeton, NJ: Princeton University Press, 2003).

Hofstadter, Richard, *The paranoid style in American politics and other essays* (New York: Knopf, 1965).

Huskinson, Benjamin L., "The missing link between evangelicals and Trump," *The American Interest*, November 23, 2018, available at https://www.the-american-interest.com/2018/11/23/the-missing-link-between-evangelicals-and-trump/, accessed June 26, 2019.

Huskinson, Benjamin L., *American creationism, creation science, and Intelligent Design in the evangelical market* (New York: Palgrave, 2020).

Ingersoll, Julie J., *Building God's kingdom: Inside the world of Christian Reconstruction* (New York: Oxford University Press, 2015).

Isserman, Maurice, and Michael Kazin, *America divided: The civil war of the 1960s* (Oxford: Oxford University Press, 1999).

Jacobs, Alan, *The Year of Our Lord 1943: Christian humanism in an age of crisis* (Oxford: Oxford University Press, 2018).

Jenkins, Philip, *Mystics and messiahs: Cults and new religions in American history* (New York: Oxford University Press, 2000).

Jones, Robert P., *The end of white Christian America* (New York: Simon & Schuster, 2016).

Joyce, Kathryn, *Quiverfull: Inside the Christian Patriarchy movement* (Boston, MA: Beacon Press, 2009).

Juergensmeyer, Mark, *Terror in the mind of God: The global rise of religious violence* (Berkeley: University of California Press, 2000).

Keillor, Garrison, *Lake Wobegon Days* (1985; London: Faber, 1997).

Kelleher, William F., *The Troubles in Ballybogoin: Memory and identity in Northern Ireland* (Ann Arbor: University of Michigan Press, 2003).

Kopp, James, *Eden within Eden: Oregon's utopian heritage* (Corvallis: Oregon State University Press, 2009).

Kunzman, Robert, *Write these laws on your children: Inside the world of conservative Christian homeschooling* (Boston, MA: Beacon Press, 2009).

Kunzman, Robert, "Homeschooling and religious fundamentalism," *International Journal of Elementary Education* 3:1 (2010), pp. 17–28.

Laats, Adam, "Forging a fundamentalist 'One Best System': Struggles over curriculum and educational philosophy for Christian day schools, 1970–1989," *History of Education Quarterly* 50:1 (2010), pp. 55–83.

"The last big frontier," *The Economist*, August 6, 2016, available at http://www.economist.com/news/united-states/21703411-movement-staunch-conservatives-and-doomsday-watchers-inland-north-west?fsrc=scn/tw_ec/the_last_big_frontier, accessed June 26, 2019.

Lewis, Andrew R., *The rights turn in conservative Christian politics: How abortion transformed the culture wars* (Cambridge: Cambridge University Press, 2017).

Limerick, Patricia Nelson, *The legacy of conquest: The unbroken past of the American West* (New York: Norton, 1987).

Lindsey, Hal, *The late great planet earth* (Grand Rapids, MI: Zondervan, 1970).

Lindsey, Hal, *The road to Holocaust* (New York: Bantam, 1990).

Lockley, Philip, "Introduction," in Philip Lockley (ed.), *Protestant communalism in the trans-Atlantic world, 1650–1850* (London: Palgrave Macmillan, 2016), pp. 1–8.

Lockley, Philip, "Mapping Protestant communalism, 1650–1850," in Philip Lockley (ed.), *Protestant communalism in the trans-Atlantic world, 1650–1850* (London: Palgrave Macmillan, 2016), pp. 25–26.

Lois, Jennifer, *Home is where the school is: The logic of homeschooling and the emotional labor of mothering* (New York: New York University Press, 2013).

Lorenz, Mike, "Wolves in sheep's clothing: Gary North, Y2K, and hidden agendas," available at http://www.sweetliberty.org/garynorth.htm, accessed June 26, 2019.

Luhrmann, T. M., *Of two minds: The growing disorder in American psychiatry* (New York: Alfred A. Knopf, 2000).

Lynerd, Benjamin T., *Republican theology: The civil religion of American evangelicals* (New York: Oxford University Press, 2014).

Macdonald, G. Jeffrey, "Secession theology runs deep in American religious, political thought," *Washington Post*, November 29, 2012, available at https://www.washingtonpost.com/national/on-faith/secession-theology-runs-deep-in-american-religious-political-history/2012/11/29/bb82bb7c-3a5c-11e2-9258-ac7c78d5c680_story.html, accessed June 26, 2019.

MacIntyre, Alasdair, *After virtue: A study in moral theory* (1981; rpt. London: Bloomsbury, 2011).

MacLean, Nancy, *Democracy in chains: The deep history of the radical right's stealth plan for America* (London: Scribe, 2017).

Malkki, Lisa, *Purity and exile: Violence, memory, and national cosmology among Hutu refugees in Tanzania* (Chicago: University of Chicago Press, 1995).

Marsden, George M., "Fundamentalism as an American phenomenon," *Church History* 46:2 (1977), pp. 215–32, reprinted in D. G. Hart (ed.), *Reckoning with the Past: Historical essays on American evangelicalism from the Institute for the Study of American Evangelicals* (Grand Rapids, MI: Baker, 1995), pp. 303–21.

Marsden, George M., *Reforming fundamentalism: Fuller Seminary and the new evangelicalism* (Grand Rapids, MI: Eerdmans, 1995).

Marsden, George M., *The twilight of the American Enlightenment: The 1950s and the crisis of liberal belief* (New York: Basic Books, 2014).

McDonagh, Ross, "The Duggar children 'liked being recognized and hate that *19 kids and counting* has been cancelled' due to molestation scandal," *The Daily Mail*, July 22, 2015, available at https://www.dailymail.co.uk/tvshowbiz/article-3171022/

Duggar-children-gutted-s-cancellation-amid-molestation-scandal.html, accessed June 26, 2019.

McGirr, Lisa, *Suburban warriors: The origins of the New American Right* (Princeton, NJ: Princeton University Press, 2001).

McVicar, Michael J., *Christian Reconstruction: R. J. Rushdoony and American religious conservatism* (Chapel Hill: University of North Carolina Press, 2015).

McVicar, Michael J., "Apostles of deceit: Ecumenism, fundamentalism, surveillance, and the contested loyalties of Protestant clergy during the Cold War," in Sylvester A. Johnson and Steven Weitzman (eds.), *The FBI and religion: Faith and national security before and after 9/11* (Oakland: University of California Press, 2017), pp. 85–107.

Melling, Philip, *Fundamentalism in America: Millennialism, identity and militant religion* (Edinburgh: Edinburgh University Press, 1999).

Menzies, James W., *True myth: C. S. Lewis and Joseph Campbell on the veracity of Christianity* (London: Lutterworth Press, 2014).

Mesaros-Winckles, Christy Ellen, "Christian patriarchy life: TLC's *19 kids and counting*," in Alena Amato Ruggerio (ed.), *Media depictions of brides, wives, and mothers* (Lanham, MD: Lexington Books, 2012), pp. 63–75.

Miles, R. E., and R. Butler, *From the Mountain Newsletter* (Spring 1985).

Miller, John J., "Back to basics," *National Review*, October 19, 2015, available at https://www. nationalreview.com/magazine/2015/10/19/back-basics-2/, accessed June 26, 2019.

Miller, Steven P., *The age of evangelicalism: America's born-again years* (New York: Oxford University Press, 2014).

Millman, Gregory, and Martine Millman, *Home schooling: A family's journey* (London: Penguin, 2008).

Mitchell, Richard G., *Dancing at Armageddon: Survivalism and chaos in modern times* (Chicago: University of Chicago Press, 2002).

Moorhead, James, *World without end: Mainstream American Protestant visions of the last things, 1880–1925* (Bloomington: Indiana University Press, 1999).

Murphy, Joseph, *Homeschooling in America: Capturing and assessing the movement* (Thousand Oaks, CA: Corwin, 2012).

Murray, John, *Principles of conduct* (London: Tyndale Press, 1957).

Murray, John, *The epistle to the Romans*, 2 vols., The New International Commentary on the New Testament (Grand Rapids, MI: Eerdmans, 1959, 1965).

Nadis, Fred, *Wonder Shows: Performing science, magic, and religion in America* (New Brunswick, NJ: Rutgers University Press, 2005).

Nicholson, Rebecca, "'The Handmaid's Tale review—timely adaptation scares with dystopian dread," *The Guardian*, April 26, 2017, available at https://www.theguardian.com/tv-and-radio/2017/apr/26/the-handmaids-tale-tv-show-hulu-review, accessed June 26, 2019.

"Of holidays and domestic violence," *The Spokesman-Review*, November 21, 2007, available at http://www.spokesman.com/blogs/boise/2007/nov/21/of-holidays-and-domestic-violence/, accessed June 26, 2019.

Olasky, Marvin, and Herbert Schlossberg, *Turning point: A Christian worldview declaration* (Wheaton, IL: Crossway, 1987).

Olson, John Kevin, and Ann C. Beck, "Religion and political realignment in the Rocky Mountain States," *Journal for the Scientific Study of Religion* 29 (1990), pp. 198–204.

Orgeron, Marsha, and Skip Elsheimer, "'Something different in science films': The Moody Institute of Science and the canned missionary movement," *The Moving Image* 7:1 (2007), pp. 1–26.

Phillips-Fein, Kim, "Conservatism: A state of the field," *Journal of American History* 98:3 (2011), pp. 723–43.

Potok, Mark, "The year in hate, 2004," available at https://www.splcenter.org/fighting-hate/intelligence-report/2005/year-hate-2004, accessed June 26, 2019.

Queen's University Belfast, "Policy and principles of ethical research," available at https://www.qub.ac.uk/home/media/Media,600198,en.pdf, accessed June 26, 2019.

Raban, Jonathan, *Bad Land: An American romance* (London: Picador, 1996).

Redford, Jeremy, Danielle Battle, Stacey Bielick, and Sarah Grady, *Homeschooling in the United States: 2012* (NCES 2016-096) (Washington, DC: United States Department of Education, 2016).

"Republican Matt Shea 'participated in act of domestic terrorism,' says report," in https://www.theguardian.com/us-news/2019/dec/20/matt-shea-domestic-terrorism-washington-state-report, accessed February 17, 2020.

Robinson, Marilynne, *Housekeeping* (1980; rpt. London: Faber, 2005).

Rogers, Daniel T., "In search of progressivism," *Reviews in American History* 10:4 (1982), pp. 113–32.

Rosin, Hanna, *God's Harvard: A Christian college on a mission to save America* (New York: Houghton Mifflin Harcourt, 2008).

Ruotsila, Markku, *Fighting fundamentalist: Carl McIntire and the politicization of American fundamentalism* (New York: Oxford University Press, 2016).

Sabean, David, *Power in the blood: Popular culture and village discourse in early modern Germany* (Cambridge: Cambridge University Press, 1988).

Sandeen, Ernest R., *The roots of fundamentalism: British and American millenarianism, 1800–1930* (Chicago: University of Chicago Press, 1970).

Schäfer, Alex R., *Countercultural conservatives: American evangelicalism from the postwar revival to the New Christian Right* (Madison: University of Wisconsin Press, 2011),

Scheper-Hughes, Nancy, *Saints, scholars and schizophrenics: Mental illness in rural Ireland* (Oakland: University of California Press, 1992).

Singer, C. Gregg, *A theological interpretation of American history* (Nutley, NJ: Craig Press, 1975).

Smith, Christian, and Melinda Lundquist Denton, *Soul searching: The religious and spiritual lives of American teenagers* (Oxford: Oxford University Press, 2005).

Smith, Christian, and David Sikkink, "Is private school privatizing?" *First Things* 92 (April 1999), pp. 16–20.

Smith, Erin A., *What would Jesus read? Popular religious books and everyday life in twentieth-century America* (Chapel Hill: University of North Carolina Press, 2015).

Somin, Ilya, "Who wants to put democracy in chains?" *Washington Post*, July 10, 2017, available at https://www.washingtonpost.com/news/volokh-conspiracy/wp/2017/07/10/who-wants-to-put-democracy-in-chains/?utm_term=.9e775df7064b, accessed June 26, 2019.

Sowards, Adam M., "Reckoning with history," in Adam M. Sowards (ed.), *Idaho's place: A new history of the Gem State* (Seattle: University of Washington Press, 2014), pp. 3–12.

Steensland, Brian, and Philip Goff, "Introduction: The new evangelical social engagement," in Brian Steensland and Philip Goff (eds.), *The new evangelical social engagement* (New York: Oxford University Press, 2014), pp. 1–30.

Stewart, Kathryn, *The Good News Club: The Christian Right's stealth assault on America's children* (New York: PublicAffairs, 2012).

Stewart, Kathryn, "Betsy DeVos and God's plan for schools," *New York Times*, December 13, 2016, available at https://www.nytimes.com/2016/12/13/opinion/betsy-devos-and-gods-plan-for-schools.html, accessed June 26, 2019.

Stroop, Christopher (Chrissy), "Is Christian homeschooling breeding a new kind of domestic terrorist?" *Playboy*, May 8, 2019, available at https://www.playboy.com/read/is-christian-homeschooling-breeding-a-new-kind-of-domestic-terrorist, accessed June 26, 2019.

Sullivan, Andrew, "Does Bill Kristol like the Taliban?" *The Dish*, March 12, 2001, available at http://dish.andrewsullivan.com/2001/03/23/does-bill-kristol-like-the-taliban/, accessed June 26, 2019.

Sullivan, Kevin, "A fortress against fear," *Washington Post*, August 27, 2016, available at https://www.washingtonpost.com/classic-apps/a-fortress-against-fear/2016/08/27/97a45992-5d60-11e6-8e45-477372e89d78_story.html?postshare=9711472462461206&tid=ss_tw-bottom, accessed June 26, 2019.

Surin, Kenneth, "*Contemptus mundi* and the disenchanted world: Bonhoeffer's 'discipline of the secret' and Adorno's 'strategy of hibernation,'" *Journal of the American Academy of Religion* 53:3 (1985), pp. 383–410.

Sutton, Matthew Avery, *American apocalypse: A history of modern evangelicalism* (Cambridge, MA: Belknap Press of Harvard University Press, 2014).

"Thank God, it's doomsday," *The Simpsons* episode 19, series 16 (2005).

"The right: A house divided," *Newsweek*, February 2, 1981.

Thompson, J. Lee, and John H. Thompson, "Ralph Connor and the Canadian identity," *Queen's Quarterly* 79:2 (1972), pp. 159–70.

Tompkins, Jane, *Sensational designs: The cultural work of American fiction, 1790–1860* (New York: Oxford University Press, 1985).

Toy, E., "'Promised land' or Armageddon? History, survivalists, and the Aryan Nations in the Pacific Northwest," *Montana: The Magazine of Western History* 36:3 (Summer 1986), pp. 80–82.

Trueman, Carl, *Histories and fallacies: Problems faced in the writing of history* (Wheaton, IL: Crossway, 2009).

Turner, Frederick Jackson, *The significance of the frontier in American history* (1894; rpt. Mansfield Centre, CT: Martino, 2014).

Tuveson, Ernest L., *Redeemer nation: The idea of America's millennial role* (Chicago: University of Chicago Press, 1968).

Usborne, David, "Nobel honour stuns Obama and the world," *The Independent*, October 10, 2009, available at https://www.independent.co.uk/news/world/americas/nobel-honour-stuns-obama-ndash-and-the-world-1800567.html, accessed June 26, 2019.

Vaca, Daniel, *Evangelicals incorporated: Books and the business of religion in America* (Cambridge, MA: Harvard University Press, 2019).

Velarde, R., "Preparing for the Apocalypse: A look at the rise of doomsday preppers," *Christian Research Journal* 36:4 (2013), available at http://www.equip.org/PDF/JAF5364.pdf, accessed June 26, 2019.

Vieux, Andrea, "The politics of homeschools: Religious conservatives and regulation requirements," *The Social Science Journal* 51:4 (2014), pp. 556–63.

Wacker, Grant, *America's pastor: Billy Graham and the shaping of a nation* (Cambridge, MA: Harvard University Press, 2014).

Waltke, Bruce K., "The Old Testament and birth control," *Christianity Today* 13:3 (November 8, 1968), p. 3.

Wellman, James K., *Evangelical vs. liberal: The clash of Christian cultures in the Pacific Northwest* (New York: Oxford University Press, 2008).

Westad, Odd Arne, *The Cold War: A world history* (London: Allen Lane, 2017).

Whitehead, John W., *Slaying dragons: The truth behind the man who defended Paula Jones* (Nashville, TN: Thomas Nelson, 2006).

William Wordsworth: The major works, ed. Stephen Gill (Oxford: Oxford University Press, 2008),

Williams, Daniel K., *God's own party: The making of the Christian Right* (New York: Oxford University Press, 2010).

Williams, Daniel K., "Prolifers of the left: Progressive evangelicals' campaign against abortion," in Brian Steensland and Philip Goff (eds.), *The new evangelical social engagement* (New York: Oxford University Press, 2014), pp. 200–20.

Williams, Daniel K., *Defenders of the unborn: The pro-life movement before Roe v. Wade* (New York: Oxford University Press, 2016).

Witt, Stephanie, and Gary Moncrief, "Religion and roll call voting in Idaho: The 1990 abortion controversy," *American Politics Quarterly 21* (1993), pp. 140–49.

Worthen, Molly, "Onward Christian soldiers," *New York Times Magazine* (September 30, 2007), available at http://www.nytimes.com/2007/09/30/magazine/30Christian-t.html?_r=1&scp=1&sq=molly%20worthen%20moscow&st=cse, accessed June 26, 2019.

Worthen, Molly, "The Chalcedon problem: Rousas John Rushdoony and the origins of Christian Reconstruction," *Church History 77*:2 (2008), pp. 399–436.

Worthen, Molly, *Apostles of reason: The crisis of authority in American evangelicalism* (New York: Oxford University Press, 2014).

"Y2K doomsday scenario," available at http://www.sullivan-county.com/nf0/fundienazis/y2k_gary.htm, accessed June 26, 2019.

Zagratzki, Uwe, "Ralph Connor, Hugh MacLennan and Alice Munro: Three Scottish-Canadian authors," *Scottish Tradition 23* (1998), pp. 3–47.

Zorn, Raymond O., *Church and kingdom* (Philadelphia, PA: Presbyterian & Reformed, 1962).

Zorn, Raymond O., *Christ triumphant: Biblical perspectives on his church and kingdom* (Edinburgh: Banner of Truth, 1997).

Index

For the benefit of digital users, indexed terms that span two pages (e.g., 52–53) may, on occasion, appear on only one of those pages.

abortion 1–3, 13–14, 42–43, 44–45, 59–60, 65–66, 79, 80–82, 83–84, 85–87, 88–89, 102, 140–41, 144–45
Adorno, Theodore 4–5, 12–13
    See also Frankfurt School
Aeschylus 111–12
Aho, James 18–19
Alfred, King 74–75
Amazon Prime 1–2, 7–8, 12, 134–35, 139–40
American Civil Liberties Union 66
"American Redoubt" 10–12, 14, 16–18, 20–21, 27–30, 31–32, 34–35, 52–53, 62–63, 116–18, 130, 132, 134–35, 139–40, 143, 144–45, 146–47, 148–49
    See also migration
American Vision 47–48, 83–86
amillennialism 58
anarchy 27–28, 44, 62–63, 67–68, 85–86
Anderson, Benedict 114–15
Anselm 74–75, 99–100, 111–12
Aquinas 111–12
Aristophanes 111–12
Aristotle 111–12
Aryan Nations 20–21
Association for Christian Classical Schools 109
Athanasius 111–12
Atwood, Margaret 60–61, 144–45
Augustine 74–75, 99–100, 110–12
Aurora, Oregon 19–20
Austen, Jane 111–12
Austin, Texas 3–4, 140–41

Bahnsen, Greg 71–74, 76, 107–8, 109–10, 140–41
Baldwin, Chuck 131–32
Balmer, Randall 60–63, 93–94, 96–97

Banner of Truth Trust 42–43, 45
Barkun, Michael 22–23, 139–40
Barzun, Jacques 4–5
Bede 111–12
Beowulf 111–12
Blodgett, Jan 129–30
Blumenthal, Max 8–9
Boethius 111–12
Boise, Idaho 16–17, 20–21
Bolsonaro, Jair 145–46
Bonners Ferry, Idaho 16–17
Bortins, Leigh A. 92–93
Bunyan, John 111–12, 119
Burke, Edmund 74–75
Bush, George W. 2–3, 62–63, 66–67, 78–79, 123–24
Butler, Richard 20–21

Cage, Nicholas 123
Callihan, Wesley 109
Calvin, John 74–75, 99–100, 111–12
Calvinism 2–3, 31–32, 40, 41–42, 45, 60–61, 73–75, 99–100, 103–4, 109–10
Canon Press 53, 80, 107–8, 114–16, 126–30, 142–43
Carpenter, Joel 121
Carson, Ben 88–89
Carter, Jimmy 65–66
Chalcedon Foundation 1–2, 24–25, 44, 65–66, 109–10
Charismatic Christianity 49–50, 71, 73–75, 88–89, 103–4
Chesterton, G. K. 74–75, 130
Chilton, David 125
Christ Church, Moscow 10, 32, 49–50, 53–56, 81–82, 116, 142–43
Christ College 109–10
Christian Booksellers Association 121–23

Christian Century 121–23
Christian Coalition 66
Christian Exodus 62–63
Christianity Today 42–43, 63–64, 69–71,
    72–73, 119–20
Church of Jesus Christ, Christian 20–21
Cicero 111–12
Clinton, Bill 27, 48–49, 66–67,
    136–37
Coeur d'Alene, Idaho 19–21, 34–35, 58,
    59–61, 85–86, 88, 130
Commoner, Barry 22–23
Confederation of Reformed Evangelical
    Churches 49–50
Connor, Ralph 119–20
Constitution of the United States of
    America 5–6, 12, 23, 28–29, 42–43, 60,
    68–69, 80–81, 85–86, 91–92, 97–98,
    132, 134–35, 142
Council for National Policy 34
Credenda Agenda 48–50, 51, 52–53,
    75–76, 77, 79, 80–81, 82, 88–89,
    109, 110–13, 114–16,
    126–27
Crossway 126–27
Cruz, Ted 62–63, 88–89

Dante Alighieri 111–12
Darwin, Charles 111–12
Defoe, Daniel 111–12
Degan, William Francis 21
DeMar, Gary 74, 109–10
democracy 5–6, 14, 41–42, 48–49, 60–61,
    67–69, 74–75, 76–77, 82, 99, 102–3,
    115–17, 142
Deneen, Patrick 140
Descartes, René 111–12
DeVos, Betsy 111–12
Dickens, Charles 111–12
Dickison, Greg 77–78, 82
Dobson, James 65–66
Dochuk, Darren 63–64
Dostoevsky, Fyodor 111–12
Dreher, Rod 7–8, 13–14, 56–57,
    111–13, 146–47
Duck Valley Indian Reservation, Nevada
    and Idaho 24
Duggar family 124

Eco, Umberto 60–61
Economist 2–3, 12
education 1–2, 54–56, 90
    "Accelerated Christian Education"
        (ACE) 91–92
    home-education 1–2, 3–4, 7–8, 14, 23,
        51, 56–57, 90–94, 95–104, 105–6,
        109–10, 112–13, 125–26, 131–32,
        140–41, 144–45
    Sonlight 113
    See also Christ College; Logos School;
        New Saint Andrews College; Patrick
        Henry College
Edwards, Jonathan 36–38, 133–34
Eliot, T. S. 74–75, 98–99, 107–8,
    136–37, 148–49
Euclid 111–12
Euripides 111–12
evangelical left 4–5, 13–14, 47
Ezekiel, Ralph S. 20–21

Falwell, Jerry 65–66
Falwell, Jerry, Jr 90–91
Family Research Council 65–66
Farron, Tim 145–46
fascism 28–29, 60–61, 93–94,
    144–45, 146
Faulkner, William 111–12
Fitzgerald, Frances 8–9, 140
Focus on the Family 65–66, 121–23
Ford, Gerald 65–66
Frame, John 42–43, 69–71
Frankfurt School 6–7, 34–35, 136–37
    See also Adorno, Theodore
Free Church of Scotland 72–73
Frykholm, Amy 123–24
Fuller Theological Seminary 63–64, 121

Gaither, Milton 95–98
Gallagher, Chet 59–60
Gentry, Kenneth 52–53, 109–10
Gill, Jill K. 18–19, 23
Goldwater, Barry 13–14, 64–65
Gordon, Charles William 119–20
Graham, Billy 37–38, 42–43, 63–64,
    79, 121–23
Grant, George 125–26
Green, Keith 121–23

Griffith, Brian 72–73
Gritz, Bo 22

Harding, Susan 30–31
HarperCollins 1–2, 12, 114,
    126–27, 128–29
Hart, D. G. 4–5, 145–46
Hayden Lake, Idaho 20–21, 33–34
Hayek, F. A. 64–65
Hedges, Chris 60–63
Heilbroner, Robert 22–23
Henry, Matthew 133–34
Herodotus 111–12
Hill, E. V. 34
Hill, Paul Jennings 80–81, 85–86,
    104–5, 140–41
Hitchens, Christopher 4–5, 12, 28–29,
    114, 127–28
Hitler, Adolph 109–10
Hobbes, Thomas 111–12
Hofstadter, Richard T. 29–30, 143–44, 146
Holocaust denial 33–34, 42, 60–61, 72–73
Holt, John 95–96
Home School Legal Defense
    Association 103–4
Homer 111–12, 128–29
House, H. Wayne 72–73
Huskinson, Benjamin 8–9, 145–46
Hyatt, Michael S. 125–26

Ice, Thomas 72–73
Ingersoll, Julie J. 8–9, 16–17, 46–47, 96–97
Irenaeus 111–12
Islam 36–37, 75, 79–80

Jefferson, Thomas 74–75
Jensen, Liz 123–24
jeremiad 6–7, 36–37, 138
Jones, Douglas 78, 109, 127–28
Jones, Paula 48–49
Journal of Christian Reconstruction 45, 71,
    74, 96–97, 99–102, 103–5, 107–8
Judaism 11–12, 36–37, 41–42,
    72–73, 132–33

Kalispell, Montana 131–32
Kamiah, Idaho 22
Keil, Wilhelm 19–20

Keillor, Garrison 19–20
Kelly, Douglas F. 103–5
Kik, J. Marcellus 40–41
Kinism 34–36, 56–57, 58, 80, 116–17,
    144–45
    See also race
Kirk, Russell 74–75
Knox, John 74–75
Kunzman, Robert 92–94

La Verkin, Utah 20
Lang, G. H. 98–99
Latter-Day Saints, Church of Jesus Christ
    of 18–19
Law, Old Testament 1–2, 5–6, 8–9, 11–12,
    17–18, 26–27, 37–38, 42, 45–46,
    60–61, 62–63, 66, 71, 85–86, 87, 88,
    132, 139–40
    See also Christian Reconstruction;
    theonomy
League of the South 54–56
Lee, Robert E. 74–75
Left Behind novels 2–3, 57–58, 118,
    123–24, 127–28
Letterman, Larry and Peg 20
Lewis, C. S. 74–75, 98–99, 107–8, 123–24,
    128–30, 141–42
libertarianism 11–12, 17–18, 27–30, 31–32,
    62–63, 64–69, 82, 87, 105–6, 113,
    131–32, 137
Lindsey, Hal 22–23, 26–27, 38–39,
    41–43, 47, 48–49, 57–58, 64–65,
    72–73, 121–23
Locke, John 111–12
Logos School 54–56, 106–13
Luther, Martin 111–12

Machiavelli, Niccolò 111–12
MacIntyre, Alasdair 147–49
Maclean, Nancy 64–65
Mann, Horace 95
Marsden, George 144–45
Marx, Karl 111–12
McDurmon, Joel 47–48, 56–57, 83–87
McVicar, Michael J. 8–9, 64–65,
    139–40
Meadows, Donella H. 22–23
Mencken, H. L. 119–20

migration 1–2, 4–6, 8–9, 10, 35–36, 51,
    52–53, 54, 74, 109–10, 116–18,
    125–26, 130, 134–35, 143, 144–45,
    146–47, 148–49
Miller, Steven P. 8–9
Miller, William 19–20
Milton, John 107–8, 111–12
Mitchel, James 20–21
Montaigne, Michel de 111–12
Montgomery, Lucy Maud 119–20
Moody Bible Institute 119–20
Moody Press 121–23
Moon, Irwin A. 119–20
moral majority 63, 65–66, 76, 136–37
Morrison, Scott 145–46
Moscow, Idaho 10, 15–16, 19–20, 23, 27,
    30, 31–32, 48–57, 58, 74–84, 88,
    106–13, 114–18, 126–30, 132–33,
    134–35, 139–40, 142–44, 146–47
Murray, Iain H. 42–43, 45–46
Murray, John 45

National Center for Education
    Statistics 92–93
National Review 107–8
Neill, A. S. 95–96
Netflix 1–2, 7–8, 12, 129–30
New Saint Andrews College 53–57, 81–82,
    109–13, 114, 115–16, 142–43
New York, State of 15–16
New York Times 7–8, 12, 17–18, 38–39, 51,
    90–91, 117–18, 131
Newsweek 65–66, 69–71
Newton, Isaac 111–12
Nietzsche, Friedrich 111–12
Nisbet, Robert 4–5
Norman, Larry 121–23
North, Gary 1–2, 4–5, 8–9, 27, 42–43,
    45, 49–50, 52, 58, 62–63, 71, 73–74,
    96–97, 99–100, 103–5, 107–8, 113,
    125–26, 139–40
Northern Ireland 143–46

Obama, Barack 2–3, 6–7, 66–67, 81–82, 140
Olasky, Marvin 107–8
Orthodox Churches 7–8, 27–28
Orthodox Presbyterian Church
    26–27, 105–6

Orwell, George 60
Oxford, University of 111–12
Oxford University Press 111–12, 126–27

paramilitarism 4–5, 27, 56–57, 60–61, 130
    See also survivalism; violence
Parks, Rosa 104–5
Patrick Henry College 62–63, 106
Paul, Ron 113
Penguin Books 1–2, 12, 17–18, 58,
    131, 134
Peretti, Frank 121–23
Perrotta, Tom 123–24
Plato 109–10, 111–12
Plutarch 111–12
Post Falls, Idaho 16–17
postmillennialism 1–2, 13–14, 15–16,
    26–27, 35–38, 39, 40–42, 44–47,
    48–50, 53–58, 74–75, 108–9, 111,
    114–15, 142–43, 146–47
Poythress, Vern 73–74
premillennialism 13–14, 35–36, 37–39, 40,
    41–43, 47–49, 56–58
Presbyterian Church (USA) 26–27
Pullman, Washington 49–50
Puritanism 6–7

Quintilian 111–12
Quiverfull movement 124

race 10, 15–16, 27–28, 33–34, 80, 92–93,
    99, 103–5, 117–18, 132–33, 139–40
    racism and racial violence 3–4, 10,
    20–21, 62–63, 74, 76–77, 141–42,
    148–49
    de-segregation of schools 68–69, 96–97,
    99, 100–1, 106
    See also Kinism
Rajneeshpuram movement 20
Ramsey, William L. 54–56
Rand, Ayn 131–32
Random House 1–2, 12, 114,
    126–27, 128–29
Rawles, James Wesley 10–12, 14, 16–18,
    27, 29–30, 31–32, 35, 48–49, 52–53,
    56–57, 58, 62–63, 87, 90–91, 130–34,
    135, 139–40
Reagan, Ronald 65–66, 121–23

Reformed Theological Seminary 64–65, 140–41
Religious Right 2–3, 4–5, 6–7, 8–9, 13–14, 24–25, 26–27, 30–31, 42–43, 47–48, 60–61, 76–77, 79, 80–81, 83–84, 90–91, 136–37
Robertson, Pat 47, 62–63, 66
Robinson, Frank Bruce 19–20
Robinson, Marilynne 31–32
Roman Catholicism 19–20, 27–28, 36–37, 103–4, 132–33, 140, 146–47
Rousseau, Jean-Jacques 111–12
Royal Bank of Scotland 46–47
Ruby Ridge, Idaho 21, 22, 51, 131–32
Ruff, Howard 22–23
Runyan, Gordon 86–87
Rushdoony, R. J. 1–2, 8–9, 24–27, 34–36, 40–47, 49–50, 52–53, 60–61, 64–65, 67–68, 69–71, 74–75, 86–87, 88, 104–5, 107–8, 109, 125, 126, 129–30, 138, 142
    and education 96–104
Rutherford Institute 66, 103–4

Sabean, David 16–17
San Diego, California 3–4, 140–41
San Luis Obispo, California 24–25
Sandpoint, Idaho 19–21
Sasse, Ben 109, 145–46
Sayers, Dorothy L. 101–2, 107–8
Schaeffer, Francis 8–9, 26–27, 40
Schaeffer, Franky 66
Schäfer, Alex 7–8
Schlossberg, Herbert 107–8
Scofield Reference Bible 37–38
Scopes trial 37–38, 63–64, 119–20, 137
"secular humanism" 6–7
Shakespeare, William 111–12
Shaw, A. R. 130
Shea, Matthew 23
Sheldon, Charles Monroe 119
Sider, Ronald J. 125
Simon & Schuster 1–2, 12, 17–18, 131, 134
Singer, C. Gregg 68–71, 74, 80, 96–97
Slavery 37–38, 54–56, 80, 83, 127–28
Smith, Erin A. 119–20, 121
Socrates 109–10
Sophocles 111–12

Southern Baptist Convention 42–43, 60–61, 62–63, 65–66
Sowards, Adam 18–19
Spenser, Edmund 111–12
Spokane, Washington 19–20, 33–34
Stalin, Joseph 109–10
Stewart, Katherine 90–91, 93–94
Stites, Idaho 48–49
Supreme Court of the United States 2–4, 42–43, 68–69, 81–82, 96–97, 119–20, 148–49
survivalism 10–11, 17–18, 20, 22, 24–25, 27, 46–47, 48–49, 52, 74, 116–17, 131–33
    See also paramilitarism; violence
Sutton, Matthew Avery 63–64, 137

Tappan, Mel 20
taxation 1–2, 65–66, 76–77, 83–84, 88–89, 100–1, 102, 105–6
Thatcher, Margaret 72–73
Thayne, Steven 23
theocracy 23, 27–28, 60, 82, 102
    See also theonomy
theonomy 1–2, 4–5, 9, 16–17, 42, 46–47, 48–49, 62–63, 64–65, 71–75, 81–82, 85–87, 88, 91–92, 96–97, 101–2, 104–6, 109–10, 113, 114–15, 116–17, 124, 125–26, 131–32, 139–41, 142–43, 144–45
    See also Christian Reconstruction; Law; Old Testament; theocracy
Theroux, Louis 22
Thoburn, Robert 96–97, 105–6
Thomas Nelson 125–26
Thucydides 111–12
Tilton, Robert 71
Tolkien, J. R. R. 74–75, 129–30
Tozer, A. W. 121
Travesser, Michael 19–20
Trewhella, Matthew J. 59–60, 85–86
Trump, Donald 2–3, 6–8, 9, 12–13, 60, 78–79, 81–82, 88–89
Turner, Frederick Jackson 119–20, 130
Tyler, Texas 52, 71, 74, 139–40

Vallecito, California 139–40
Van Creveld, Martin 4–5

Van Til, Cornelius 44, 74–75,
    99–100, 108–9
violence 3–4, 5–6, 24–25, 26–28, 59–61,
    62–63, 76–77, 80–81, 85–86, 87, 88,
    100–1, 104–5, 140–43
    See also race: racism and racial violence
Virgil 111–12
Vitruvius 111–12
Volker Fund, the William Volker Charities
    Fund 64–65, 96–97

Waco, Texas 51, 131–32
Walden Media 123–24
Wasco County, Oregon 20
Washington Post 2–3, 12
Weaver, Randy 21–22
Welles, Orson 121–23
Westminster Seminary California 73–74
Westminster Theological Journal 24,
    69–71, 121
Westminster Theological Seminary 45,
    71, 73–74
Westover, Tara 93–94
Weyrich, Paul M. 136–37

Whitehead, John W. 48–49, 66, 103–4
Wigglesworth, Michael 36–37
Wilkins, Steve 54–56, 127–28
Williams, Daniel K. 8–9
Wilson, Douglas 10–11, 29–30, 32, 35,
    48–53, 54–58, 72–73, 74–83,
    85–87, 106–13, 114–16, 117–18,
    121–23, 126–29, 132–33, 134–35,
    139–40, 142–43
Wilson, Jim 49–50, 127–28
Wilson, N. D. 78–79, 127–30
Wilson, Nancy 127–28
Winthrop, John 36–37
Wise, Jesse 92–93
Wise Bauer, Susan 92–93
Wodehouse, P. G. 127–28, 130
Wordsworth, William 138
Worthen, Molly 42–43, 46–47, 91–92,
    113, 139–40

Y2K crisis 27, 46–47, 48–49,
    51–53, 125–26
Yeats, W. B. 148–49
Young, William P. 123–24